Toby

ABOUT THE BOOK

Toby Rawlinson was one of the most endearingly eccentric, fearless, inventive, ingenious individuals that has ever lent excitement to the conduct of any war.

Being highly individualistic, he constantly by-passed military bureaucracy and succeeded in pulling off feats of unequalled bravery, as well as deploying his creative genius to invent highly efficient methods and devices that effectively dealt with the enemy in the Great War.

Toby and the Duke of Westminster and a bunch of fellow madcaps all dashed off to the Front in their Rolls-Royces with their chauffeurs to the astonishment of both sides. So began a tense and engaging series of adventures of espionage and death-defying escapades through Europe which eventually took him to the Middle East.

He devised a new gun for the British to repay German mortar fire, modified a stethoscope to detect Zeppelins, dashed off to Turkey for a spell in prison after adventures in Persia where he scared off a vast Russian-armed detachment with a cardboard tank.

Exciting and compelling, his inexhaustible talent for getting into and out of sticky situations makes him prime material for a really thrilling ripping yarn in the *Boy's Own Paper* tradition.

ABOUT THE AUTHOR

Major A J Smithers was born in 1919 and served in France, West Africa and the Far East during the War and subsequently as Deputy Assistant Adjutant General War Crimes. Since then he has published biographies of Sir Horace Smith-Dorrien, Sir John Monash, Lord Kitchener and a history of the Kaffir Wars.

Toby (Rawlingson, alfred)
A Real Life Ripping Yarn

A. J. Smithers

Gordon & Cremonesi

Designed by Heather Gordon
Set in 12 on 13 point Baskerville
by Input Typesetting Ltd., London
Printed in Great Britain by litho at The Anchor Press Ltd
and bound by Wm Brendon & Son Ltd
both of Tiptree, Essex

British Library Cataloguing in Publication Data

Smithers, Alan Jack
    Toby.
    1. Rawlinson, Toby   2. European War, 1914–18 – Biography
    1. Title
    940.4'81'41   DA574.R/   78-40403

LCCN:78-040403
ISBN: 0-86033-069-9

Gordon & Cremonesi Publishers
London and New York
New River House
34 Seymour House
London N8 0BE

Contents

Introduction

The shattering events that followed upon the retreat from Mons, which was succeeded by the series of battles culminating in the first battle of Ypres, have distracted attention from the important operations of large British forces in Belgium and off its shores during much the same period of the First World War. To tell of this story is to tell how Germany, by incredible exertions, managed to raise a new and formidable army in the north while the clash of arms on which the attention of an anxious world was riveted echoed along the valley of the Aisne; how Britain and France, determined to resist the German onslaught towards the defenceless Channel ports, deliberately diverted the last trained troops to the Low Countries and scraped together from their empty store-houses the means to equip an army to hold Antwerp – with the object of preserving a sally-port from which, one day, Germany might be outflanked; how the Royal Navy, rich in untrained men but poverty-stricken in practically everything else needful for such an enterprise, took over the functions of army and air force alike; and how, for a time, the chances seemed nicely balanced between a German army marching to Abbeville and the Western Front reaching the sea near the Dutch border. These things were seen by a small body of men unique in military history.

It came about as follows. At the outbreak of war in August 1914 the British Expeditionary Force (BEF) was sadly deficient in motor-cars. An appeal to the Royal Automobile Club (RAC) for members who were willing to go to France with their cars and to place these and themselves at the disposal of the Army met with an immediate and enthusiastic answer. Of the many volunteers only twenty-five were selected and these included some of the toughest middle-aged men of means in the country. The three most colourful characters were the immensely rich Duke of Westminster (always addressed or referred to by his friends as Bendor, the name he shared with his grandfather's Derby winner); Frederic Coleman, an American citizen cast in the mould of Teddy Roosevelt; and Toby Rawlinson, a former cavalry officer who had gone on to become one of the most famous racing drivers of the day. For some years past he had been managing director of a firm near Paris which designed and built the fastest cars in the business, and, as most motor-racing was then carried out on ordinary roads, he had an encyclopaedic knowledge of the highways of northern France and Belgium. The War Office had assured him that at forty-seven he was too old to be of any use to the Army. Toby's response was to take his Hudson racing car, specially imported from Detroit for the 1914 Isle of Man TT race, but not used, owing to a mechanical fault; drive it to Southampton at a steady eighty miles per hour; and take charge of the RAC party. Most of them already knew each other, and, as they all knew that Toby was the most experienced driver–mechanic among them and knew inside out the region to which they were going, he was readily accepted as leader. The men with whom he had served as subaltern of horse were, for the most part, now general officers, and his elder brother, Henry, was known to be earmarked for command of a division.

The careers of the volunteer drivers lasted only for a few months, but without them the communications of the Army would have been seriously prejudiced. Many of their activities went far beyond those expected of civilians: Toby Rawlinson, for example, feeling that he was unprotected in the open bucket seat of a car built for speed and deficient of both windscreen and hood, bought a pair of machine-guns at a shop in Cannon Street (with no greater formality than if he had been buying a tin of tobacco). The use he made of them will presently appear. The Germans, had he fallen into their hands, would, as he well knew, have been perfectly within their rights to have shot him as a *franc-tireur*.

The battles along the Belgian coast were, in fact, critical to the final result of the entire war. They pointed a forgotten lesson by harking back to the unfairly despised eighteenth-century co-operation between soldier and ship, and they showed how right Napoleon had been in his curt comment to his generals, "Ask of me anything but time." It was time that these actions gained, and time, in the autumn of 1914, was the most necessary and most expensive asset of all. With a little shifting of the luck, 1914 could very easily have been 1940.

Chapter One

Between Dunkirk and the gap, far to the east, where the waters of the Scheldt pour themselves into the sea stretch the monotonous sand-dunes of the Belgian coast, with a maze of water-courses and sluices keeping the head of the hinterland above water. This dismal region had long been a fundamental concern of those charged with the defence of Britain: Edward III had defeated the French at Sluys; Cromwell's red-coats under Sir William Lockhart of the Lea had trounced the reputedly invincible Spanish infantry at Dunkirk Dunes; and for centuries the names of Dunkirk, the traditional nest of privateers, and Antwerp, the "pistol pointed at the heart of England", were as likely to have been written on the hearts of England's ministers as Calais was reputed to have been inscribed on that of Queen Mary Tudor. The creation of a sovereign Belgian state in 1830, largely as a result of the exertions of Talleyrand and Palmerston, had, so men hoped, at least drawn the charge from it.

The emergence of a powerful and truculent German Empire after 1870 stimulated the small trading kingdom to give thought to its defences, and the engineer Brialmont was entrusted with the design and building of the best fortresses that the plans and resources of the late nineteenth century could contrive. Chief among his memorials were the chain of works which engirthed the key cities of Liège, Namur and Antwerp. In August 1914 the last-named had grown to house a population of more than 400,000, but, even so, competent judges still reckoned its defences to be amongst the strongest in Europe. Unfortunately, despite the native courage of the people, Belgium regarded her army but lightly and, in the fashion of commercial nations, its equipment and training were sadly neglected. Since Marlborough had extinguished the Spanish Netherlands at Oudenarde, the country had on many occasions been the unwilling provider of battlefields for more powerful neighbours, but only at Waterloo had Dutch–Belgic troops fought as a national entity, and that encounter had done little to enhance their martial reputation.

Though the Belgians were not a military nation, they were fortunate, when the German invasion eventually came, to have at their head a soldier–king, the valiant Albert I, whose consort, Queen Elizabeth, possessed a heart as high as his own. Long devotion to the arts of peace, however, had denied him the sword he so needed; only the shield remained and that was soon to be riven. The immense 420-millimetre mortars, tailor-made for their task in the Austrian Skoda works, smashed Liège into a heap of smoking rubble on 16 August and performed the same pulverizing office for Namur six days later. On the morrow of this last calamity the few divisions that made up the BEF were locked in battle at Mons.

The plans for organizing and despatching abroad the BEF had been worked out with meticulous care, but it soon became apparent that there was one glaring deficiency in these plans. Like all armies of the day, the BEF depended almost entirely on animal transport, and the fact that the motor-car had become an efficient piece of machinery had been largely overlooked. In a war of movement such as the Great War was going to be, a modern form of the galloper was plainly needed, and, in a country well furnished with good roads, the motor-car was indispensable. Within a matter of days, the War Office requested the attendance of Julian Orde, the secretary of the RAC, in order to ascertain whether his organization could provide enough vehicles, complete with drivers, to undertake this essential work. They could be offered neither rank nor pay nor equipment, but must provide themselves with khaki uniform devoid of badges. The Club would provide distinguishing armlets.

Orde had already been bombarded with inquiries by his more adventurous members as to how they could make themselves useful, and this was something better than any of them had bargained for. The difficulty was not to find volunteers but to pacify those who, for one reason or another, were not selected. Eventually twenty-five members and twenty-five cars passed the tests prescribed for them by the Club. All were middle-aged men, most of them possessed of substantial private means, and all were famous sportsmen. The most distinguished was the Duke of Westminster, who was spoiling for a fight; a claim by him to be included together with a fine Rolls-Royce and the most accomplished chauffeur in the country could hardly be resisted. According to his third wife, he welcomed the war as it saved him from the disagreeable necessity of fighting a duel with a French nobleman whose wife he had compromised. There were racing drivers of distinction, including Oscar Morrison, Jimmy Radley and

C. D. Baker-Carr, there were men who were celebrated big-game hunters and explorers, and a number of ex-officers who were trying to conceal their mortification at having been told by their services that they were too old to be of any use in the war, and there was an American writer, Frederic Coleman. Amongst the first in the queue was Toby Rawlinson. He was forty-seven years old, former officer in the Seventeenth Lancers and renowned as a polo-player, motor-racing driver and aeroplane pilot. For some years past he had lived in Paris, where he was managing director of a British-owned firm which manufactured, so he said, the best racing cars in the world. He spoke perfect idiomatic French and, as a result of his road-racing experience, knew every road, bridge, track and hostelry between Le Havre and Brussels. In addition to that, he owned the fastest car in the country, a Hudson which he had imported from Detroit. The vehicle consisted of a powerful engine, a chassis of immense strength and, superimposed upon it, a tiny aluminium body with two narrow seats. Its appearance eloquently explained why the French for a car of this kind is *un torpedo*. His personal kit went easily into a small suitcase, but the Hudson was provided with every conceivable spare part, including four extra wheels. It had neither windscreen nor hood, and Toby, wrapped in a leather coat and with helmet, goggles and heavy cavalry moustache, assumed, when driving, the aspect of a determined walrus. On the day that Namur surrendered, the party of London clubmen and their cars made the passage to Le Havre.

On disembarkation, Toby mustered his command and instructed them as to the route to be taken to their destination at Amiens, which they reached at tea-time. There General Robb, General Officer Commanding, Lines of Communication, informed them that a battle was going on at Mons and that the Commander-in-Chief urgently needed half a dozen of the cars. The Duke, Coleman and Toby, with three others, set off at once along the Roman road through Villers Bretonneux, Peronne, St Quentin and Le Cateau, names still of no significance save to those who lived there. Before St Quentin they encountered the first trickle of refugees, which was soon to grow to a flood. The road became choked with the sad columns: old farm-horses slowly plodded on between the shafts of even older carts piled high with every form of household article, useful and useless alike, the children and the very old seated where they could; pedestrians pushed along wheelbarrows, drove donkeys and carried what there was no room for elsewhere. Among the many were old people who had done the same thing in 1870, and young ones who did not understand why they were doing it at all, save for the fact that they must escape the Germans. From them Toby and his companions learned the impossible truth: the BEF was in full retreat and, it seemed, by process of deduction, in very real danger of annihilation. Toby spent the night in the bucket seat of his car, exquisitely uncomfortable and registering a vow (later made good) that before darkness fell again he would have a blanket even if he had to steal one. Stiff and cross, he drove into Le Cateau; there he met Powell, the Duke's chauffeur, who took him to the room above a shop where his master had found a bed of sorts. The two drivers took coffee together; Powell drank his in the Duke's Rolls, from which he refused to be separated. They then sought out General Headquarters (GHQ), where Toby was given a staff major for passenger and told to go and find General Sordet and the French Cavalry Corps. From all accounts German Uhlan patrols were everywhere, and Toby drove with his pistol on his knee.

At a crossroads not far from Avesnes—about twenty-five miles east of Le Cateau—they met the head of Sordet's column, something like 20,000 horsemen spread out over many miles of road. They were plainly very weary but slowly they made their way towards the west, where they were to help sustain the British left against the next German onslaught. Toby was particularly struck by the ages of the French generals, any one of whom could have given him ten years and some of them, from their looks, more than twenty. The staff officer had a long conversation with General Sordet and they returned to Le Cateau, where the Duke, recognizing the sound of the Hudson's engine, leaned from his window and invited Toby up. There he found Francis Grenfell, an old friend of them both, with a couple of bullet-holes in him but still capable of adding much to their information.

They were all of them cavalrymen. Grenfell had received his wounds charging at the head of his squadron of the Ninth Lancers, and the Duke, after leaving Eton, had served for a time with the Blues. He had been mentioned in dispatches for his work as aide-de-camp to Lord Roberts in South Africa and had missed the DSO (Distinguished Service Order), then usually taken to stand for "Dukes' Sons Only", probably by reason of the fact that his father had died young and Bendor was a duke already.

Eventually Toby took his leave, armed with his little pink billeting order, to find out where he was to sleep that night. It was already dark when he presented himself at the cottage designated for him and he explained the cause of his presence to the good-looking lady, whom he elegantly described as "between the ages". He soon realized that her obvious alarm could be explained by the fact that the verb *coucher* is surprisingly imprecise for a French word, but after he had explained that he was of a chastity *à tout épreuvre* and, moreover, to the last degree fatigued, his involuntary hostess summoned her sister and the pair instantly and gratefully produced an admirable omelette and vast quantities of excellent coffee. One of them resigned her bed to him and Toby fell into a deep sleep, only to be aroused by what seemed to be the entire army loosing off its rifles at a low-flying German aeroplane. For the next few days he and his little racer were kept more than fully employed in carrying staff officers in all directions and at great speed with the invariable object of trying to ascertain where everybody was.

At this period of the war the word "Uhlan" was in every mouth, as it had been in 1870, and beyond doubt the countryside was alive with small parties of enemy cavalry. The only troops on the left of the BEF were French Territorials, whom Toby indulgently described as very respectable elderly gentlemen, recently called up and unmistakably nervous. On several occasions he nearly fell foul of their tendency to shoot at anything unfamiliar before troubling themselves to identify it.

He was in Landrecies when the Germans attacked the town and there the little car narrowly escaped receiving its quietus. As he sat in the bucket seat, the rim of which rose no higher than the small of the back, awaiting his passenger, the cry went up, "Clear the road—a battery is coming at the gallop." There is no more heart-lifting sight and sound in the world than a well-handled battery of field-guns moving at speed, but it is not a thing to be met in a narrow road. As the troop-horses charged towards him, nostrils distended and eyes rolling wildly, and the guns swung and bounced about behind them, Toby took the only course open to him. Alongside the road ran a railway line, separated by a line of kerbstones a couple of feet high. Before he could think, Toby jumped out, started the engine, leapt back into his seat, swung the car round and charged the kerb. The little Hudson erupted into the air and landed on the upper level just as the first gun appeared in the road, but agonizing noises indicated that the experience had not improved it. The damage demanded a workshop where battered components could be straightened out and the various rents soldered. To most motorists the task would have seemed an impossible one, but Toby Rawlinson was not easily daunted. When the Army Service Corps (ASC) major in charge of the transport brusquely told him that he must shift for himself, Toby acquired some lengths of clothes-line from the laundry and cunningly rove them into a short rope. The major's sergeant proved more accommodating than his chief, and aided by him Toby hooked his tow onto the rear of the last lorry of a passing column and set out for the south. For a time all was well, but after a short interval the driver lost his way and was seen to be heading for a battery of artillery which was shooting straight at them. Toby, powerless to influence events, took the ungrateful course of firing his pistol into the back of his tug, whereupon the driver stopped instantly. Though the guns were in action a couple of hundred yards ahead of them, Toby found time to speak to his errant driver with eloquence. In the end the lorry was made to swing wide over a ditch, the little racer still bounding in its wake, and they drove back across a field until they mounted the road again. None of the other lorries was to be seen, and Toby constrained the chastened driver to haul him to Guise, where there was a garage of which he knew. The clothes-line snubbed and tore at the car and it says much for the strength and reliability of the 1914 Hudson that they arrived intact.

Once in Guise, Toby found the garage he sought and, tired though he was, set to work to mend his beloved car. In a little over an hour it was fit for the road again, and he drove back, bringing the first news of the action at Landrecies, to St Quentin, where in his racing days he had once rented a room above a baker's shop. The baker had been called up, but his wife gave Toby a great reception and he spent the night curled up under the shop counter.

The noise of battle continued to roll south, leaving the sand-dunes deserted. The Belgian army, five divisions strong, trickled into Antwerp, which stood alone as the last defensible place in the kingdom. Thirty forts ringed it, in two lines, and beyond these the German cavalry rode up and down the country in small parties. Ghent was held by armed civilians and the main German armies were marching away, towards Paris and the Marne. For a space the old cockpit of Europe, the region where the outcome of the war was (in the beliefs and plans of the participants) to have been swiftly decided, was empty. Orders were sent to the Burgomaster of Ostend not to attempt to defend his town, but to send all the weapons of his Civic Guard—ancient Comblain rifles which fired a single lead ball—into Antwerp, where they might be of more use. (The British Royal Marine Brigade, which had been there since the 26th, was, for no obvious reason, sent home on the 31st.) Every first-line French soldier was being whipped in to join General Maunoury's Sixth Army forming around Paris. As the BEF marched towards the Marne, there were few khaki figures left in the Low Countries. The fate of Belgium was not going to be decided there.

Though, for the time being, the armies seemed to have lost interest in the sea coast, the admiralties of the Allies had never lifted their gaze from this vital area. In London, maritime affairs ranged far beyond the dispositions of great battle fleets, which were now of minor importance, and comprehended many aspects of sea warfare, some traditional and others entirely new. Since the revival of the Navy under Robert Blake and his contemporaries, the main reason for the existence of a fleet had been to provide squadrons of great ships which were capable of sinking, burning and destroying the squadrons of potential enemies. The Grand Fleet, now safely in its harbour at Scapa Flow, had a sufficient margin of superiority over the Kaiser's High Seas Fleet to make a general action something to be welcomed rather than a matter for apprehension, but the possibility of it in the immediate future seemed remote. The other traditional activity, the hunting down of isolated enemy units and commerce-raiders, was proceeding reasonably satisfactorily. The last field of activity, the holding out of a hand to the Army, seemed to offer little scope, more especially so as the Army was drawing further and further away from the friendly sea. In any event, the Royal Navy was not equipped for a land-supporting role. Its ships were designed to fight other ships on blue water and, apart from some gunboats on the China station (whose crews had been taken from them to complete the company of HMS *Triumph*), there were no bombarding vessels in commission. The type had been allowed to fall into obsolescence since the Crimean War and was represented only by three monitors under construction for Brazil that had been purchased from that well-disposed government even though there was no obvious use for them. There were, however, two grave novel problems. The submarine was already a weapon efficient enough to be taken extremely seriously and the Zeppelin was an unknown quantity. So long as the submarines could be kept operating from their home port of Cuxhaven, they might be contained; if they were to be able to work out of Ostend and Zeebrugge, they would become infinitely more formidable. Practically every serviceable military aircraft was already in France, and, as a result, the Admiralty was requested to take over responsibility for the air defence of the homeland.

The First Lord, Winston Churchill, had seen this coming for some time and, by an adroit use of funds voted to the Navy for rather vague purposes, he had built up a naval air arm of some fifty machines, the design of which had been hastened forward partly by reason of the great interest taken in the Schneider Trophy races. Plainly, these aircraft must have their base as near the enemy as possible, preferably somewhere across the Channel: for one thing, this would be far more convenient for the destruction of Zeppelins, which, since they could fly far higher than any heavier-than-air machine, were really vulnerable only while they were on the ground. Churchill cast covetous eyes on Dunkirk.

Almost embarrassing to the Navy was the number of ardent young men who wore its uniform but for whom no present use could

15

be found. The Crystal Palace, the camp at Betteshanger, Kent, and a number of seaport towns were filled with recruits of the Royal Naval Volunteer Reserve (RNVS) for whom there were no ships. The very words "Naval brigade" were like a trumpet call in the ears of men brought up during the long Victorian peace, and conjured up visions of horny-handed men in white duck and sennit hats brandishing cutlasses and storming through mangrove swamps to relieve legations or punish cannibal chiefs in the Queen's name. The works of G. A. Henty and the adventures of Mr Kingston's "Three Midshipmen" abounded with them, and, more recently, the exploits of the field-gun crews performing feats of incredible strength and agility at the White City had introduced the Naval brigades to an even larger audience. If the young recruits of the RNVS could not serve with the Fleet, Naval brigades they should be. In addition to the volunteers, there was also in the country a brigade of genuine Royal Marines, reservists for the most part but trained and experienced men.

The Army was in a less happy case. The last formed Regular division, the Sixth, was on its way to France, and the Seventh, made up of troops brought home from garrisons overseas, was still forming. The bulk of the Territorial Force was still in the country, but would not be released so long as the faintest possibility of invasion remained. The greatest shortage was in artillery. Churchill had ideas about that and approached the Secretary of State for War. His military staff officer, Major Ollivant, had suggested that a dozen British batteries be shipped back from India and replaced by batteries from the Territorial Force. These could provide the gains which would transform the Naval brigades from makeshift infantry into a genuine Royal Naval division. What did Lord Kitchener think? Lord Kitchener thought it a splendid idea; and in the event did not limit himself to a mere dozen batteries but effected the exchange of thirty-one batteries and thirty-nine battalions. When Churchill observed that he supposed he could now count on the dozen batteries for his Naval division, Lord Kitchener gracelessly rubbed his hands with glee and announced that he was going to keep every one of them to form three more Regular divisions.

Nevertheless, when General Joffre, on 16 September, asked the War Office to provide a brigade of Marines to reinforce the tiny garrison of Dunkirk and Lord Kitchener passed on the request to Churchill, the invitation was accepted with alacrity. This was the opportunity to get the naval aeroplanes well forward, and allowed the Admiralty to do something to fill the vacuum in the plains of Belgium and northern France. Lord Kitchener grudgingly agreed to add one regiment of Yeomanry cavalry, the Oxfordshire Hussars, in which Churchill held a commission as Major. Ollivant, now promoted Lieutenant-Colonel, was still fertile of suggestions. With his chief's approval, he denuded the London streets of fifty motor omnibuses and requisitioned as many lorries as he could find, bearing such homely names as Harrods, and Waring and Gillow. The Marines, conspicuous in their postman-blue uniforms topped with the peakless naval cap bearing the crown and laurel, moved into Dunkirk and travelled in comparative luxury to show the flag in defenceless Ypres, Lille, Tournai and Douai. They were not equipped to fight a serious battle, but were expected to be more than a match for any German cavalry they might encounter. In fact they encountered none, but their mere appearance was heartening.

Chapter Two

In turning aside to take a broader view and to consider how the Admiralty in London reacted to events in the plains of Belgium and northern France, we have anticipated events. We must now return to Toby Rawlinson, whom we left sleeping the sleep of the exhausted on a diminutive mattress under the counter of the baker's shop in St Quentin.

At 3 p.m. he was awakened and ordered to report at once to GHQ. His immediate task was to carry an officer to Noyon by way of La Fère, the name of which was familiar to most British as the "La Fère of putrid memory", of which Robert Louis Stevenson had written with much feeling in *An Inland Voyage*. The distance was about thirty-two miles and he complained bitterly of a five-minute delay, which made him take forty-eight minutes to complete the journey. Toby's racer was achieving some notoriety as being the fastest, if the least comfortable, of the RAC contingent. His billeting order was cancelled before he had had time to find out what fate had in store for him this time, and he was bidden to return at once to St Quentin with a packet for GHQ.

The journey back, through Ham, was very different from the scurry down a fairly empty road which he had enjoyed earlier. The roar of artillery from the north, where General Smith-Dorrien was fighting a battle around Le Cateau, was plain to hear, and weary refugees cluttered the road. By the time Toby reached GHQ again, it was obvious to him that the retreat was continuing, and, practical man that he was, he decided to get a decent night's sleep while he still had the chance. His friend the baker's wife gave him the use of her bed, announcing that she intended to keep the shop open all night in order to sell what remained of her stock to the worn-out troops who were already trickling into the town.

In the morning he was again set to work as a kind of independent reconnoitring patrol, scouring the roads to the north for information and then to the west once more to find out what had become of the French cavalry. It was not quite the task the RAC had contemplated, but none of the owner-drivers considered this a matter for complaint. The fog of war was complete. The Hudson swept round to Roye and then on a further ten miles to Rosières, but there was neither sign nor news of Sordet's cavalry. These Toby eventually found near the village of Mons-en-Chaussée, where some of them had been engaged against the Uhlans all through the day. The village itself was held by the Germans and General Sordet was heard to express his intention of "storming" it. As the storming of a village by cavalry was something outside his experience, Toby decided that he could justifiably spare a little time to watch the operation. It proved to be well worth a short delay. Several batteries of seventy-five-millimetre guns took ground and began to play upon the village with high explosive at a rate of fire far greater than anything he had ever known; as the village disintegrated under his interested gaze, squadron after squadron rose into line and began to advance upon it at the trot. All of a sudden the trot changed to a gallop, bugles rang out from end to end of the line with "that glorious call, so dear to the ears of every cavalry soldier—the 'Charge' ". The avenging horsemen of France roared forward in a cloud of dust, the ground quaking to the thunder of thousands of hoofs, while the guns continued drum-fire over their heads. As they approached the village the cavalry divided, one wing swerving round either side, while a proportion of them rode straight down the main street. The gunners craftily fired a few rounds of shrapnel for the benefit of any of the erstwhile defenders who might be vacating the place rearwards. Toby waited until the cavalry returned, bringing some prisoners with them, and, after expressing his congratulations, drove back to Noyon.

The following day, the 29th, he accompanied GHQ on its next move, to the palace of Compiègne. Even in its vast echoing rooms and galleries, now resounding to the hammers of signallers nailing up festoons of wire in the place where Napoleon III and the Empress Eugénie had married, there was no room for a civilian. Toby philosophically parked his car under a tree outside and curled up, his feet amongst the pedals, his shoulders in the mechanic's bucket seat, and a waterproof sheet, mysteriously acquired, draped over all. The next night, however, he was more fortunate. In desperation to find somewhere more comfortable to sleep he marched up to the front door of a large house standing back from the road in its grounds immediately opposite the hotel and rang the bell. It was answered by an elderly major-domo. When Toby asked apologetically if he could be directed to some place where he might obtain a meal and a bed, he received the unexpected reply, "Here, Sir, in this house you can find all you need. I will at once open the gates and you can drive your car in and put it in the garage." He went on to explain that he was alone in the house, his master having left, and that he was sure that it would be his wish that everything possible be furnished of which *les braves alliés* might stand in need. A beautifully cooked steak, a bottle of unexceptionable claret, a steaming bath and a luxurious French bed followed. In the morning, Toby wrote a grateful note to the owner, though he doubted whether it would ever come into his hands.

GHQ's next move was to Dammartin, on arrival at which Toby, after a journey during which he distinguished himself by storming past a Rolls containing Sir John French and covering it with dust, found himself with nothing to do. He therefore set off moodily to find himself a dwelling-place. Dammartin lies on the outskirts of the Forêt d'Ermenonville and was a very popular weekend resort for the richer Parisians. Of the many small and extremely chic villas Toby found one, the Villa Coquette, unoccupied and promptly moved in. He found it redolent of femininity and decorated with many pictures of two extremely beautiful and obviously Parisian ladies, some of them depicting the subjects elegantly gowned while others showed them not gowned at all. It soon dawned on Toby that he was the tenant of a high-class and very exclusive miniature brothel. This in no way discomposed him, for the furnishings were admirable in every respect and the deserted farms adjoining were well stocked with chicken and eggs. Toby, as one would expect, was a good plain cook, and before long he was joined by another RAC member, Borritt by name, whose Rolls had recently been used by Sir Douglas Haig. Word soon got around of the civilized life there and it was not long before Bendor arrived, accompanied by Hugh Dawnay of the Life Guards; a couple of generals were also dinner guests and Toby, in his capacity of *chef de cuisine*, was so carried away by his work that he forgot to leave any dinner for himself.

The life of a volunteer driver, however, was more than a motoring holiday interspersed with picnics. During the afternoon of 31 August, a car arrived at GHQ riddled with bullet-holes and soaked in blood. It had blundered into a patrol of Uhlans, who had shot the mechanic dead and mortally wounded the driver. This brave man had, however, managed to drive the car to a place of safety before he died, and the third occupant had brought it in to Dammartin. Toby began to wonder whether a .455-inch revolver was really an adequate weapon in the circumstances and began to formulate certain plans. He spent the next couple of days driving far and wide following rumours of

German cavalry, but, probably mercifully, encountered none.

On 2 September GHQ began to pack its bags again for a further move south. News had come in of the great cavalry fight at Nèry, but there remained a gap of some nine miles between them and Sir Douglas Haig's First Corps. It was strongly rumoured that German cavalry had infiltrated into the space between, but there was no reliable information to·be had. Once again, Toby was sent for. Would he be game to drive through the night across the gap and ascertain the truth of the matter? Another car, containing a staff officer, would be coming too, but Toby was to act as guide. At 11.30 p.m. he was ready to move off and the other car arrived, a superb open Rolls-Royce. It did not take long to recognize the driver: the Duke was coming and his passenger was Hugh Dawnay. Bendor was at the wheel himself, for this was not the kind of adventure that should be delegated to a paid employee. Besides, it promised excitement.

The moon was rising and it was agreed that Toby should drive without lights, the Rolls following as far behind as it could stay without losing sight of him. They would avoid the main highway and stick to the by-roads. Even the Hudson could not gather much pace under those conditions, and Toby drove with his ears stretched and his pistol ready to hand. The moment came, as he half expected it to, when he heard the stamp of a horse in a field alongside the road. Reasoning that an explanation of his civilian status might not be the best course, Toby left the car and went to investigate, creeping quietly through the ditch. Fortunately there was nothing to fear: the horse turned out to belong to a party of refugees who had bivouacked there for the night. The remainder of the journey passed without event, and they reached the château where Haig was lodged. Dawnay went to make his report while the cars drew up on the grass by the roadside and their drivers prepared to spend there what remained of the night. Bendor, who had dined well, bade his friend "Good night", but Toby, who had dined not at all, went into the château to forage. It was one of his luckier days, for he emerged the richer by an excellent ham and some croissants wrapped in a napkin, plus a quantity of much-needed plates and cutlery, which, as he explained later, he had saved from the Germans. At daylight the Duke, who now had a good understanding of these things, produced thermos flasks of coffee and they breakfasted very adequately.

Later that day, after Toby had been bidden to accompany the Ninth Lancers and had nearly stampeded that famous regiment when, driving over a bank, the mud-shield over the fly-wheel had bent and caused ear-splitting noises (a mishap which Toby rectified by borrowing a Lancer's weapon and driving its heel into the engine), he was ordered to go at once to Paris, taking an officer to General Galliéni, and then bring the officer back to Melun. It was impressed upon him that speed was essential, but, naturally enough, he was not sufficiently in the confidence of the High Command to be told that the battle of the Marne was about to begin. It was a nightmare of a drive through roads congested with military traffic and refugees who were streaming into the safety of the capital. Wealthy Parisians, by contrast, were doing their utmost to get out of the city. The government was already on the way to Bordeaux, and great crowds were thronging the Gare d'Austerlitz, the station that serves the south. Toby's little car threaded its way through the mob to Galliéni's headquarters at the Invalides, an oasis of calm after the storms outside. After a long wait in the car, during which he gained a good deal of information from passing officers about what was afoot, his passenger returned and they set off for Melun.

They arrived at the town late at night and Toby found himself a bed in a house given over to some staff officers and the RAC members. All the next day he was busy driving various officers along the lines of the French army, in order to make them familiar with the dispositions of the troops covering Paris, and he found that a kind of spy-mania was widespread. At Lagny there was an incident which pointed a danger that nobody had expected: a French sentry, unimpressed by the passes produced to him, lunged at Toby's companion, his bayonet passing between the cross-belt of his Sam Browne and the shoulder-strap. Toby's roar brought the sergeant of the guard at a run. He explained that he had for some time believed the sentry to be mad and that this exhibition persuaded him that his suspicions had been well grounded.

On the way back to Melun, Toby found himself on familiar ground, for the Château de Ferrières, the seat of the head of the Rothschild family, was a place at which he had been a frequent guest in the past. As they were both tired and hungry, it seemed foolish for him and his passenger to pass by without paying a call. Once again, Fortune smiled: Baron Edouard had gone, but his steward, who knew Toby well, remained in residence and enthusiastically produced a dinner fit for a Rothschild. At its conclusion, the Visitors' Book was handed to them, and Toby took pleasure in showing his companion some of the entries in it. The château had been the headquarters of the King of Prussia in 1870, and the first signatures were those of the two future German emperors, followed by those of Otto von Bismarck and von Moltke. Two less exalted ones were added, together with a few words of appreciation for the admirable refection served during the battle of the Marne. The old steward's last, kindly office to Toby before he left was to furnish him with a hamper stocked with every delicacy the château could provide. Melun proved far less welcoming. It was packed to bursting and the only shelter offered to Toby was a chicken-house. In his own words, "as the dew was heavy I soon had the chickens out of that and there I spent not only that night but all the nights I was in Melun until the advance began again".

In his adversity he found a companion. As he left GHQ in the morning with an officer who had to be got to the new base at St Nazaire with the least possible delay, he observed a figure dressed in the blue capote and red trousers of a French private soldier sitting disconsolately on the parapet outside and addressing his mournful gaze up towards the windows. There seemed to Toby something familiar about him, and, as Toby passed, the dejected soldier looked him straight in the eye. It was his old, very wealthy friend Jimmy Rothschild, who had received his calling-up papers. Toby unfeelingly asked what the devil he was doing in that get-up, and Jimmy replied that he was very unhappy and wanted a posting to Sir John French's staff, where his linguistic talents could be more usefully employed. Toby set himself to pulling such strings as lay to his hand.

The little Hudson covered 150 miles that day, all of it on roads well to the rear of the front, and he was fortunate enough to be able to put his passenger on a train at Chartres. This brought him back to Melun in sufficient time to be able to add a blanket and a mattress to the limited amenities of his chicken-house. On the morrow he was sent off to Third Corps, on the left of the British line, where he met an old friend and school-fellow, Stanley Maude, later to be the victor of Mesopotamia. Practically everybody Toby met in the higher reaches of the BEF was, it seems, an Old Etonian. He impressed on Maude how useful would be Jimmy Rothschild's intimate knowledge of the country around them, and what an excellent fellow he would be to have in the Headquarters Mess. It was not long before he found himself a member of it. That night the fowls returned to the chicken-house, as Toby had no sooner reached Melun again than he was once more sent on his travels, this time to the headquarters of General Maunoury, with whose Sixth Army he was ordered to remain, as the advance was about to begin.

He found the Sixth Army in a village on the outskirts of the great Forêt de Bondy, once the hunting-ground of the kings of France and also a notable haunt of highwaymen. He remained with Maunoury throughout the battle, to see the sword of France flash once more as that general lunged for the sac of the octopus whose strongest tentacle was feeling its way between the twin objectives of Paris and Verdun. If Toby had not been already an ardent francophile, the sights and sounds of these hot days of late summer would have made one of him. The Sixth Army was far from being a *corps d'élite*, having been hastily cobbled together by Joffre from whatever formations— battered regular, colonial and territorial alike—he could find. They bore themselves, however, in a fashion that would have done credit to the Old Guard as they strode towards the grey columns of von Kluck and von Bülow, their long bayonets glittering in the sun.

The BEF, in concert with them, marched forward across the Petit Morin, and GHQ moved to Coulommiers, where Toby rejoined it on 11 September. He took with him the blanket that he had used in the chicken-house, and left for the owner a civil note to the effect that his (Toby's) need for it appeared the greater. His new billet was in the house of a doctor, but he spent little time there. TheDuke had come back also, bringing with him great quantities of provisions from Paris, and had established himself fittingly in a house in the town. Toby enjoyed there many excellent dinners, which, as he wistfully observed, "excelled by a thousand times the modest entertainments which we had succeeded in providing in the Villa Coquette". Bendor was not a duke for nothing.

Toby's war very nearly came to an abrupt end at this time. Driving from La Ferté Jouarre to Meaux, it is necessary to cross the Marne by the bridge at Trilport and the bridge lies at the bottom of a long hill. Toby sailed confidently down it in the dawn light at a steady seventy m.p.h. and was already half-way along the causeway which leads onto the bridge when he became aware that the first arch was no longer there. It was far too late to stop; the only courses open to him were to try and leap the gap or to turn down the steep slope of the embankment. He elected for the latter, closing his eyes as he turned, convinced that this was the end. The descent was, so he says, "sensational and acrobatic" and he could hardly believe it when the car finally skidded to a halt, undamaged, on the river bank. He pondered to himself that he had been right in believing that it really was impossible to capsize the vehicle. One wonders how many modern cars would stand up to such punishment as Toby's little Hudson endured. People hurrying up informed him that the bridge had been blown only the previous evening; already the remains of seven cars were piled up half in and half out of the water.

Toby remained with GHQ throughout the advance to the Aisne, and during the long, hard battle for the Chemin des Dames he was employed mostly in driving to and from the various French formations engaged there. Several times he drove through the streets of abandoned Soissons, and he was a spectator on the famous occasion when the Zouaves crossed the river under murderous shell-fire, by the single remaining girder of the railway bridge.

The war of movement now paused. The RAC drivers were quartered in a small house in Fère-en-Tardenois, the current location of GHQ, and their mess, as may be imagined, was a very cheerful one. The only disagreeable feature was that the weather had now broken and the Hudson was not designed for long journeys in driving rain. The fact that cars were regularly shot at in woods by German stragglers, well armed, hungry and desperate, was regarded as no more than a minor nuisance. The Duke moved into the town, where he took a house and once more put his staff to work to provide suitable meals for his friends. His ebullience was, however, much tempered by news of the death of his half-brother, Percy Wyndham, at Soupir during the fighting over the Aisne.

After about a week, during which he had had some good pheasant shooting, Toby was invited to take a King's Messenger to London. This was the opportunity for which he had been waiting, and from "the well-known firm of Le Personne and Co. of Cannon Street" he bought two Colt machine-guns of the pattern that had been used by the Yeomanry in South Africa, together with a great quantity of ammunition. The Colt was not a weapon used in the British service; it was belt-fed, air-cooled, and terminated in a pistol-grip, so it could easily be fired by one hand. Toby took one of them back to France with him and drove to Fère in a more confident frame of mind, wishing for nothing better than an encounter with the Uhlan patrols or cars occupied by Germans in disguise, a danger of which he had been warned at Le Havre. As it was dark when he reached the Oise, he dined and passed the night at the château of another Rothschild, Robert, at Laversine. The next day was spent with ASC mechanics in earnest consultation about the fitting of the machine-gun on the car. They made a very workmanlike job of it.

Back at GHQ there was a message waiting for him. His brother, Sir Henry Rawlinson, had arrived in France to assume temporary command of the Fourth Division in the absence of General Snow, who was incapacitated after a fall from his horse. Henry wished to see Toby at once. Toby drove to the Château de la Carrière l'Évêque, where divisional headquarters were situated, and passed a pleasant week shooting partridges. At the end of the week, on 2 October, Henry took his younger brother into his confidence. He had been appointed by his old patron Lord Kitchener to command a new corps, to be called the Fourth, made up of the Seventh Division and Sir Julian Byng's Third Cavalry Division, both in England. The plan was for the corps to land at Belgian ports and raise the siege of Antwerp. Would Toby drive him there? Toby would.

Chapter Three

Although the main stream of the war had flowed away from Belgium, a good deal of miscellaneous activity had taken place in that unhappy country. Back on 24 August, King Albert, like the brave man and faithful ally he was, had caused a reconnaissance to be undertaken in order to find out what was happening in the wake of the German armies. The information came back that a gap had opened up between Louvain and Brussels, and he wasted no time in taking what advantage he could of this development. On the following day the five divisions of the Belgian field army, flanked by its only force of cavalry, sallied out and began to make encouraging progress. There was no question of taking the tiger by the tail, for such an operation could have been beyond the King's strength, but at least he would give it a sharp nip in the ankle. On the 26th, the day on which Sir Horace Smith-Dorrien's Second Corps turned on its pursuers at Le Cateau, the Belgians were fighting their way forward, but when the news arrived that the retreat of the British and French armies had been resumed King Albert took the only possible course and fell back to his fortress. Honour did not require that he should bring about the destruction of his only army to no purpose. Even though he had been denied a victory, the King's bold stroke had given von Moltke furiously to think, and the German Ninth Reserve Corps and Sixth Division were detained for the time being in face of Antwerp.

On 9 September, when the battle of the Marne was at its height, King Albert struck again. His intelligence had correctly informed him that both these enemy formations were on the move to join their main body, and he was opposed only by some Landwehr and Ersatz units, which were in no way superior to his own force. This time he left two divisions in the citadel and thrust towards Aerschot with his remaining three and his cavalry. The leading elements of the Belgian army actually entered Aerschot and it was not until the Sixth Division was brought back into the fight that the Belgian offensive was halted and the army withdrew to Antwerp for the last time. From the German point of view it had been a near-run thing. The Ninth Reserve Corps had been halted at Brussels and the Fifteenth held up on its way from Alsace. The absence of these powerful reinforcements was not felt on the Marne but their appearance during the battle of the Aisne after some prodigious marches came just in time to dash the cup of absolute victory from Joffre's lips. If they could have been held up for another day the results for the Germans would have been devastating. The Belgian contribution to this situation has tended to be overlooked and King Albert has generally not received the credit he deserved. It may well have been anger at the hardihood of the commander of an army that he reckoned less even than the British that stung the Kaiser into his order of 12 September that Antwerp be taken at once regardless of the cost.

As soon as it became apparent that events on the Aisne had reached a stalemate, the men responsible for the conduct of the war began again to direct their attention to the theatre where it had started. Exactly a week after the Kaiser's order, the Royal Marine Brigade and the Oxfordshire Hussars disembarked at Dunkirk in response to the request of General Joffre that, "owing to the new German movements towards the north of France ... all available troops should be sent there and to Calais to act effectively and constantly against the enemy's communications and thus hinder their operations in that region". The threat was no imaginary one. The German army was known to possess an enormous force of cavalry, highly trained, excellently equipped and so far little engaged. If they were directed at once on the Channel ports, even with Antwerp still untaken in their rear, they could enter them almost unopposed. Only a few French Territorials stood in their way. General Aston of the Royal Marines was given command with orders to avoid a pitched battle but to bluff the enemy so far as he could into believing his force to be substantial and to do such things as cut railway lines and demonstrate noisily. He could do no more. Lord Kitchener had no soldiers to spare. The Admiralty also had other things to think about, for on 22 September came the news of the sinkings of the three old cruisers *Aboukir*, *Hogue* and *Cressy* by a submarine in the Broad Fourteens with the loss of nearly 1,500 lives. In spite of this tragedy, Churchill would not be deflected from his purpose and the Naval brigades were put under orders to stand by to relieve the Belgian stronghold.

On 28 September the Skoda mortars began to range on the city;

three days later the first two forts had been obliterated. The next morning the British ambassador to Belgium, Sir Francis Villiers, telegraphed to London that the Belgian government had accepted the advice of its Superior War Council that the King should march out of Antwerp with the field army on 3 October and by way of Ghent seek to join up with the French. The government would move to Ostend and the Queen would accompany it. Although the Council assured Sir Francis that the garrison troops left behind were capable of continuing resistance for five or six days more, he took leave to doubt whether they would do so once everybody had abandoned them.

Churchill conferred with Lord Kitchener and Sir Edward Grey, all of them having received the news with consternation. Liège and Namur had been shocks, but their fall was comprehensible once the power of the mortars was understood. Antwerp was quite another matter. The inner ring of forts were old, but the outer ones were reckoned as good as any in Europe. Apart from artillery, the Belgian forces alone were at least equal to the investing army. The emotional ties to "gallant little Belgium" could not be underrated, for there was no denying that, although Britain had gone to war on Belgium's behalf, she had done precious little in the military field for her small ally. The ministers concocted a cable to the ambassador, instructing him to urge on the Belgian government the importance to the common cause of keeping Antwerp an inviolate fortress on the German flank and promising instant dispatch of the Marine Brigade. It happened that Churchill was due in Dunkirk the next day, and the Cabinet readily agreed that he should offer the heartening addition of his energetic presence to the Antwerp garrison. All the French could offer was to send two Territorial divisions to Ostend. Churchill reached the beleaguered city at 3 p.m on the 4th, for the railway to Ostend was still unmolested. As he was being taken by the Prime Minister, de Broqueville, for audience with the King, the Marines began to arrive. General Paris, who had succeeded to the command five days earlier, when Sir John Aston had been sent home sick, was ordered to take up positions at once as far forward as possible in order to demonstrate to the weary Belgian soldiers that they had not been deserted by everybody. He found the field-works between the forts to be very poor: "troughs rather than trenches" was one description. Nevertheless, his middle-aged Marines, looking oddly un-English in their round hats and blue uniforms, set to work with pick and shovel to make what they could of them. On the same day the first of the Naval brigades were marching down the gang-planks at Dunkirk. In appearance they were even odder than the Marines, the men wearing ordinary naval "square-rig" with antiquated leather equipment and cap-ribbons bearing such legends as "RNVR Eastbourne". Each man carried a bandolier containing 120 rounds of ammunition, and the brigades had a number of Maxim machine-guns. Their officers, among them Rupert Brooke and "Oc" Asquith, the Prime Minister's son, wore either Navy blue or Army khaki, depending upon what they happened to have possessed when the brigades were formed. Very few were either sailors or soldiers by profession. The training of most had been limited to an annual camp or two supplemented by what they had been able to pick up during the last few weeks between spells of guard duty and the like. All the same, there were no others. They entrained at once for Antwerp and began to arrive there during the 5th. By the following morning they too were digging ditches and making sand-bagged machine-gun positions.

4 October had been an eventful day. During its last hours General von der Marwitz had issued orders to three full corps of German cavalry for a general offensive to "break down the weakening resistance of the enemy by operating against his flank and rear, to block all the railways leading from Paris and the lower Seine, and to destroy completely the railways from the lower Somme and the coastal railways near Abbeville". Some hours earlier, Churchill, still immured, had received a message from Lord Kitchener:

> Am arranging expeditionary force for relief of Antwerp as follows:—British force 7th Division, 18,000 men, 63 guns under General Capper. Cavalry Division 4,000 men, 12 guns, under General Byng, to arrive at Zeebrugge 6th and 7th October ... French force Territorial Division, 15,000 men, proper complement of guns and 2 squadrons, General Roy, to arrive Ostend 6th to 9th October. Fusiliers Marine Brigade, 8,000 men, under Rear Admiral Ron'arch. Grand total 53,000 men.

It sounded a lot of men, as indeed it was. Nobody in the Allied camp was aware that Germany had already raised four completely fresh corps, totalling eight divisions, who were preparing to join the five divisions already besieging Antwerp.

The last noteworthy event of 4 October was the departure from La Carrière L'Évêque of the two Rawlinson brothers and their entourage. Borritt drove Sir Henry in his Rolls, with Bendor following in another. It was not the open one of his earlier adventures but, as Toby explained, "a covered Rolls which he had, I think, picked up in Paris, as he had sent his open car to obtain supplies with which they were to re-join us in Belgium". This was the fashion of waging war proper to dukes, reminiscent of the way in which Marshal the Duke of Vendôme had ordered his affairs in the same area some two centuries before.

It was dark, well before four o'clock in the morning, when the two cars began to be loaded up. The two Rolls-Royces were to proceed directly to Amiens by way of Compiègne and Breteuil, as prescribed by Toby, who had first to make a detour of eight miles to pick up his kit from Fère; but he reckoned that if he took the direct road from there to Amiens – a matter of about seventy-five miles – he would, by hard driving, just about be able to catch up the others at their destination.

Toby scorched to Fère, where he packed in the little Hudson all his kit. Then, adjusting his machine-gun on its forward mounting, as there were the usual rumours of German cavalry patrols, he set off. At Compiègne he learnt that the others had passed that way an hour earlier, for Bendor also had a taste for fast driving and his Rolls was faster than its appearance might have suggested; he learnt also that Uhlans had been seen on the Montdidier road and slipped a belt of cartridges through the feed-block in hopeful anticipation. Between Compiègne and Montdidier the recent presence of enemy troops proclaimed itself: the countryside was deserted, farm-houses were in ruins and not so much as a chicken was to be seen. Beyond Montdidier, Toby fell in with the Third Cavalry Brigade, heading westward, and passed the time of day with General Vaughan, whom he had known long ago as a subaltern of Hussars. He reached Amiens without further incident, and drove straight to the Hôtel du Rhin, where he had to meet the others. It may not have been entirely due to good management, but he had timed his entrance to perfection: they were just sitting down to luncheon. The German advanced troops had in fact briefly occupied Amiens, but the French had driven them out again before they had had the chance to do any mischief and the Hôtel du Rhin had survived unscathed.

After the meal Toby took himself off to make inquiries about the safety or otherwise of the various roads open to them. Information was confused but alarming, and it was manifest that none of the direct routes could be guaranteed free from Uhlans. Toby might have taken chances himself, but he was not going to risk his important elder brother; he obviously stood in some awe of him, for throughout his chronicles, although he refers to his friends nearly always by their familiar names, Sir Henry is invariably "the General". His inquiries completed, Toby reported back that the only safe way was to drive to the sea at Boulogne and then follow the coast through Calais and Dunkirk to Ostend, where Fourth Corps Headquarters was to be set up. It meant going round two sides of a triangle and covering more than 300 miles over roads which were everywhere barricaded and manned by sentries, of whom he had already had experience. The event was every bit as bad as the anticipation: time after time they were stopped, rigorously examined and their passes checked. Sir Henry's red-banded and gold-laced cap, far from being a talisman, merely led some to believe that he was a German in disguise. They reached Dunkirk at 6 p.m. and, while Sir Henry was closeted with officials, Toby and the Duke were left in an empty office at French headquarters. On the absent owner's desk stood a heap of blank military passes; the eyes of the Duke and Toby met. Toby nodded. Without a word they each grabbed a handful of passes, appended illegible signatures and passed the official rubber stamp back and forth. By the time the owner returned their pockets were stuffed with passes which, as Toby wrote with suitable meiosis, "considerably simplified the remainder of our journey".

For Toby the drive nearly finished soon after they had left Dunkirk. Bendor managed to pick up a puncture and Sir Henry, who did not share his brother's enthusiasm for the open Hudson, continued in another car. Toby remained behind to help change the tyres and, when this had been done, he and Bendor set off in pursuit. Toby was the leader and "very naturally put on a bit of extra pace". The road was a rough one, but this did not deter him from keeping up a steady fifty m.p.h., with the Duke maintaining the same speed a furlong behind where the dust thinned out. As they roared through a small village about ten miles short of Ostend, Toby discovered, too late, that a series of deep gutters crossed the road at right angles. The front tyres of the long-suffering Hudson hit the edge of the first with a violent impact and one of the front wheels detached itself completely from the axle, bouncing high into the air and careering through the village on its own. Even Toby's experience had not comprehended the driving of a car at high speed between rows of houses in a narrow street with gutter after gutter lying in ambush and with only three wheels. As he fought with the steering wheel, the car slewed sideways and they continued the journey broadside on with a trail of sparks coming from the *pavé* as the axle of the missing wheel dragged across the sets. The inhabitants dashed from their houses, fearing an onslaught by German batteries, and, when they saw Toby's spectacular progress, returned within doors even faster than they had emerged. His attempts to keep the vehicle under some sort of control were masterly, for the car avoided coming into collision with any of the houses and he contrived to bring it to a standstill before it could overturn and kill him. The wheel which had started the trouble was recovered from a field 150 yards further on. To the end of his days Toby never knew for certain exactly how he had survived. By a merciful dispensation of Providence no great harm was done, and when the wheel had been recovered the two men forced it back on again. The little car could be driven, though the steering was inevitably erratic, and Toby let the others go on ahead as he slowly made his way to Ostend. There he left the car in a garage to have the axle straightened while he went to report himself to his brother in his temporary corps headquarters at Ostend railway station.

The town was full of gloomy stories about the state of affairs in Antwerp, but the Seventh and the Third Cavalry Divisions were now coming ashore and it was strongly felt that the situation would undergo a radical change as soon as they could take the field and move north-eastwards to thrash the besiegers. The Seventh was the last division of the old Regular Army and every man was a trained soldier; in a short time it would give proof of what the British army of 1914 was made of, though few would survive to tell of it. Toby, however, had no time to ponder on these things, for the car demanded most of his attention. His brother intended to use it and its driver to scour the countryside and find out what was happening, for nothing else could travel at the pace of the Hudson and he knew Toby to be a faithful and accurate observer. On the 5th—the day on which von der Marwitz began to move his 40,000 horsemen towards the coast—Sir Henry shifted his corps headquarters to the ancient town of Bruges, on the road to Antwerp. Toby passed the entire day breathing down the necks of harassed Belgian garage mechanics, fuming at being kept away from all the excitement. The job was a major one and it was not until the morning of the 7th that it was completed. By then Sir Henry had gone on to Antwerp itself to confer with Churchill, who, for all practical purposes, appeared to be commanding the garrison.

As soon as his car had been returned to him, Toby drove it to corps headquarters, leaving it in charge of a Belgian sentry as he went in to seek his brother. He had hardly entered the building when a rattle of musketry which he instantly recognized came from the street below. Toby rushed down and found his car surrounded by a crowd while every window had its face peering from it; people were lying in the gutters, "women were screaming at full pitch and fainting in droves. It appeared that 'certain young men' had desired to show off their military knowledge and to explain the working of the gun to the assembled multitude." They had in this been successful and had opened fire on the adjoining houses at the rate of 400 rounds a minute. Fortunately for everybody, the gun had been cocked up at a high angle on its mounting and most of the rain of bullets had gone tearing over the roof-tops. Toby, who ought to have known better than to have left it loaded, collapsed with laughter at the sight of two stout ladies who had swooned as the first burst tore a hole in the plaster wall between their respective windows and whose bulk made their removal a matter of some difficulty. The young men responsible for the incident melted away.

Sir Henry Rawlinson was still in Antwerp the following morning and there were apprehensions about his safety. The French representative in Bruges was General Pau, a splendid old veteran of 1870 who had lost an arm fighting the Prussians before the German Empire existed. News of his unease about both the British Corps Commander and Churchill came to Toby's ears; he was none too happy about the situation himself, for it was on that day that the German Fourth Cavalry Corps had passed through Ypres, thus winning for themselves the distinction of being the only German soldiers to have passed through the Menin Gate not as prisoners. Toby went to the Hôtel de Commerce, where he knew General Pau to be lodged, and offered to drive to Antwerp by way of Ghent to see if the road were safe for the return journey of the two important passengers. General Pau gladly accepted; Toby withdrew to the hotel restaurant, where he knew he would find some of the RAC drivers, and asked whether anybody would come with him. He did not like doing it, for he much preferred to have his adventures alone, but the General had pointed out that there was a very real prospect of a fight with the German cavalry and no man could both drive the Hudson flat out and work the machine-gun as well. Toby, having reluctantly agreed to take someone along, was obliged to limit his choice of volunteers to those who, in addition to their other talents, were competent machine-gunners. It happened that there was in the restaurant a man who had exactly the right expertise. Lord Edward Grosvenor, in addition to being Bendor's uncle, was a trained Royal Naval Air Service (RNAS) pilot and therefore knew all about machine-guns. He was also, "like all the Grosvenors, absolutely fearless, a splendid fellow in every way and a most amusing and agreeable companion". Indeed, his only drawback was that he was also corpulent and not ideally suited to the mechanic's bucket seat of the Hudson. However, it would have been futile to attempt to argue with Ned Grosvenor, and with the assistance of some of the other drivers his well-knit frame was intruded into the car, where he inspected the unfamiliar pattern of gun knowledgeably. A little before midnight the two set off under a bright moon down the road to Ghent, twenty-five miles away. They made their way through barricades without difficulty, for passes were no longer a problem, and reached the town at about 1 a.m. In Ghent they made inquiries for definite news, as opposed to rumour, of German cavalry in the neighbourhood. Ghent was on tenterhooks, for the knowledge that some big movement of the German horse was taking place was common, and there was no lack of men who were expecting the field-grey columns to debouch into the town at any moment. There was, however, general agreement that no patrols had been seen upon the main road to Antwerp, though there were many accounts of their presence in other directions. Toby and Lord Edward drove on.

Ten miles or so beyond Ghent, the road crosses a heath with many shrubs and thickets crowding close on the carriageway; it was an ideal spot for an ambush. Toby was not a nervous man, but on the principle of safety-first he drove the car off the road and extinguished the lights while Lord Edward swung the gun to and fro for the benefit of any unseen eyes. The shadows moved as no shadow should on a still night; Toby fingered his pistol and moved a few paces to one side, watching and listening. Grosvenor curled his index finger round the trigger of the Colt and took first pressure. Still nothing happened. While Toby was hesitating, uncertain what to do, the lights of motor-cars coming from the direction of Antwerp appeared in the distance. The driver of the leading car seemed to catch sight of them and halted about a hundred yards away, the others behind following suit. Toby felt tolerably sure that this must be his brother and party coming back but knew that it might equally well be a German patrol, armed to the teeth and swift to open fire. He moved cautiously towards the cars and loudly whistled "a certain family call which my brother and myself had been in the habit of using as children". To his intense relief, he heard a familiar voice call out: "It's all right; it's Toby." Churchill and Sir Henry had come thus far in safety. On such small things depended great ones: if the Rawlinson boys had not had their private call, Toby might have walked on and been fired on by a nervous escort. If that had happened, Lord Edward would, without doubt, have riddled the occupants of the cars, Churchill and Sir Henry included, before there was time to draw breath. However, all was well. Sir Henry gave a succinct account of the deteriorating situation in Antwerp, how the forts were being systematically destroyed and the city was preparing for evacuation. The Hudson led them back to Bruges and Churchill went home.

He would have plenty of things with which to busy himself at the Admiralty, even without the problems presented by the conduct of the war at sea. Antwerp was plainly tottering to its fall; even before he had left the city the smell of burning oil from the refineries was permeating everything. The port could not be used for any purpose, as access to it is by way of the Scheldt, the mouth of which is in Holland, and the Dutch claimed that for the Allies to use it infringed their neutrality. When the Belgians and the British force came to withdraw, if withdraw they could, there was no line that could poss-

ibly be held east of the Yser. Rawlinson's corps could not be employed offensively and it would have its work cut out to cover the
retreat of the others. There must be transports at hand in case a
hurried embarkation was forced upon them; there must be ships
available to bombard the German army once the remnant of the
Belgians had reached the Yser, exhausted and almost without guns.
From where were these ships to come? The Royal Navy had no
vessels designed to shell targets ashore; neither had the French.
Probably the only navy in the world which had not lost sight of their
usefulness was the Japanese, which had used them at Port Arthur ten
years before. There were old battleships in plenty, but they were
made for the open sea and drew a lot of water; there were probably,
however, a few old gunboats remaining, relics of the days of the
fortress-mania which had followed Napoleon III's development of
Cherbourg. The shallow draft of these vessels would make it possible
for them to lie inside the Nieuport Bank and the Grote Rede, but
could they be got there in time? Could they weather a Channel gale
in autumn? Was there ammunition to be had for their ancient guns?
Churchill had much to think about as he boarded HMS *Attentive* at
Ostend. There were just a few small crumbs of comfort. Admiral
Oliver, with a team of four men and a Belgian Boy Scout, had
managed to disable thirty-eight ships in the port by placing explosive
charges in vital parts of their engines; at any rate the Germans would
not get them. And the pilots of the RNAS were not going to leave
without having a dash at the Zeppelin sheds at Düsseldorf while they
were still in range.

Sir Henry Rawlinson was well aware of all the factors on which
Churchill was exercising his mind, but his own responsibilities were
pressing and his status rather obscure. The Fourth Corps was, presumably, a part of the BEF and under the orders of Sir John French.
The rest of the BEF, however, was far away and still in the process of
moving back from the Aisne. Between it and Rawlinson lay not only
many miles of France and Belgium but also strong German armies,
which it would have to fight and overcome before it could join him.
Sir John had been last heard of at Fère and could not possibly be
seized of the situation in Flanders. General Foch had, since 24 September, been acting as Joffre's deputy in the north, but precise news
of his dispositions was not available to Fourth Corps. It was known
that the new French Tenth Army was fighting a hard battle between
Arras and Douai, but, again, details were lacking. Sir Henry saw
only one thing for it: he sent for Toby.

Once more a racing car would be found the most useful of vehicles. Toby was to go to Sir John French's GHQ, deliver the despatch
entrusted to him and come back at the greatest possible speed. He

made a quick calculation: the distance would be a round trip of just about 600 miles; it was still the morning of the 8th and the despatch was not yet ready (nor had his adventures the previous night given him much time for sleep, but that did not come into his calculations); if he left at 6 p.m. that same day, he informed his brother, he would be back by the morning of the 10th. If he did not turn up then, Henry might give up the idea of ever seeing him again. His unfeeling elder, however, told him to start as soon as the despatch was handed to him and not to travel alone. Toby never argued with Sir Henry and routed out Borritt for what he later said was "that sensational drive, a great deal the hardest and most difficult one which I have ever been called on to undertake". In a quiet way, Toby succeeded in organizing things in his own fashion and it was not until 6 p.m. that the Hudson left Bruges, carrying two helmeted and goggled middle-aged gentlemen, and petrol for more than 400 miles. As they drove, Borritt received instruction on the workings of the Colt machine-gun.

Chapter Four

For a little while we must leave the two motorists driving through the cold and darkness of an autumn night, and turn aside to see what was the state of affairs in Antwerp when Churchill and Sir Henry Rawlinson left it. The Belgian troops, after fighting day and night for so long, were exhausted. The great shells were now falling on the forts of the inner ring and, as with the more modern ones of the outer defences, no more than half a dozen were needed to reduce them to a rubble of masonry and twisted steel. The old Krupp guns with which they were armed barked back for as long as they could, but they were quite useless against the superior weight of metal. To complete the agony of the city, the water supply had now been destroyed. General Paris had, by order of Churchill, been placed in command of the naval contingents as well as his own brigade, but for want of proper signal facilities it was impossible for him to exercise effective supervision. The only good thing was that the city was still not cut off from the world outside. For some reason the German cavalry had failed to raid and destroy the railway lines, as they could easily have done, and traffic was continuous. A steady stream of wounded and refugees flowed south-westwards out of the postern gate while such help as the Navy could afford entered by the same way. The two armoured trains of Lieutenant-Commander Littlejohn and the Belgian Captain Servais steamed into the town and added their quota to the fire of the defenders. By noon on the 6th the Royal Marines and the Naval brigades were in position straddling the Antwerp–Lierre road between Contich and Vremde. Only the Marines were capable of manoeuvre, but the amateur sailors could be trusted to give a respectable account of themselves from behind fixed defences. Ghent had some time previously been taken over by a Belgian brigade. There had been a last attack by King Albert's field army during the night of 5–6 October, but it had ended in failure; the men were incapable of further effort and it was resolved that the best divisions be moved at once to the left bank of the Scheldt, as, other considerations apart, communications had to be kept open. The divisions in question left their positions in the line at about the same time as Churchill and Sir Henry drove out.

There now remained in the city only the scratch British Force, the Second Belgian Division and the fortress troops; facing them were five German divisions, one of them also consisting of marines. Far more formidable, however, were the mighty guns, whose fire continued unabated. Throughout the weary hours of 7 October fort after fort crumbled; civilians fled by the thousand to the sanctuary of neutral Holland or to the open country in the general direction of Ghent. That same day two officers of the RNAS in their small aeroplane made the long flight to Düsseldorf and managed to blow up the airship sheds which housed a Zeppelin; on the return flight they bombed the railway station at Cologne. It was a brave feat but it could be no more than a gesture. In the night the Naval forces were withdrawn, tired, low in ammunition and entirely without water, they crossed the Scheldt by the light of the burning houses and made for the lifeline of the railway. The French marines were detraining at Ghent and two brigades of the Seventh Division were on the way to join them with a couple of batteries. The bulk of the Belgian army had already moved from its camp across the Scheldt to positions between Ghent and Ostend, leaving rear-guards at various points to help cover the withdrawal from Antwerp, and were being strongly attacked around Lokeren. The Belgian defenders, fully alive to the importance of maintaining their positions, fought stoutly and would not be moved.

The last hours of the stricken city presented a scene of appalling confusion. The population of 400,000 had been greatly swollen by refugees from the countryside who had sought safety behind its defences. Now they, together with countless numbers of the original residents, were trying to get out. The narrow streets were crammed with panic-stricken civilians, making the movement of formed military bodies impossible, and the railway stations were swarming with them. As darkness began to fall, the spectacle was lit up by the flames coming from the great oil refineries, which had been put to the torch rather than allow their precious contents to fall into the hands of a hated enemy. In many places the burning oil had crawled across streets and open spaces, from which rose the smell of the roasting horse and cattle carcasses engulfed by it. Here and there groups of people, lit by the flickering flames into the likeness of demons, could be observed dashing through the seas of fire. The Marine Brigade, the only British formation with any semblance of a staff, made its way in good order to the south-western corner of the city, where the Second Naval Brigade and the Drake Battalion of the First Brigade soon joined them. They marched alongside the river, between blazing oil tanks, to the smoke-covered bridge at Burght, shells still crashing down in all directions. Once across the river they continued on to Beveren Waes, on the main railway line to Bruges, where they were given the erroneous information that the Belgian defences at Lokeren had been driven in and the Germans were advancing on St Nicholas. The weary men were, as a result, diverted to St Gilles-Waes, near the Dutch frontier, and on the way they were caught up in the main stream of refugees and the Second Belgian Division pouring over the St Anne Bridge. All order was lost and the troops were swept along with the mob until the station was reached. At St Gilles-Waes station they entrained and were soon in Ostend.

The other two Naval battalions were less fortunate. After much delay, they reached St Gilles-Waes station eight hours after the last of their comrades had left; and, hearing that the line was cut and that the Germans were advancing on them, and knowing how hopeless it was to think of fighting a way through to Ostend, the senior officer present decided to follow the example of Bourbaki in 1870 and seek internment rather than capitulate. 1,500 men marched the few miles to the Dutch frontier, where all, save for two officers and about forty men who refused to cross, marched into captivity. The irony of it was that the report of the cutting of the line and of the German advance had been only partially true. A train containing a Marine battalion had indeed been attacked; the Marines had leapt out to fight, but had been swamped by the mass of fugitives with them and all but 150 had been captured; the Germans had withdrawn at once, apparently in the belief that a strong Belgian force was on their heels. The truth of the matter was that a force of several thousand Belgians had, with the greatest chivalry, given up some earlier trains to the British and were retreating on foot. They were nowhere near and in no shape to fight a battle, but the news of their existence was enough. A Belgian officer who understood such things eventually drove the train to Ostend. There was still one train behind it that also got through safely. Such was the fog of war.

Although the fall of Antwerp had been inevitable for some time, the five days gained by the arrival of the Royal Naval Division had been of critical importance. As a result the Belgian army lived to fight another day and, in the end, to return home victorious. The fine British Fourth Corps now stood in the path between the new German armies and the Channel ports. If Antwerp had capitulated on the 3rd, it is hard to see how the Germans could have been kept from taking Dunkirk, in artillery range of Calais, or, indeed, from reaching the lower Somme. There is a memorial on the banks of the Thames by the boundary of the City of London testifying for all time to Belgium's gratitude to Great Britain. A companion piece in Brussels would not be out of place.

On 10 October, according to an American correspondent present at the time, the German Marine Division marched into Antwerp, with bands playing, to receive the sword of its brave governor. In London, execration was heaped upon the First Lord; but today the main dock of Antwerp proudly bears the name Churchill. The remnant of the Royal Naval Division went back to its camps around Deal and Walmer to await the day when it would be put once more into battle, on the Gallipoli peninsula, where it was to have even less chance of success than it had enjoyed at Antwerp.

All of this, of course, was hidden from Toby and Borritt as the Hudson bore them swiftly over the long French roads in their search for the Commander-in Chief, though both of them had a shrewd idea of what was likely to happen. Between Bruges and Dunkirk they encountered no Uhlans and Toby put his foot down on the accelerator as hard as he dared. The Belgian mechanics had done a good job and the car seemed none the worse for its misadventure. Borritt, who was accustomed to the shelter and luxury of his limousine, appreciated the car's good points but could not, with the cold wind whistling past his frozen cheeks, bring himself whole-heartedly to share in Toby's enthusiasm for it.

In some nameless place to the south of Nieuport, it had once more proved its robustness. Deliberately they were travelling on the by-roads, which are narrow and serpentine, but they had still man-aged to keep up a good speed; Borritt had seen no reason to expect anything untoward when, suddenly, his driver bellowed, "Look out!" and swerved violently into a dry ditch on the outskirts of a village. Toby, who had the ability to keep a keen eye on all his surrroundings when travelling at sixty, had seen something that he did not like. A flash of weak sunlight had touched a fast moving object at the far end of the village and shown a glint of metal; some sort of a car was about and the fact that it had turned sharply off the road into the trees did not inspire confidence. For half an hour the two men remained in the ditch, Toby with field-glasses to his eyes and Borritt with the pistol-grip of the Colt firmly in his hand. No sign of movement came and they prepared to sell their lives dearly. This was not the situation the RAC had contemplated when asking for volunteer drivers, but it was too late to think about that now; if the German cavalry came clattering down the village street, they would have to fight their way through machine-gun fire until they emerged again to find the corpses of two well-connected English civilians and with them a small racing car. At last movement came; several Belgian children came out into the road and began to skip. This was enough for Toby, who swung the engine into life and drove his long-suffering car over the lip of the ditch into the street, with Borritt standing unsteadily on his feet to display his khaki uniform. Almost at the same moment, an armoured car drove out of its lair to confront them, the gunner repaying the compliment by standing up so that they could see his uniform of Belgian blue. Relieved handshakes followed and the armoured vehicle led them to Nieuport, where the lock bridge was opened to allow them to pass. The driver was firm that they must on no account travel by the obvious short route, by way of either Ypres, Cassel or St Omer, as the entire district in that direction was alive with enemy horse. He was quite right.

When, after a night's hard driving, with thick fog making the going exceptionally difficult between Abbeville and Amiens, they arrived at Fère, it was to find that Sir John French and GHQ had left for Abbeville by train half an hour earlier. Wearily retracing their steps, it was 2.30 p.m. by the time that they drew up outside the Commander-in-Chief's house. Toby was at once ushered into the presence and handed over his despatch; as a civilian, he was uninhibited by rank from impressing on Sir John that his orders were to take back an answer without delay. Sir John, after one look at Toby, told him firmly that he was to go and get some sleep first and handed him over to an old friend, Brigadier-General Sir William Lambton. Toby and Billy Lambton had (inevitably, one feels) been at Eton together. Lambton led the exhausted Toby to his own bed and swore to wake him at 5.30 p.m. Toby does not say what happened to Borritt; presumably somebody found him a bed somewhere.

Lambton did his duty and called Toby at 5.30. They went to the Chief's room, where a large map of the coast and the hinterland from Antwerp to Amiens was spread out on a table. Sir John, having read the news brought by Toby, now had a grasp of the situation in Belgium and hazarded the opinion that Fourth Corps would probably have to re-embark in the transports which were hovering off the coast against that eventuality. He said that he was very doubtful whether Toby could make the return trip safely as the whole of the country he would have to cross was, for all practical purposes, in enemy hands. For that reason he refused to entrust him with any written document but took him to the map and expounded in detail the exact movements that he intended to make during the next few days with each of his divisions. Toby was ordered to repeat what he had been told; he did it well but, reasonably enough, he explained that he could not answer for every detail remaining in his mind for a matter of days and asked whether he might not have a map on which he would make cabbalistic markings charged with meaning for him but senseless to anybody else. Sir John refused, but compromised by handing him one marked with what his Intelligence Staff believed to be the German position at that day. Toby addressed himself to memorizing the identities of the British formations opposed to those shown on his map. They seemed very few.

Sir John then commented on the badgeless state of Toby's uniform and asked to be shown whatever passes he carried. On reading them Sir John observed, very sensibly, that they were no credentials at all, and that if he were to be captured – a very probable state of affairs – he would in all likelihood be shot as a spy. As Sir John knew, both of them being cavalrymen, Toby had resigned his commission outright many years ago and did not even enjoy the status of a Reserve officer. However, there are times when expediency must outrank the proprieties and Sir John dubbed Toby colonel. For all the validity of the appointment he might have created him a duke or a bishop, but this was not a time for niceness about such things and Toby had the advantage of looking as a colonel should. Documents were made out for the newly-constituted field-officer and a counterpart in French was drawn up and signed by Colonel Huguet, the Head of the French Mission. There was no commission for Borritt. He stoically accepted the metamorphosed Toby in crowns, stars, red tabs and gold-leafed cap without inquiring whence these adornments had come. When Toby explained the probability of capture on the way back, he took some comfort from the situation. As a civilian driver he might have expected honourable captivity, but as a civilian operating a machine-gun, and a privately-owned one at that, he could anticipate the worst. It could only be hoped that, if they were to be taken, Toby's martial cloak would cover them both.

Toby explained in general terms the purport of the messages with which he had been charged. There stuck particularly in his memory the phrase "the British Expeditionary Force would be in occupation of a line extending from Aire to Béthune on October 11th". There was a good deal of unfounded optimism about at the time and even Foch was writing to his chief that "if you approve and Sir John French agrees, I propose to advance our left [the Tenth Army] by Lille to the Scheldt at Tournai or at Orchies, the British moving in the direction of Lille and to the north of that town, and forming line from Tournai through Courtrai. In this way all the French, British and Belgian detachments would be united on the left banks of either the Scheldt or the Lys." Subsequent events were different.

Toby, however, was concerned only to deliver his message before some vital part of it slipped his memory. The drive back to Ostend by the same road that they had used before was untroubled and they arrived at Ostend station in the early hours of the 10th, just as he had said he would.

He went straight in to Sir Henry, who was too preoccupied with other things to inquire about his younger brother's strange plumage. Toby recited his message with commendable accuracy, while Borritt went thankfully back to his limousine. The trains containing the Marines and the Naval brigades were beginning to arrive, with refugees and other passengers piled up on the roof, sitting on the buffers and clinging to the sides. Toby observed to himself that it was a good job there were no tunnels on the way. News of the missing units was scanty and it was not until long afterwards that the ignominious fate of the bulk of the First Naval Brigade became known.

With the benefit of Toby's news, Sir Henry Rawlinson was at last able to formulate a definite plan. His Seventh and Third Cavalry Divisions were still to the south-east of Bruges, where they were well placed both to guard the retreat of the former Antwerp garrison along the coast and to block any advance by the German troops (now formally constituted as the Fourth Army) in that direction. As soon as the move was completed, Fourth Corps would fall back on the unimportant little town of Ypres in order to link up with the main body of the BEF on the Aire–Béthune line, Admiral Ron'arch's marines would come back to Dixmude, and the Belgian army would establish itself northwards to the sea on the line of the Yser, with the French Forty-Second Division to back them up. The three cavalry corps of von der Marwitz had shot their bolt: the French Twenty-First Corps had effectively halted them on the Lorette heights, and de Mitry's cavalry corps (the one previously commanded by Sordet) had completed the task. They were now facing the BEF between Armentières and Bailleul and no longer need be taken into consideration by Sir Henry.

While Toby was still living in limited comfort at Ostend railway station, Bendor arrived to greet him. Sir Henry entrusted to them a task for which they were admirably suited and in which they were both now experienced. Corps Headquarters was to leave Ostend and a new abode was needed somewhere about Thorout. Toby and the Duke were to go and select it. They took a wide detour around the countryside and eventually hit upon the Château of Wynendael; it was not the first time the old walls had seen the arrival of British soldiers, for this was the place where, two centuries earlier, the Jacobite General Webb had defeated the French force sent to intercept an important convoy on its way to Marlborough while he was besieging

Lille. They inspected the castle-like building, approved the large, well-furnished rooms, noted that it was now supplied with electric light and decided that it would do. "Exactly the class of Headquarters which we were seeking", was Toby's verdict. The owner was away and the place in charge of a steward who lacked a sense of history and demurred at the suggestion that it be taken over. Toby's red tabs were, however, too strong for him and he was warned to have things ready for their return on the following day. Back in Ostend, the harbingers thoughtfully added to their resources two excellent taxicabs which had come from Antwerp and whose drivers were temporarily unemployed. Bendor accepted the task of filling them to capacity with provisions and hiring them for an indefinite period. The drivers were only too willing and they and their vehicles remained attached to Corps Headquarters until the following spring.

Next day, the two men returned to Wynendael and made themselves at home. The steward, whose objections seemed to have been overcome, served them not only with an excellent dinner but also with some quite remarkable claret. The same night Toby had one of the taxicabs cleared out and its load replaced with a supply of the wine for their future use. Unfortunately, neither he nor the Duke was in possession of sufficient ready cash to pay for it; Toby, therefore, wrote out a receipt which contained an undertaking to make payment on its presentation. Four years later, after the Armistice, the owner presented it to the War Office. Toby speculated about the payment, if any, made for the rest of the contents of the cellar by the German army which arrived a few days later.

The news that came into Wynendael was not reassuring. The two British divisions were withdrawing by way of Thielt with 60,000 Germans on their heels and there was no information to be had about the whereabouts of the main body of the BEF. In the morning they received the even more disquieting news from Sir Julian Byng that he was in touch with German cavalry to the east and even to the south of Ypres. Plainly Corps Headquarters could not remain where it was for much longer and later that night orders arrived that it should move behind the walls of Ypres itself. Toby slept on the floor in front of a blazing fire in the room in which his brother was working, for Sir Henry had said that he wanted to be taken to Roulers as soon as he had finished. He had no let-up all through that night, and at dawn, having taken time only for a quick shave, he ordered his young brother out.

They travelled as before, with Toby and his gun-car in front and the General trying to get a little sleep in the Rolls of the faithful Borritt. They drove fast and the two cars were in the square of Roulers before sunrise on a morning of bitter cold. The town was seething with excitement and full of troops, many of whom had made fires on the cobbles in order to keep warm. Horse-drawn wagons were moving in all directions, their iron tyres crashing over the *pavé*; groups of men were brewing tea while others, dead to the world, slept on the stones. Toby inquired the way to General Capper's headquarters, and, on arriving there, was told that they had only just arrived and that most of the staff were still asleep. Forgetting for the moment that he was now a colonel, Toby bounded up the stairs and had the General out of his bed with no more ceremony than he had wasted on the chickens at Melun. General Capper hurried down, pulling a greatcoat over his pyjamas, while Toby told him acidly that his corps commander had been denied the luxury of any sleep at all. This was not quite fair, for "Tommy" Capper was the best of generals and the last man to spare himself at need; however, there was no time to inquire as to how Sir Henry would have benefited if his subordinate commander had not snatched a little rest while he could and Toby was not invited to remain during the interview. Instead he went off again in search of Borritt and coffee, returning in time to collect Sir Henry as he left the house. Sir Henry Rawlinson was not a choleric man, but he was obviously angry, and by degrees Toby learnt the cause to be his dissatisfaction at the speed with which the division had made its withdrawal. He had just given peremptory orders to Capper to get his men on the move at once and to be clear of the town by eight o'clock. They then moved on to see Sir Julian Byng at the headquarters of his Third Cavalry Division. Here Toby found himself amongst friends, who gave him the interesting information that the right flank of Fourth Corps was completely in the air. It did not seem to worry them greatly, for everybody was in tremendous spirits; nobody, however, congratulated Toby on his promotion, if such it was, or even seemed to notice.

Sir Henry, on leaving Byng, told Toby that he had another job for him. He was to go back along the Seventh Division's line of retreat and to keep driving until he encountered Germans: having done that, he was to take a careful note of what kind of troops they were, what were their numbers and what sort of pace they appeared to be making. Once he had armed himself with this information, he was to drive back as if all the fiends in the pit were behind him. He was to be at pains to be in Roulers by 8 a.m.; once there, he was to make sure that Sir Henry's orders about the move by the Seventh Division had been obeyed; and then he was to report back to Ypres.

Toby permitted himself the comment that it seemed a fair morning's work, then swung the engine and climbed into the car. All along the road he came across stragglers from the Seventh Division, strolling along without a care in the world and aiming to join up with their units in Roulers. Toby stopped to speak to every one, making forcefully the point that this was not a quiet walking tour, that the division had already left Roulers for Zonnebeke and Ypres, and that nothing but a little space remained between them and the Uhlans. The pace of most quickened perceptibly. At Pitten, a couple of miles short of Thielt, the road was blocked by the closed gates of a level-crossing; they remained obstinately shut against him as train after train, each festooned with refugees, crawled slowly past towards the west. Toby could only smoke cigarette after cigarette and swear bloodcurdlingly. At last the gates opened and he drove into Thielt. From that point on it was unquestionably tiger country; Thielt appeared to be a city of the dead. He drove slowly into the square, turning the car and taking up a good tactical position at a corner from which he could drive back again fast if he were given the chance. He moved the machine-gun from its position on the bonnet to another mounting on the stern which he had had put there for just such an eventuality as this. It was an uneasy posture, for several roads led in to the square, along any of which the Germans might come at any moment. The car was backed onto a pavement so that it would have some degree of concealment and only the tail-end and the gun jutted out. Toby waited; it was just 7.20 and he had to be back in Roulers by eight. He reckoned he could allow them another ten minutes, so he lit one more cigarette. Not a mouse stirred, though he had strongly the sensation that many eyes were watching him from behind closed shutters.

At 7.25 he heard the unmistakable clatter of many horses' hoofs, and at the far end of the square a patrol of ten German cavalrymen rode into view; they were moving only at a walk and when they reached the Mairie, half-way down one side of the square, they halted. The leader and some of the men dismounted and entered the building. Before Toby had decided what he should do, the head of a much larger body appeared, riding down the road from Ghent. A full squadron rode into the square and they halted in the same place, their leaders also entering the Mairie. Before they were inside, yet a third party rode in, this time by the Bruges road and much nearer to Toby. The first two parties had not spotted him, but this one could not fail to do so and that very soon.

Toby thought fast. The better part of two squadrons were at his mercy, for his machine-gun could have put a thousand rounds into them before they would have recovered from the surprise. He would have had no difficulty in outdistancing them in his racer, and would have been in little danger from the wild musketry with which alone they could have pursued him. His engine was still running and his hand was on the pistol-grip of the gun. The decision whether or not to press the trigger was an agonizing one; a part of his mind assured him that it would be a breach of duty to ignore the opportunity of inflicting the maximum damage on the King's enemies, but another part was less certain. The war was still young and, so far as the armies were concerned, it had so far been fairly decently conducted; the real beastliness was yet to come. It offended every instinct to kill unsuspecting men, something more like murder than a lawful act of war. There were also two other factors in Toby's mind. Though motor-cars had long since supplanted horses in his affections, he had been brought up in the life of a Lancer regiment; if he fired then it was certain that some of the stream of nickel-jacketed bullets would tear into the innocent horses, reducing many to a bloody, screaming pulp. Toby simply could not bring himself to do it; it might have been different if he had had to shoot his way out of a tight corner, but that was not the case at that moment. Also, if he did use the machine-gun, he could be quite certain that, after he had escaped, the furious Uhlans would wreak a terrible vengeance upon the Belgian civilians. The loss to the enemy of a score of hussars was not worth it. Toby put his Hudson into gear, gently let in the clutch and slipped away.

He passed the same stragglers on the road back and added to his exhortations to get a move on, though by now it was too late to be of much use. Nothing out of the way happened as he sped back to Ypres. Roulers was empty of troops, though his tidy mind was offended by the masses of litter they had left behind them. Back at Ypres, he rendered a full report of his adventures to Sir Henry, whom he found standing in the square outside the beautiful thirteenth-century Cloth Hall. Both his divisions were coming back now, the cavalry on the left extending itself to join hands with the Belgians, and the Seventh covering the town and looking out hopefully for signs of the main body of the BEF.

Chapter Five

As Toby emerged from the little car in the shadow of the Cloth Hall, a number of momentous events were taking place around him. General Pulteney's Third Corps was beginning to detrain at St Omer, the Second had become bogged down in heavy to-and-fro fighting among the mining villages and slag-heaps behind Armentières, and Sir Douglas Haig's First Corps was still on its travels from the Aisne. Only Allenby's Cavalry Corps was, so it was thought, in any position to prolong the line to the south, but that, too, was completely out of touch with the defenders of Ypres.

The situation to the north was almost equally obscure. The sorely-tried Belgian army was now in some sort of position behind the Yser, almost without guns and dependent for its last reinforcement on the 16,000 men who had escaped from Namur more than six weeks before and had been transported by the French navy to Cherbourg. The line ran roughly from the dunes at Nieuport to Dixmude, where Admiral Ron'arch's marine brigade lay, to Boesinghe, nearly four miles north of Ypres. Thirty miles of utter flatness were held by six weak and exhausted divisions, with only the Fusiliers Marins to help, and against this were directed the eight fresh German divisions, rich in artillery of every kind. King Albert had established his headquarters at Furnes, where the Queen insisted on remaining at his side, and prepared to meet the onslaught as best he could, but the ability of his troops to continue an effective resistance against such odds was much in question. General Joffre and his deputy shared with Sir John French the happy illusion that no substantial German force could exist in face of Ypres and were busying themselves with planning impossible offensives towards Lille and Tournai. King Albert had no such dreams. Ostend and Zeebrugge had gone, their port installations left intact—to the anger of the Royal Navy—on the implausible ground that they would probably be needed before long for further landings. Determined to cling on to the last few acres of his kingdom, the gallant Albert sent a message to the Admiralty asking for a warship to lie off his coast and bring her heavy guns to bear on the invaders. He was pushing on a door already wide open.

Churchill had wasted no moment in making his plans. The only bombarding vessels in the service, the three ex-Brazilian monitors, each armed with two six-inch and two 4·7-inch guns, were being rapidly prepared for battle; the orders had, in fact, gone out two days previously, and all three were on their way to Dover when the anguished call from a fainting ally arrived. The ships' captains, however, in common with everyone else in the Royal Navy, had no experience of using ships' guns against a landward target, which made it difficult to know how those guns would perform. Added to this, there was the threat of German submarine activity. In crossing the Channel, both *Severn* and *Humber* were attacked by torpedo, but they succeeded, thanks partly to their shallow draft, in reaching the great harbour unscathed. Churchill was determined that everything possible should be done for the neglected Belgians. This was partly for reasons of creditable emotion and partly because their disappearance from the battlefield—an eventuality that their weary and disorganized state made increasingly likely—would leave a gaping hole, which no other troops were at hand to fill, at the extremity of the line. The French Forty-Second Division had not yet come into the picture and the French Ninth Corps, which was to play such a robust part in the coming battle for Ypres, was still far away.

The Royal Navy took its new duty extremely seriously, and a new command, that of "The Rear-Admiral Commanding the Dover Patrol and Senior Naval Officer, Dover", charged solely with covering the Belgian flank, was constituted under Rear-Admiral the Hon. H. L. A. Hood. Hood, by common consent an outstanding officer, had prior to this been Naval Secretary to the First Lord and the force could not have been in better hands. On the 16th a message arrived at the Admiralty from Joffre, now alive to the situation in the north, that the three German divisions released from before Antwerp, together with the eight of the new Fourth Army, were swarming towards the Belgian line, and he besought Churchill to send ships to smite them from the sea. It was a pleasure to the First Lord to be able to assure him that the monitors, escorted by a destroyer flotilla, were already on their way.

All of a sudden the weather took a hand. During the night of 16–17 October an autumn gale sprang up and a gale in the straits at that time of year is not a small matter. The monitors could not possibly live in it with their low freeboards, and as a substitute twenty-four light cruisers and destroyers were got under way. A German flotilla of four destroyers was despatched to head off these intruders but the Royal Navy had a short way with such as these. All four were sunk without having achieved anything. An attempt to take Dixmude by a *coup de main* failed equally disastrously under the cool musketry of Ron'arch's highly-trained marines. In case the monitors should prove insufficient, two elderly battleships, *Queen* and *Implacable*, were ordered to Dunkirk from Portsmouth.

Admiral Hood landed from his flagship at Nieuport in the early hours of the 18th and went to see things for himself. It did not look too reassuring; the Belgian divisions were on a line following the left bank of the Yser from Nieuport to Dixmude, with outposts beyond it at Lombartzyde, Rattevalle, at the crossing-point of the Bruges Canal and at Mannekensvere, where the main road from Brussels comes in. In a plain as flat as a billiards table and hopelessly cut up by dykes and streams, no defence works worth the name were possible. The Germans were plainly poised for an attack on Nieuport itself and there the Navy could help. Unfortunately, all along the coast of west Flanders are sand dunes—not mere gentle undulations of the kind that fringe the Royal St George's Golf Club on the opposite shore, but hills rising to fifty feet or more above sea level and blocking the view landward from out at sea. The gunnery control of seagoing ships (as well as that of the monitors, which arrived later in the day) could do nothing to remove the difficulty and, in the absence of any form of communication between ship and shore, fire could only be blind, aimed by map, compass and faith. Even so, it was a great deal better than no fire at all. As the Germans advanced across the polder by the sea, the guns of the flotilla thundered and shells bigger by far than any fired by land batteries began to fall around them. Black columns from common shell and yellow from lyddite spurted up around Lombartzyde and Mannekensvere; the German battery just established on the sea's edge at Westende was hammered by the destroyers and the Belgians felt that no longer were they quite alone. The naval six-inch shell weighs 112 pounds, and, although its fragmentation was intended to smash ships and not to kill men, it is a powerful inhibition to movement in the open.

All through 19 October the battle raged along the seashore; some of the Belgian advanced posts were swamped by numbers and urgent appeals came in for the fire to be increased. Battleships, monitors, cruisers and destroyers continued to pound away until their ammunition stocks dwindled. At Hood's suggestion, old and less valuable ships were sent to him to replace the good, modern cruisers, which were sitting ducks for any enterprising submarine. The ships sent made up the oddest fleet ever to sail under the White Ensign, but they could throw their shells as far as required, and they drew so little water that a submarine would have to surface to get at them. The survivors of Queen Victoria's navy were soon in action against her grandson's army and the enemy batteries at Blokhuis Farm and Westende Bains found them no subject for ridicule.

By morning on the 20th there were no Belgian positions beyond the Yser. The fine German army of 1914 was not to be checked by the fire of a few ships and could still be prodigal of men and material. Lombartzyde was lost and at Tervate (about half-way between Nieuport and Dixmude) the river was crossed and German infantry began to dig in. Next day, the Belgians pushed an officer's patrol into Lombartzyde and brought back prisoners, who spoke with awe of the effect of the ships' gunnery. The old vessels redoubled their activities and, under the curtain of their shells, Lombartzyde was regained by the heartened Belgian infantry. And now the floods began to rise. Slowly the waters crept around the German boots, rising imperceptibly until batteries of heavy howitzers found themselves trapped and incapable of movement. Water-logged earth proved even more effectual than scorched earth, and the ancient, desperate expedient had once more brought relief to King Albert's sorely-tried soldiers. The French marines had stood like a stone wall in Dixmude despite crippling losses; the Forty-Second Division, after a futile attack at Nieuport, had arrived to thicken up the southern flank; and Sir Douglas Haig's First Corps was beginning to march into what would soon be known for ever as the Salient.

Sir Douglas himself had visited Rawlinson at Ypres on the 18th and was coolly disdainful of what he found there.

> I was amused with Rawlinson's staff. His General Staff consists of two Regulars, R. A. K. Montgomery R.A. and Dallas, who had a bad sun-stroke in India, from War Office. Amery, the writer of "The Times History of the South African War", was in charge of his Intelligence Section, while Toby Rawlinson (his brother) acted as Mess President. The latter is now graded as Colonel, though he left the 17th Lancers as a subaltern. Joe Laycock and the Duke of Westminster were A D Cs. There were 2 or 3 other officers about who in peace time were connected with motors or polo ponies. I should prefer for serious business to have on my Staff more trained officers of the Regular Army.

This was less than charitable or even fair; Sir Douglas's Corps was the pre-war Aldershot Command and contained the only complete trained Staff in the BEF. Most of the other corps commanders had been compelled to assemble and train their staffs as they went along, but at least they had been provided with the necessary officers. Rawlinson had been furnished with no staff at all. (Dallas had been picked up almost by accident, having been sent by Kitchener to Antwerp and having no duties to perform after the fall of the city.) Though Sir Henry Rawlinson did not fit exactly into the mould of most pre-1914 general officers, he did not of his own choice select a staff so idiosyncratic.

The duties of Mess President took up only a very small part of Toby's time, for he and his motor-car spent the whole of the battle known as First Ypres acting as his brother's corps cavalry. Sir Henry was, in fact, in almost total ignorance of everything that was happening other than he could discover at first hand. He had been given an absurd order by Sir John French to attack towards Menin on the 19th, and had wisely abandoned the enterprise when he realized that the German strength was far greater than anything Sir John had contemplated; he knew that two French Territorial divisions covered by de Mitry's cavalry corps were supposed to be taking over the line between Ypres and Dixmude, but he had had no contact with them. He knew that Allenby's cavalry were also supposed to be linking up with him to the south in the general direction of Mount Kemmel and Messines, but that exhausted his knowledge in that direction. Much more had to be learnt about these critical matters, and Toby was the only man fit to be entrusted with the task of finding out.

During the 14th, Sir Julian Byng's cavalry were assigned the task of taking ground to the north of the city to join hands with the French, the Belgians or whatever other allies they might find between Ypres and the sea. The Seventh Division, still almost without casualties, except for stragglers in the course of its retreat, was in line to the east, to cover the city and to join hands with Third Corps as soon as it put in an appearance. Until that should happen, the right flank was in the air, but nothing could be done about it. Toby was bidden to drive to Poperinghe to find some suitable place for Corps Headquarters. First he tried the Château de Lovie, where the old Baron and Baroness were still in residence with their numerous family. They declined to move, but dined Toby royally, footmen attending him in white gloves. Sir Henry came to the conclusion that it was not quite the place he was seeking and bade his brother to try again. The next choice was a substantial but firmly shuttered house in Poperinghe itself. Toby, properly equipped with requisitioning order, approached the municipality only to be told that, as the owner was away, it was quite out of the question for him to be permitted to force an entry. Even when further inquiries elicited the information that the house belonged to a German gentleman who had recently returned to the Fatherland, they continued obdurate. Toby detailed a few passing soldiers to help him break down the door, while a disapproving party of officials stood by, making copious notes of the damage he did. The house served as Corps Headquarters for the next ten days. There was a considerable, and by no means fanciful, spy scare at the time, and Toby learnt of one instance of how the German intelligence worked. An officer walking across the square in Ypres noticed a pigeon circling overhead; when it appeared to have got its bearings, it landed on the roof of one of the old houses which still stood there, walked along the gutter and halted by a dormer window, out of which a hand reached and swiftly grabbed it. The officer reported what he had seen and a squad of military police paid the house a visit. There they found a party of Germans with a loft of carrier pigeons, with which they were keeping up a regular communication with General von Beseler's headquarters. As Toby succinctly put it, "this ingenious and very effective system of furnishing information, it is needless to record, they did not live to continue".

At about this time intelligence was received that de Mitry and the two French Territorial divisions were moving into their allotted position somewhere about the Forest of Houthulst, between the Belgian right at Dixmude and Byng's cavalrymen. No details were available and, as the reports from the other direction compelled the view that the big German attack could not be far off, Toby was sent to find them and to report exactly where they were and what they were doing. With an Intelligence officer for passenger and with copious ammunition for his machine-gun, he drove north through Poelcapelle and Staden towards Cortemark. They came upon one of the Territorial divisions, whose bearing did not impress Toby with confidence in their ability or willingness to stand and fight. Toby spoke scathingly of them as excessively equipped with facial hair and paunches; they were, for the most part, middle-aged men, fathers of families, who had long since finished their period of conscript service and now, to their astonishment, found themselves recalled for duty.

De Mitry's cavalry, however, had been a *corps d'élite* before the war and had given an excellent account of themselves since, though they had been grossly overworked. Toby encountered the first small parties of them south of the Roulers–Cortemark road and was given the information that two of the four divisions were in position, dismounted, some distance to the north, and that they were being attacked all along the front. This was not good news, for the French cavalry of 1914 were trained to fight only from the saddle, and their *mousqueton*, the only firearm they carried, was about as lethal as a rook-rifle. Furthermore their huge boots and brass helmets made them slow-moving on foot. However, he had to find them, and as heavy firing was audible from a wood about a mile to the north of the road he turned the Hudson in that direction.

After a while Toby and his passenger found themselves travelling along a narrow sunken lane which ended at an isolated cottage whose garden, clearly, formed a part of the firing line. Beyond lay a field of vegetables half a mile wide and beyond that again was the wood itself. Bullets were whistling and cracking over their heads as Toby and his companion left the car in order to see what was happening. In front of the cottage there was a long view of a mile or more in either direction and wherever they looked they saw the incongruous figures of dragoons and cuirassiers falling back. Toby's first thought was to turn the car for a quick getaway, a purpose which he accomplished by driving it through the garden and swinging it round. Then, from a position behind a bush, he set to work with his machine-gun, firing belt after belt into the German position on the edge of the wood. After expending about 2,000 rounds in this fashion, he noticed the leaves in front of him to be moving in a way that no leaves should, so he transferred his attention to these; enthusiasm at the chance to use his gun against a real target got the better of him and he "browned" the greater part of the field in the hope of flushing out some at least of its presumed occupants. None appeared and, as the German bullets were coming thicker and faster, Toby decided that it was time to go. As the car drove back up the sunken lane, grey figures rose up from behind every clump, some less than fifty yards away, and the return journey was enlivened by a clatter of ill-directed musketry. They made their way back through numbers of the cavalrymen, some of whom were travelling on hands and knees, with Toby, "full of pride and folly", refusing either to stoop down or to drive fast. It was fortunate for him that the German Fourth Army was largely made up of young volunteers whose musketry training had been very incomplete. After a little they stopped, and from the vantage point of a haystack he and the Intelligence officer watched the German infantry coming across the road. Reckoning that he had carried out his task, Toby returned to Ypres as fast as the Hudson would go and reported that "the enemy were advancing at a rate which would clear the country of opposition over a distance of 10 miles a day and that there were no troops on that flank which were capable of holding up the advance".

Next morning Sir Henry sent him back again to find out how far the retirement had gone, what the cavalry were up to and what had become of the Territorial divisions. At first, the only French he could find was a small patrol near Dixmude; their leader told him airily that there were five cavalry divisions in that part of the country but they had all "retired" and he would find their headquarters in the Forest of Houthulst, some ten miles further south. With this unpromising information, Toby decided to go and see whether the Territorials were in any better case. He found them around Staden, a couple of miles east of the forest, and was not immediately captivated by what he saw. The "respectable elderly gentlemen" were engaged in the digging of trenches, which Toby had to admit were not at all badly sited, but a more critical examination revealed that this was not their major activity. The digging was perfunctory and a great mass of transport wagons was drawn up close behind in order to facilitate a quick departure. Every vehicle, Toby noted, was ready facing homewards so that not a moment should be lost when the time came. When, soon afterwards, the entire division decamped, it advanced as its reason the fact that "les ennemis ont tiré sur nous". He quitted them in disgust and drove back to look for de Mitry.

At an inn in the forest he came upon the General and his staff; de Mitry was a fine soldier in the old tradition of Lasalle and Murat and his command comprehended five fine divisions of regular horse. For once, Toby found him in despair, the days of storming villages long forgotten. Toby explained the purpose of his call and asked pertinently what this large force was doing, adding some information of his own about the activities he had observed on the previous day. At this the natural reserve of the Saumur graduate broke down and "he danced about with a wealth of gesticulation and a variety of forcible expressions which were typically French". The whole truth came out when, in reply to Toby's direct question, de Mitry permitted himself the indecorous answer of "Nom de Dieu, ils foutent le camp", which Toby bowdlerized into "By God, they are running away."

Sick at heart he returned once more to Ypres to add this awful news to Sir Henry's other burdens. Mercifully, that same night the dykes were opened and the immediate danger passed. On his next journey north he was able to see the accumulating waters and to learn that the Germans were abandoning many of their drowned positions. For the rest of the war one heavy battery, forsaken and abandoned, was a well-known landmark.

On 20 October the vanguard of Haig's First Corps began to reach the line and to take up its position on the left of Byng's cavalry between Ypres and the Forest of Mouthulst. It was not a moment too soon, and on the following day Haig attacked north-east towards Poelcapelle, still ignorant of the overwhelming strength of the enemy. Sir Henry Rawlinson seized the opportunity of doing something to help create a flank in the south and moved the Third Cavalry Division down towards Messines, where he hoped they would be able to join forces with Allenby's horsemen, still fighting their way forward from around La Bassée. He desired that Toby should go with them, so that his speed and mobility could be used to bring the two formations into touch with each other, but Toby had become a casualty. It came about as follows.

After his visit to de Mitry, Toby had returned to the German gentleman's house in Poperinghe for food and a brief rest. In his room he had poured out a healing draught of whisky, which he topped up from a bottle of Vichy water which stood on the mantelpiece. It tasted rather nasty but Toby was in no mood to be hypercritical—Vichy water is not the ideal accompaniment to good Scotch at the best of times—and he finished his frugal meal before retiring to bed. On waking next morning he felt very ill indeed, "with a green sweat breaking out all over me", but made his way to the car and drove to his usual place outside the Cloth Hall to await the next summons. Once there, he pulled the waterproof sheet over his head and lost consciousness. The next thing he knew was that somebody was standing over him saying, "What the devil is the matter? You look like death." Toby mustered up enough strength to reply that this was an entirely accurate description of the way he felt, and soon after, a doctor arrived and took him back to Poperinghe. There the bottle of Vichy water was examined and found to contain "a carbolic disinfectant of extraordinary strength". He was dosed with "all conceivable and inconceivable purges", subjected to indignities with a stomach-pump and "it was not until two or three days later that a very green-looking and tottering shadow took the little gun-car out again". To the end of his days Toby was never certain whether or not he had been booby-trapped.

In spite of this, he soon reported himself to Sir Julian Byng at Wytschaete and was taken to the summit of Kemmel Hill, from where the entire Salient unfolds like some giant sand-table. Sir Julian explained that he urgently needed information about Allenby's whereabouts and pointed out that large numbers of von der Marwitz's raiding cavalry were about the place, trapped between the two wings of the British cavalry formations. The woods around Kemmel and Ploegsteert were believed to be sheltering many of them and all the roads to the south and east were said to be barred. The two men studied the landscape; there was no sign of life anywhere, nor did any sound reach them from the plain below, in spite of the still air. Toby, made wise by past experience, commented on the ominous absence of any peasant working his fields; Sir Julian took the point, but his need of news was desperate and he asked Toby to drive south-eastwards towards Wulverghem and see what he could find that way. It was an exceedingly dangerous assignment for one man in an unarmoured racing-car, but Toby did not hesitate. Still feeling ill, he drove off up a farm track leading in the general direction of Wulverghem and Messines.

Before he reached the village Toby ran into trouble. The track was of slippery clay without a trace of metalling and the driving wheels of the Hudson began to spin uselessly; soon he was completely bogged. The fields on either side were of deep ploughland and offered him no help. For a moment he sat disconsolately in the mud-splattered car and considered giving up his task and walking home. Then he began to lecture himself on the theme that "it is well for the man who goes first to have some resource" and got out to see what could be done. Less than a furlong ahead he spotted by the roadside a heap of gravel, obviously intended for road repairs. He ran joyfully to it, stripping off his expensive leather driving coat as he went, and then spread out the coat on the slimy ground. After filling it with as much gravel as he could carry, he staggered with it back to the car; it did the trick and he managed to turn the car without too much difficulty. On the principle that negative information is always useful, he drove back to report to Byng that there was no life on the Wulverghem road; he found him drinking coffee at a table set by the roadside outside a café on the slope commanding the valley between Kemmel Hill and Neuve Église. The fact that he presented a splendid target to any of the Germans who were certainly nearby weighed not at all with him against the desirability of seeing for himself the advance of his division.

He sent Toby off again almost at once, this time to take a Gunner officer up the road towards Neuve Église to reconnoitre the best artillery positions should the ridge opposite be held by the enemy. (The ridge rises to a height of about 250 feet, not much more than half of that of Kemmel, but still a considerable eminence for Flanders. Neuve Église is about half-way up it.) Nothing happened, but while he was waiting Toby noticed some houses alongside the road in the valley which "looked as if they might contain Germans" and also, half-way up the side of the ridge, an isolated cottage, beyond which, he conjectured, there might very well be a road-block. He could not see as much as he would have liked, because the road was overhung with trees, so he obtained Byng's permission to go back up the road, alone this time, and see what lay at the top. The trip seemed likely to be no more than routine but it turned out to be the most adventurous even in Toby's career.

Toby drove cautiously down into the valley until he came within sight of the houses he had noticed; he stopped about a furlong from them. They were the conventional type of two-storied Belgian cottage with dormer windows projecting from the upper floor; no sound or movement came from them, but to Toby's experienced eye they had an air of very recent occupation. To test his theory, he sighted the Colt on each window in turn and loosed off a belt of 250 rounds. The impact of his bullets made a very satisfactory noise as they smashed the windows and brought down a shower of tiles, but nothing more dramatic happened. Toby decided to move on. He crept slowly up the road towards the cottage, steering with one hand and holding the pistol-grip of his gun with the other, and as he cleared the overhanging trees he caught sight of the object he had expected to see. A substantial barricade of earth four feet six inches high and made in two overlapping parts completely blocked the road; luckily he was by then abreast of the cottage, and he swung the car sharply to his left behind it. There he waited, as dusk fell. It seemed that no one had noticed him or had paid attention to the racket made by the machine-gun. He therefore produced his field-glasses and took stock of the situation.

The barricade was 160 yards from him. (He paced it out after the war.) To the right, about a mile away, he could see small parties of British troops on the lower slopes of Kemmel Hill, while to his left he could see the square tower of Neuve Église. Equally plain were the Germans with several machine-guns on its roof. Toby repeated his drill of Thielt, moving the gun to its rear mounting and backing the car until only its tail and the muzzle of the gun could be seen from the barricade. This accomplished, he settled down to wait again. After a few minutes a German officer strolled out from behind the barricade and examined the country to the south through his glasses; apparently he saw the same British soldiers as Toby had noticed, for he called out something, which Toby could not catch, to his men behind the earthwork and a motor-cyclist emerged at once. The officer spoke to him, pointed in the direction of the troops, and then made an unmistakable gesture towards the church tower. There could be no doubt but that he was ordering the man to take the information which would bring down fire on British soldiers and Toby felt no compunction this time about becoming a combatant. As the soldier saluted, Toby pressed the trigger, "clenched my teeth and kept the shower of bullets going until they were both down and lay quite still". For a full minute he continued to watch the barrier, ready to fire again at anything which might appear, but no movement came; presently he saw a small dust-cloud rising from behind it, from which he drew the conclusion that the defenders were off.

Having transferred the gun to its usual bow-chaser position, Toby backed out into the road and charged the barricade, "with my finger on the trigger and my heart in my mouth". There was nobody there. He stopped for a moment to make sure that his two victims were quite dead ("as I might have been able to do something for them") and, as there was no room for doubt on that score, he thoughtfully cut a new German great-coat from the back of the motor-cycle, "as it could be of no further service to its late owner but would be very acceptable to me during the cold nights and long drives I was then experiencing". Then he set out in pursuit, having made a mental note that the machine-gunners had disappeared from the church tower of Neuve Église. From the top of the hill he could see no trace of the departing Uhlans, save for a little dust still hanging in the air. He deduced, correctly, that they must have gone down the long slope towards Messines, a course that even the Hudson could not follow. Still hopeful of cutting them off, Toby drove down the Messines road as fast as his car would take him, again with one hand for the wheel and the other for his gun. It was not long before he caught sight of them, a full squadron of Uhlans galloping at a speed which should have broken their horses' hearts. In order to make them improve even on this performance. Toby fired short bursts at them. "I had not any hope of hitting them at the speed at which I was moving, but was determined to keep them on the run, as that was a spectacle which afforded me the utmost satisfaction." As the exhilaration of the chase died down, however, he began furiously to think about what he should do next. Even Toby was not sufficiently sanguine to believe that he could destroy or capture an entire squadron of regular cavalry single-handed; he was heading away from his friends at a fast speed, and if the squadron leader were to recover his wits and turn about the little car would be swamped by a hundred horsemen. It was clearly time to bring the escapade to an end and go home. As he was preparing to do so, luck gave him an unexpected bonus. One of the riders at the rear of the column was suddenly shoved off the road by the press of numbers and, from a distance of 100 yards, Toby "distinctly saw the horse turn completely over as he lost his footing". Horse and man disappeared, upside down, into what turned out to be an exceptionally deep and muddy ditch, while the remainder of the squadron galloped on. Toby pulled up and was greeted by the sight of four horse-shoes glittering in the air; there was no trace of the rider. He was underneath, down in the ditch, with his leg pinned between the saddle and the bank. Toby advanced menacingly on him, pistol in hand, but it soon became plain that there was no fight left in the miserable object. The horse was kicking furiously, squashing the unfortunate man with its body at every writhe, and Toby, "at some considerable risk of being kicked by the horse", hauled him out. It required some effort and success was not achieved until one of the man's legs slid out of its boot, which remained under the animal. Toby heartlessly refused to waste time in rescuing the boot, but piled his victim into the mechanic's seat and headed back towards Ypres with tangible evidence of what had happened. He had a little difficulty in passing some of the Allies' road-blocks with a palpable German at his side, but eventually, before midnight, he reached his usual parking place by the Cloth Hall. He and his Hudson were well-known to Fourth Corps by now, and most people were aware that he was missing. As he drove between the fires lit in the Grote Markt, a roar of cheering went up which brought Sir Henry to the window of his office on the first floor of the great building. In reply to his testy inquiry as to what was going on, a voice bellowed out, "It's all right, sir. He's back and he's got a prisoner." As Toby later put it, "Having got a good grip from my brother's hand, I drove straight on to Poperinghe and had a good night's rest without, on this occasion, drinking any of the Vichy water on the mantelpiece."

"Late one afternoon somewhere in the neighbourhood of Kemmel Hill", Toby completed his primary task; the vedettes of John Vaughan's Third Cavalry Brigade and the little Hudson met, and at last the right of the line before Ypres had something more solid than air upon which to rest. As had been the case with the arrival of the First Corps in the north, the junction did not come a moment too soon. As the floods were rising before Dixmude, so was the Allied line becoming thicker and stronger; yet it did not approach in power the forces now massed against it and of which the tireless pilots of the RFC brought daily tidings. The line ran drunkenly from Nieuport to Ypres, around the edge of the Salient, which at that time bellied out to include Langemarck, Broodseinde, Gheluvelt and Zandvoorde, where it doubled back westwards to Hollebeke. From Hollebeke it continued direct to Messines, leaving Wytschaete well inside the line, and then south, in front of Ploegsteert to La Bassée and beyond. When Sir Douglas Haig's First Corps marched in, the Seventh Division was moved south to the lower hinge of the Salient and opposite the point where a new German army, commanded by General von Fabeck and with six divisions and a powerful artillery, was being interposed. North of Zonnebeke there now stood the French Ninth Corps, in place of the feeble defence which Toby had encountered. Byng's and Allenby's dismounted cavalry carried the line to its junction with Pulteney's Third Corps. Toby's journeys were now shorter but even more frequent (he became one of the most well-known sights of Ypres, though who he was and what his functions were generally unknown), and he had an unrivalled view of the Old Army as it went into its last and greatest fight. The Seventh Division had been made up of 400 officers and about 12,000 men when it had detrained at Bruges three weeks earlier; the storm broke upon it in the early hours of 23 October, by which date it had already lost 162 officers and 4,340 men. By the time it was withdrawn from the line at the end of the month, only forty-four officers and 2,336 men remained on their feet. The line remained unbroken.

For Toby it was a time of heartache; not a day passed without his visiting several units, and scarcely a visit passed without his hearing of the death or mutilation of old friends. Years later he still found himself unable to write of it.

Ypres saw the last of him before the great battle had reached its climax. On 27 October Sir Henry was ordered to hand over what was left of his shattered but victorious Fourth Corps to Sir Douglas Haig and to go home. Toby, masterless, went with him. The Duke of Westminster, not being *persona gratissima* with Haig, left also and joined the Navy, which gave him command of a squadron of armoured cars.

Toby recovered some of his spirits during the journey home, for it turned into a triumphal progress. The car, with a German helmet lashed on each front mudguard, was mobbed in Boulogne and even more enthusiasm was shown for his reassuring "Ça tient toujours" to every anxious question about the state of affairs in the Salient. Much the same thing happened as he drove along the Old Kent Road, where his *Pickelhauben* produced equal interest. He went at once for a rest at the home of Borritt, but its proximity to Salisbury Plain drew him to be present with Sir Henry at the inspection of the Eighth Division and he devoted most of his leave to watching the RFC exercising in the novel art of artillery spotting. On 6 November the brothers returned to France.

Chapter Six

They arrived back in the forward area on 12 November, the day after the first battle of Ypres officially came to an end. Sir Henry's Fourth Corps had been reconstituted after its brief disbandment and now comprised his old Seventh Division, brought by fresh drafts to a strength of over 7,000, and the Eighth. The latter was the last Regular division of all, put together by Kitchener from battalions gathered in from the uttermost garrisons. The Third Cavalry Division, battered almost to pieces but triumphant, had gone to join the Cavalry Corps and would not return. Its new sector was to the south, in the plain of the Lys around Armentières, sandwiched between the Third Corps on the north and the newly-arrived Indian Corps of General Willcocks to the south. There the Rawlinsons had many friends, for their connection with India was of long standing. Their father, the first baronet and also named Henry, had been a major-general in the service of the East India Company and had been a member of the last board of directors when that venerable institution was wound up. His fame, however, lay in the fact that he had served in the wild places of Persia and the Middle East, in the course of which he had become the first great Assyriologist. (His translation of the Behistun Inscription had provided the key to the ancient cuneiform script.) He had returned home to marry late in life (he had been born in 1810) and from him his sons had inherited an enthusiasm for India and things Indian. Both Sir Henry and Toby had spent much of their careers there and the former had been a member of the military family of Lord Roberts, to whom he was devoted. They had a third brother, who became a parson.

Trench warfare had now begun in earnest and "trench" was the modish word of the moment. From official sources came trench boots, trench periscopes and, occasionally, trench boards. The military outfitters in London purveyed trench-coats, trench-daggers, trench-waders and so on. There also appeared, fortuitously, trench-feet and trench-fever, for this was the coldest and wettest winter of the century so far. Articles with good Crimean names, such as cardigans and Balaclava helmets, appeared once more on the battlefield, and even older memories were stirred by an issue of hairy goatskin jerkins which made their wearers look like Ancient Britons. For all that, they were very welcome and highly prized, for possession of one of these after the smooth leather variety became general marked a man out as a 1914 soldier.

Toby, still in his colonel's disguise, was spared the worst rigours, but even so his lot was not a happy one. The château on the outskirts of Merville which served as Corps Headquarters contained a hot-water system which appeared to date from the early Bronze Age. As it did not work, Toby was bidden to employ his mechanical talents in putting it to rights; but discovering it to be the most "infernally complicated and rotten" system that he had ever come across, he could do little to it. It came as a relief to find that some unknown genius had kindled the fires with the boilers empty and that they were burst beyond repair. The best that Toby could do was to botch up the windmill and pumps so that at least they had a supply of cold water. In intervals between grappling with the plumbing he once more took on his function of Mess President, for the great forest of Nieppe was only a mile away and Toby was a dead shot with any sort of firearm. He had no luck with the deer but pheasant figured regularly on the Corps Headquarters menu. To add to his pleasure Lieutenant-Commander The Duke of Westminster RNVR arrived shortly afterwards with his armoured cars and established himself in another, probably better appointed, château some fifteen miles to the north, and "many a good dinner and cheery evening was spent there, which I most thoroughly enjoyed".

Life, however, held more for Toby than plumbing and pheasants. The front had quietened down for the winter, but the German long-range artillery galled the men in the trenches day in and day out. The British guns which could reach far enough to reply were few and ammunition was scarce. The daily dribble of casualties became accepted as a fact of life about which it was impossible to do anything. Before long, however, things suddenly became very much worse. No army had started out equipped for the siege-warfare forced upon them by long trench lines, but the Germans had been quicker off the mark than the others. Batteries of the heavy mortars known as *Minenwerfer* (mine-throwers) appeared for the first time; they had no pretensions to accuracy, but lobbed great canisters of explosive high into the air, whence they descended to explode with a deafening roar;

where the mine landed in a trench the defenders who escaped the blast were, more often than not, buried alive, for a single mine could obliterate an entire traverse. Quite apart from the casualties the mines caused, they depressed even the stoutest spirits and there was no means of retaliation.

The problem was, of course, not confined to the front of the Fourth Corps, and every general pressed into service such masters of improvisation as he could find. Contraptions of all kinds began to appear—spring-guns, catapults and every form of ballista and wild-ass. Sir John French consulted his friend Moore, an American engineer. Sir Henry Rawlinson consulted his brother Toby. They agreed that mortars probably existed, for they had been made in large numbers and of all shapes and sizes for the bombardment of Sebastopol sixty years before. The bomb-ketch had been one of the standard weapons of the Royal Navy until the advent of steam and had done valuable work during the eighteenth and early nineteenth centuries. Toby had useful friends in the engineering world, many of them in France. It was his suggestion that he should go and find mortars and bring them into action.

He drove to Paris and went at once to see Colonel Chauchat, the head of the Arsenal at Puteaux, whom he knew well. Chauchat had just completed his design for a light automatic, which was to be issued in large numbers to the French infantry. It was not his fault that the factories made many of them so badly that when, years later, they were issued to the Americans, they refused to accept them and demanded the Lewis. Chauchat received Toby cordially and listened to his problem. He came up with the best solution possible. Certainly there were mortars stowed away in the recesses of the French arsenals and museums; they were, of course, all of great antiquity, some indeed going back to the days of Villars and Marlborough, but something might be made of them. He armed Toby with the necessary piece of paper and suggested that he begin his search at Versailles.

There Toby saw a sight that made him rub his eyes: every conceivable kind of mortar ever used by the French in war was there. Each piece was beautifully made, cast from the very finest gun-metal, and, he was assured, great quantities of cast-iron spherical bombs were held to go with them. Having earmarked a few of the most promising for his purpose, Toby went to call on General Galliéni, the governor of Paris. The veteran general did not restrict himself to permitting Toby to take what he wanted, but gave him *carte-blanche* to use the Versailles ranges for his experiments and placed two young engineer officers at his disposal to help.

Now the real problems began. First there was the question of a propellant. Mortars have not changed much throughout the ages: they consist of a tube which cannot be varied very much from an angle of about forty-five degrees and are loaded from the muzzle. Differing ranges are obtained by varying the strength of the propelling charge. All the old guns were, of course, designed to be used with black powder and emitted a cloud of smoke on being fired. If that were to happen in the line, they would never have the opportunity of firing again, for the smoke would draw on them the retaliation of every artillery weapon in range. Some sort of smokeless charge was needed, but modern smokeless explosive differs from the old powder more than in degree. Put simply, black powder explodes: when the spark ignites it, it burns comparatively slowly in the process of converting itself into gas. Cordite and the other modern successors detonate: the whole charge goes off instantly with stunning violence. The art of gun-barrel proofing is based on an understanding of this. Worse still, from Toby's point of view, the old mortars were worn and had never been bored with mathematical accuracy; there was a good deal of "windage" between the walls of the tube and the outside of the bomb passing through it. It did not matter much with black powder, for the worst it could cause in that case was some loss of power and accuracy. With cordite, the gases would rush past the projectile and probably leave it in the barrel, even if they failed to blow it up where it sat. All this Toby knew very well, but he was a thoroughly practical engineer and not easily daunted. If the bombs did not fit the bore, they must be made to fit. He set off for Paris with four six-inch mortars, the smallest size, each bearing the escutcheon of Louis Philippe. They had been cast at Douai in 1847. With them he took 100 of the spherical bombs and made immediately for the workshops of the old motor-car company. The spheres of most of the bombs were imperfect; this obstacle he overcame by fitting each with "a species of wooden shoe or cup into which the bomb was bolted". This device, together with metal rings which expanded and acted as gas-checks when the charge was fired, proved promising. Next, some sort of fuse was necessary, for a bomb is not of much use unless it bursts at the right moment. Toby made fuses. They had to be percussion fuses, operated by their striking something solid, so the next problem was to ensure that the bomb would hit the ground fuse first. This part of the task was rich in ingenuity: first he tried links of chain attached to the tail to keep the missile from revolving in the air. It worked fairly well but was obviously not the right answer. The correct one came up partly by accident: the wooden cup was fastened to the bomb by a long bolt and, when the cup was destroyed by the blast, the bolt stopped it from spinning. With this discovery Toby felt ready to begin practical tests, and on 28 November he returned to

Merville with all his paraphernalia.

There was a large audience of generals, staff officers and professional gunners waiting to watch the performance and Toby understandably felt apprehension. The mortars were set up in a ploughed field fifty yards from the road; along its edge ran a deep and very muddy ditch, into which many of the spectators fell. Flags were run out about 300 yards away and Toby's Frenchmen began the bombardment.

> We were able to keep up quite a decent rate of fire from our little battery. The direction and accuracy of range left a great deal to be desired but the bombs went off all right and the importance of the explosions astonished everyone. Great chunks of the field were blown in all directions and any trench or parapet in the vicinity would most certainly have been utterly destroyed. More important still, no bomb failed to explode; and none exploded before, or in any other place than when and where they were intended to. Nor did any mortar burst.

There was still a long way to go, but it was a start. The demonstration had proved that the old mortars could be used with smokeless powder; it remained to be shown that they had range and hitting power enough to be of service. Toby was told to go back to Paris and persevere, a grant of £100 being voted for the purpose.

Once back in the capital, Toby carried out another raid on the museums. A specimen of each kind of mortar there was removed to his workshop for renovation: there were more of the six-inch variety already used, which two men could carry; a nine-inch model which required a bearer party of ten; and two monsters which weighed several tons. Each was painstakingly rebored with modern machinery to precise tolerances. The job was well done and even the exacting Toby was pleased with the result. (He was not a comfortable person for whom to work: of his French assistants, two were killed during trials and a third had half of his face blown off.) Now it remained to fabricate proper projectiles, for the would-be spherical bombs were clearly not good enough. Amongst his other accomplishments Toby had a gift for wood-carving. With loving care he turned out a wooden mock-up of a shell for each calibre of mortar and then supervised the casting of them in steel. He decided to try the first test on the biggest mortar of them all, the thirteen-inch giant which had, in all probability, been constructed to smash the Malakoff.

The test, alas, was a disaster. After the plunger of the electric exploder had been depressed, there was a roar like a major earth-quake and the whole party was flung violently to the ground; after they had recovered themselves, they found, in place of the pit in which the mortar had stood, a vast, smoke-filled crater at the bottom of which could be discerned several large masses of gun-metal. An hour later, when the team had transferred their attention to another and smaller mortar, a cortège was seen to be approaching from the direction of the town a mile and a half away. It comprised four men pushing a hand-cart on which reposed a large, heavy lump of what was plainly gun-metal, and it was escorted by a very excited civilian who appeared to be in the throes of some sort of a fit. As they drew nearer, Toby recognized without difficulty that they were bringing him a part of the muzzle of the great mortar. It turned out that the great chunk of gun-metal had demolished an outstandingly vener-able tree that was the pride of the town and that stood near the café of which the excited bearer of the news was the proprietor. Toby, influenced equally by considerations of security and common pru-dence, denied that the mortar had been despatched by him and pointed out that the mortars with which he and his assistants were occupied were far too small to have been responsible. He neverthe-less offered to give the mortar a meticulous examination. Only half convinced, but not being anxious to push the thing for another hour, they partly accepted the offer and returned whence they had come. As soon as they were out of sight, all hands turned to and filled in the crater, with the meteorite at the bottom of it.

The shells for the six-inch weapon were far more satisfactory, and by a long process of trial and error one was finally produced which weighed ninety pounds, more than half the weight of the gun itself, and contained three times as much explosive as the shell of a seventy-five-millimetre gun. The nine-inch model, with an early pat-tern of shell weighing fifty pounds, attained a range of nearly a mile and, when fired into a wood, blew up the trees by the roots. Reluc-tantly, however, Toby came to the conclusion that it was too cum-bersome and did not pursue it further. A good number of the small model would be more serviceable and needed far less diversification of everything.

Throughout all this time Toby was coming near to disproving the famous observation of Sir Boyde Roche that "not being a bird, he could not be in two places at the same time". There was the factory in Paris and the depot at Merville, where mortar crews were in training, to supervise, and frequent visits to General Galliéni and his Chief of Staff, General Clergerie, were necessary, to keep them informed of progress. Toby became a firm friend of Clergerie and learnt from him a good deal about the anti-aircraft defences of Paris;

this information was to come in useful later. From Paris to Merville by road is all of 150 miles and many long, solitary journeys through the freezing December nights could not be avoided. As often as not it snowed, and Toby learned to dread one particular hill between Doullens and St Pol: this caught the wind to such an extent that "nine times out of ten it was a sheet of ice".

On the last night of November, whilst he was working in the bitter cold of the château at Merville, there came a message direct from GHQ that the King was coming to luncheon there next day and would be bringing with him President Poincaré, Generals Joffre and Foch and other highly placed dignitaries. Toby was very sensible of the honour done to his brother's corps but could have wished that another day had been chosen, as there was nothing more than a few tins of corned beef in the Mess larder. The mortars and everything to do with them were hastily put aside, and at the first streak of dawn the Mess President was out in the forest with his gun and a trusted companion. They hoped for a deer but the game was coy and the undergrowth thick. In the end they came back with six pheasants from which some sort of refection was prepared, so upholding the reputation of Fourth Corps. There was no pheasant left for Toby, but he had the honour of being presented to the King. As there was nothing for him to do whilst his superiors were in conclave, Toby wandered outside to inspect Joffre's splendid limousine, which he knew to be driven by an old friend, the famous racing driver Ballot. The King's car was drawn up to lead the procession, and, as it moved off, Ballot pulled towards the centre of the road to follow it. As he did so, another car coming up from behind tried to cut in front and collided heavily with the rear end of Joffre's vehicle. Joffre, black as thunder, lowered his window and thrust out his head. His controlled rages were famous throughout the French army and Toby waited with interest to listen to what he might have to say to the culprit. All of a sudden the old man's face became wreathed in smiles as he saw what had happened. The Prince of Wales, driving a big Daimler, had got out of control on the slippery road and could not have avoided the impact. Joffre smilingly waved him on, but Ballot, who knew only that some cretin had rammed him from behind, let down his window and addressed the Prince in words that come naturally to a French racing driver in such circumstances. Toby said firmly that it was all Ballot's fault for pulling out without making sure that the road was clear. The Prince in all probability heard nothing of it, which was a pity, for Ballot was an accomplished man the strength of whose language was equalled only by his anguish when he learnt the identity of his victim. Toby went back to Paris and ballistics.

The French authorities had done much for him but their own

needs were such that they could not keep up a supply of explosives. Toby therefore travelled to London to lay his case before the committee which dealt with such matters. There he was told that His Majesty's Government had, for many years past, acknowledged the existence of two kinds of explosive only: those approved by the committee and the rest. This was at the time of the great shell famine, which was to culminate in Sir John French turning to the Press for aid and thus causing great scandal. In something like despair, Toby sought out Lord Moulton, the committee chairman, who furnished him with samples of several different kinds of explosive. Toby took them gratefully back to France and the experiments continued. The production of shell-casings was coming on well enough, but more and more explosive was needed.

Toby went back to London and Lord Moulton, who armed him with authority to demand an explanation of why he could not have what he needed. In due time he was summoned to appear. Toby now was pretty expert in the chemistry of explosives and well able to present his own case, but the atmosphere as he entered the room was bitterly hostile. It was "an august assembly of some twenty venerable representatives of both services". He wanted ammonal, a well-known explosive and much used later in the war; the committee was going to demonstrate why he should not have it. A large register divided into columns was produced and Toby read it over the shoulder of the clerk who held it. In the first column various explosives were named and in the following ones their characteristics analysed. The last column stated "Authorized" or "Unauthorized". Ammonal was "Unauthorized". Toby demanded to know why; he received the plain answer "Hydroscopicity", which is to say, "a tendency to absorb water". Of this quality of ammonal Toby was aware. The next sentence seemed to win his case for him: "on account of its hydroscopicity, this explosive could not be considered as safe to store in His Majesty's magazines for any period in excess of seven years". Toby patiently explained that such a contingency was not probable in present circumstances, and Lord Moulton undertook to provide twenty tons of ammonal within a fortnight. There was, apparently, no crushing shortage of explosives in the winter of 1914–15; much of it merely lacked official approval.

The supply of explosives being organized, Toby turned his attention to shells. The workshop in which the cases were being made did not have the capacity to turn them out in sufficient numbers and steel was running short. The difficulty over the first part was enhanced by the fact that every Frenchman capable of work was already employed and not a man was to be spared for this relatively unimportant project. Toby soon found his factory, through the good offices of an old colleague in the motor industry; M Ribeyrolles, and managed to recruit for it a number of Belgian workers who claimed to have been steel-founders in the Ardennes. Not all of them gave proof of the skill they claimed but they were adequate. After several false starts, Toby got his steel. His spies discovered that there were large quantities of it in Switzerland that had been made in Germany before the war and were now left on the hands of the stockholders. The motor company bought the lot and it gave Toby some pleasure to see the metal, clearly identifiable to the expert eye as the product of a firm in Westphalia, being prepared for use against the country of its origin.

Just after Christmas, Toby, "for some reason which I forget", found himself driving from GHQ at St Omer with Robert de Rothschild, who was employed in some capacity with the Eighth Division, in thick snow. As night fell they managed to lose their way somewhere about Hesdin, where the hills were frozen and slippery. After having many times been forced to get out and push, they eventually stumbled into Abbeville at about two o'clock in the morning, exhausted and perished. The Hotel Tête de Boeuf was full and they passed what remained of the night in armchairs before setting off again early for Rothschild's château at Laversine. After a nightmare journey through snowdrifts, they arrived and spent a luxurious night before continuing the journey to Paris and another Rothschild residence, in the Avenue Marigny, opposite the Elysée.

On the morning after their arrival in Paris, Toby, who had not been feeling at all well for some days past, woke with a raging fever. The Rothschilds' doctor was hurriedly summoned and announced that Toby had congestion of the lungs, brought on by the terrible night drives in the open racer, coupled with extreme overwork. It was a month before he was on his feet again and, as he readily agreed, if he had not been where he was when he fell ill it would most probably have been the end of his time in France, if not of his time on earth. Happily, the production of all the essentials for the mortars was now organized and M Ribeyrolles saw to it that it continued. To the Army, Toby did not officially exist, so no question of Medical Boards arose, and on 28 January he was in Merville again. He had no business to be back at duty without a period of convalescence, but Sir Henry had telegraphed that the authorities had called for another test and that it had been fixed for that day.

He left Paris late on the 27th and drove through the night, arriving at Corps Headquarters soon after dawn. The trials were to begin at 2 p.m.

The gathering was one of particular distinction, headed by the Master-General of the Ordnance himself, Sir Stanley von Donop. Toby spent the morning supervising arrangements, and after the party had finished their luncheon he was satisfied that all was in order. However, one complication arose immediately. The spokesman for the examiners sought out Toby and said that he was to take rather elaborate precautions with such unpredictable weapons and, in particular, was to withdraw all the crews once laying was completed and fire the batteries by electric exploder from a safe distance. Toby had made no arrangements to do so and explained that the only things available on the ground were friction tubes. The friction tube is a simple device which creates a spark when a pin is pulled out by means of an attached wire. Rather grudgingly, he was told to go ahead.

The mortars were loaded and laid, the friction tubes inserted in the vents and the wires led back behind the parapet where the party was standing. At a signal, Toby gave a sharp pull on the wire leading to the first gun. To his horror, instead of the familiar "Crack" of the discharge, the entire mortar turned majestically over and pointed directly at the parapet. He had not made allowance for the fact that the bomb was so heavy in proportion to the weight of the piece that it took only a small strain to unbalance it. As the pin had stuck in the tube, no dire consequence followed and the audience, being gunners, knew that if it did not go off immediately it would not go off at all. All the same, enthusiasm seemed to be sparing as Toby was ordered to try again. The next attempt met with better success and the watchers saw some very pretty shooting. Range and accuracy were better than Toby had dared to expect and it was officially pronounced that one round would have killed any man above ground within a radius of 250 yards from the point of impact. The examiners were satisfied and Toby was delighted. Next day, not surprisingly, he went down with pleurisy. "This, however, lasted only a week and on 5 February I went back to Paris to get the foundry going." The mortars were "approved" and their next appearance would be on the battlefield.

Chapter Seven

So successful were the tests that they became an embarrassment to the inventor. The Master-General officially approved the new weapon under the name of the "Toby" mortar and demanded that forty of them, with 3,000 shells, be made ready at the earliest possible moment. The thing was, of course, done, but not without some difficulties. The motor-works attended skilfully to the reboring of gun after gun as they were disinterred from the vaults in which they had slumbered for so long, but the shells were another matter. Many of the Belgian workmen lacked the skills of which they had vaunted themselves and Toby was forced to spend much precious time in the foundry to "watch the colour of the 'blast' in our steel furnaces in order to make sure that the molten metal was 'drawn off' at exactly the right moment. The metal had then to be poured into the moulds with the greatest care, and our first efforts were far from being as successful as could have been desired." Each shell then had to be tested for flaws and its thickness checked before it was handed over to the machinists to be turned to the exact size to fit the barrel. Meanwhile the training of the gunners continued at Merville, and there again Toby's personal supervision was essential. He came to know the road between that place and Paris as well as he knew his own face.

Day and night the work on the mortars continued, and by 9 May, the date on which the attack on Aubers Ridge was to take place, all was ready. Forty-four Toby mortars with well-trained crews of British soldiers were mustered at Merville and a stream of motor-lorries came in from Paris carrying every possible round of ammunition for them. During the nights which preceded the battle Toby and his second-in-command, Richard Grosvenor (another of Bendor's cousins), were out digging pits for the guns and shelters for their teams. It was hard and dangerous work under a steady rain of German star-shells, and under constant sniping. One working-party lost seven men in a single night, for the mortars were to be well up close to the front-line trenches. The big battery of thirty-two mortars lay only seventy yards behind the front parapet with a sunken cart-track running between the two; to the rear there was no cover at all. When the work was complete there were eleven compartments, each save one housing three mortars, and all cunningly constructed. Every shell had to be carried up by hand, and, somehow, it had all to be done without exciting suspicion.

The barrage was timed to open at 5 a.m. on 9 May. Toby and Dick Grosvenor were to be in charge of the main battery, with the smaller one, consisting of the remaining dozen mortars, away on the left and in the charge of a subaltern. At the last minute Toby was sent for and asked whether some of his guns could be made sufficiently mobile to move forward for the consolidation phase after the attack had succeeded. A quick trip to Paris brought back four pairs of old wheels for which axles were made on the spot. Eight other pairs of wheels and axles followed for the platforms upon which the shells were to be carried forward. He was back with his battery before dawn, having left the car in a ruined farm not far behind.

At first light, everything received a final check; charges were carefully weighed out and packed in their little muslin bags. Fuses were set for various ranges (Toby had not been satisfied with his percussion fuses and had created workable time-fuses from an obsolete model donated by the French artillery), every man was moved to his action station and they sat down to watch the hands moving towards the hour of five. Toby did not like the look of the enemy trenches; though there was nothing visible his usually reliable sixth sense divined movement and it was disquieting when, contrary to habit, the German field-guns began to shell the parapet. There was, however, no great weight of metal falling and, on the dot of five, the Toby mortars roared out. Toby and Grosvenor watched through their glasses from a very exposed position in front. What they saw was "most satisfactory, for our heavy bombs were coming over with the greatest regularity and were falling on, or just beyond, the enemy's parapet. As each one burst great clouds of earth were being thrown up, in the midst of which were to be seen portions of Germans and even machine-guns whilst gaps were also appearing in the parapet itself."

This state of affairs, however, did not last for long; the German gunners, who may well, through the agency of spies, have had some inkling of what was afoot, began to get their location. In a thunder of smoke and flames, part of the parapet by Toby erupted into the air and a sudden pain shot through his right arm and shoulder. He saw Grosvenor lying on the ground a few yards away and made his way over to him.

Grosvenor, who had had all the wind knocked out of him, peevishly inquired whether he still had two legs; Toby was able to set his mind at rest on this score and received in return an assurance that his own arm appeared perfectly undamaged. Having both come to the conclusion that their injuries were not mortal, the two men returned to their places on the parapet. The mortars were still banging away and it was clear that the ninety-pound bombs were doing a lot of damage and that they were

> establishing a "funk" behind the opposite parapet. This was brought home to me when I saw a German officer—a very brave man and they had plenty of them—leap on to the crest of the parapet; then, turning his back to us, he obviously exhorted his men to stand fast, showing them at the same time that he himself was without fear. I am glad to say that, after exposing himself to every shell and bullet for some minutes, he at length jumped down again in safety, having very nobly done his duty.

So far no shells had actually landed in Toby's battery, though it was obvious that the German guns were diligently searching for it. The fire was kept up with great regularity until the moment came when the barrage plan required that the range be increased. Toby went back to the parapet to continue his observation of the fall of the shells, leaving Grosvenor to superintend the mounting of four guns on their carriages to go forward with the attack. He watched with approval "our great shells, which looked splendid as they turned over and over in the air, shining brightly in the early morning sun". Clouds of earth and mud continued to rise, this time a good 200 yards beyond the enemy front line. At this moment, however, the German gunners found them; within a few minutes shells began to fall in ever-increasing numbers around the pits from which the mortars were doing their work. He saw with dismay mortar after mortar being blown up, masses of earth shooting into the air and the stretcher-bearers carrying his wounded men to the rear. The mortar fire slackened and soon it became plain that the battery had shot its bolt, except for Grosvenor's four pieces, which he could see being lifted on to the carriages and moving away to their start line.

Zero hour was very near now and the order was given to set up the ladders. At last the whistles blew all along the line and khaki figures in flat-topped caps moved out into the open, their bayonets gleaming. As they emerged from cover the German machine-guns opened up from a distance of between three and four hundred yards. Men fell in swathes; others at once took their places, only to be cut down in their turn. The artillery bombardment continued to fall on the enemy second-line trenches to prevent the arrival of reinforcements, but, from the German point of view, there were men enough in the front line already.

Toby walked back to see how Grosvenor was getting on, accompanied by Douglas Uzielli, a member of the Stock Exchange and older than he who, having been consistently rejected for service, had attached himself to Fourth Corps as an interpreter. Toby, usually sparing with his praise, described him as "one of the bravest men I have ever seen. There was no expedition of danger for which he did not volunteer, whether it was a night raid into No Man's Land or a working-party digging under fire at night he was always there. On this occasion, when a forlorn hope of mortars was to be dragged along with the first line of the attack, there he was again, encouraging everyone and as happy as he could be to be in the thick of it." Something of the same sort might have been said about his commander.

The battery position was in a sorry state. The eleven neat compartments had been blown into one great crater at the bottom of which lay a jumble of broken mortars, shells and corpses. Only three of the original thirty-two remained intact and Toby set to work to load, aim and fire them himself with only Uzielli to help. The attack was still going in, the artillery support was, in all conscience, feeble enough, and every little might help. German shells, however, continued to search the area and it soon became apparent that the two men were wasting their time. Toby came to the sensible conclusion that he could do no more than wait there for orders, so he curled himself up and went to sleep, shells notwithstanding. Quite the worst of these was the kind that everybody called a "Jack Johnson", from the dense and very black cloud that accompanied its explosion. After a decent period of rest, Toby awoke and occupied himself by "studying the flight of these great projectiles". At a little before noon, having dozed off again, he was sharply awakened by a gun which seemed to be fired in his ear; a British eighteen-pounder had been man-handled across the fields and had taken up a position right beside his lair. As he surmised they would, the Germans drew the conclusion that the Toby mortars were in action again and soon shells of all sizes were "falling all round the work like hailstones in a storm". Toby thought it only common prudence to crawl out and seek refuge in a nearby drain on his way back to the original front-line trench. "I had only gone a few yards when something happened, and from that time onwards my recollections are very vague." What the onlookers saw was a heavy fire being opened on the old mortar position, an occurrence that pleased them as they believed the enemy to be wasting shells on an empty hole in the ground. From it there suddenly came a figure, running from the deserted battery towards the front trench. "They were in no way surprised when a great black shell burst quite close to the running figure and blew it high into the air in a cloud of mud and earth. They were, however, very much surprised indeed when, after a few minutes, the figure arose again; and then, walking quietly and unconcernedly upright, as if taking a stroll down Bond Street on a summer morning, reached the parapet without further injury."

Toby, sublimely unaware of what he was doing, continued on down the communication trench and, without a word to anybody, walked back the two miles or so to the farm where he had left the car. He started the engine, drove to Corps Headquarters and had a quiet sleep in the sun on the lawn there. Refreshed by this, he got up, made his way to his room and went to bed. "I have a hazy recollection of seeing my brother next day, and of telling him that I didn't feel right and that everything seemed to be in a mist." Sir Henry immediately sent him home, without reporting him a casualty, since, officially, Toby did not exist. "At home I got a good rest, though I don't remember very much about that either."

Aubers Ridge had been another heroic failure, nearly 10,000 men being lost for no tangible gain. The Army was still learning its trade; the official history speaks with feeling of the weakness of the British artillery and the paltry effect of the forty-minute barrage which preceded the attack. The men of later attacking battles would have thought it laughable were it not for the tragic results in the loss of irreplaceable trained soldiers. The Toby mortars were used again in small batches, particularly at Hill 60, but Aubers Ridge was the scene of their only appearance in large numbers. The excellent modern weapon invented by Sir Wilfrid Stokes was soon to appear and the mortar was to become, as it still remains, the most useful close support weapon that infantry can ask. Toby Rawlinson should not be denied the status of godfather, or at least that of accoucheur.

The rest and quiet which were his portion for the next six weeks soon pulled him round and he began to speculate on his further employment. On 20 June a staff officer came to see him with a written message from Lord Kitchener. Toby's excitement at opening it soon evaporated in incredulity: it told him, in sharp terms, that he had no right to consider himself an officer as, "whatever passes might be granted in the field on special occasions, the War Office alone had the right of granting commissions". Toby was bitterly angry, not so much at the content of the message as at its brusqueness. His innocent little charade had deceived nobody—except, perhaps, Sir Douglas Haig, and he had not intended to keep it up after his return home.

In a wave of disgust at such treatment after all his unpaid exertions, he decided to follow the example of his friend Bendor. Metaphorically shaking off the dust of the War Office, he crossed Whitehall and entered the Admiralty. Within the hour he emerged as a duly-commissioned Lieutenant-Commander RNVR and with the command of an armoured-car squadron. The metamorphosis involved no great difficulty as armoured-car officers were a part of the Royal Naval Division and wore khaki. His RAC uniform did perfectly well, shorn of stars and crowns but embellished instead with the two and a half rings of gold lace that denoted his new rank. There was still one sacrifice demanded of him: Toby marched into his barber and suffered the removal of the moustache which had been his companion since adolescence. Though a naked upper lip changed his appearance considerably, he never really assumed the likeness of a man of seafaring antecedents. That, however, did not greatly matter and soon he was hard at work training his driver–mechanics and gunners as thoroughly as he knew how.

Then there came a day when he was summoned to the Admiralty by no less a person than the new First Lord, A. J. Balfour, who desired him to meet Admiral Sir Percy Scott. Toby had found a new career.

Chapter Eight

Toby had little difficulty in guessing the nature of the duties about to be imposed on him. War had suddenly come directly to London and London did not like it. For centuries the capital had been spared any contact with an enemy; the last time Londoners had experienced battle on their own threshold had been nearly three centuries before, when the London trained bands had repulsed Rupert's raiding horsemen at Turnham Green. Londoners had trembled in their shoes during the 1745 rebellion and had known some bad moments when Bonaparte's Grande Armée had concentrated at Boulogne, but nothing had ever happened to come between the citizens and the innocent occupation of making money since times so remote that all memory of them had long faded. The concept of the fortified town, familiar to every burgess of Europe, was unknown; from Magdeburg to Metz cities had been besieged and stormed so often that tribal recollections were strong and even a kind of drill, to be carried out when an enemy army appeared before the ramparts, lurked at the back of every continental mind. Within the lifetime of men not yet old, even mighty Paris herself had been encircled and bombarded, with many of her famous buildings put to the torch in the subsequent civil commotion. Of all great cities, London alone was practically undefended, and it was a cruel shock when the lesson was given that the sheltered days were over.

Such feeble defence as existed was entirely the creation of Churchill when First Lord of the Admiralty. When the risk of attack by Zeppelins had first been mooted, Kitchener had made it very clear that it was useless to look to the Army for relief; its own weakness in artillery, dreadfully shown up by every battle since the Aisne, made it quite out of the question for him to divert a single gun or gunner from the task of beating the German army in the field; if the result was that London had to suffer, then suffer it must. Those in authority, and whose posts of duty were in the capital, accepted this stoically. The best Churchill could furnish was a section of two three-inch naval guns on high-angle mountings, crewed by regulars from the Royal Marine Artillery, at the Tower. He was, however, able to supplement them with auxiliaries.

An Anti-Aircraft Corps of the RNVR was called into being very early in the war under Commodore Murray Sueter RN. No such thing as an anti-aircraft gun existed or was even projected, nor was there any form of doctrine on the subject. For a start, however, a number of searchlights were taken away from the fixed defences of various naval harbours and entrusted to the staff of the Office of Works, who were for that purpose sworn in as special constables. Other civil servants were able to join the corps, for it existed only on a part-time basis between the hours of 6 p.m. and 6 a.m. Soon all were enlisted as seamen and some very remarkable weapons were produced for them to man. On the roof of Gresham College was mounted a one-inch pom-pom, captured from the Boers in 1899 and almost worn out. One of the crew, Charles ffoulkes (during daylight hours Master of the Tower Armouries), wrote that they were given a strong warning not to use it for practice purposes more than was absolutely essential, for it might break and no spare parts existed.

There were similar weapons, elsewhere in London, but the guns of the Marines, though not made for the job, were the only ones that could hope to be of the slightest use. Their range was considerable, their projectiles were fused to burst in the air, and, indeed, some of the same pattern were still in service in 1939. The rest were not merely useless but a positive danger; their shells were made to explode, if they would explode at all, only on impact, and unless, contrary to most expectations, they struck some hard part of a Zeppelin (the gas-bag would be far too soft), they would go off on hitting whatever they first met on the way down. On 31 May 1915 the first Zeppelin raid came and, to the surprise only of those who knew nothing about them, the defences proved themselves completely otiose. Only five people were killed and fourteen hurt; the bombs were little more efficient than the defending guns and the damage to buildings was insignificant. This was not, however, the point, for a howl of affronted anger went up from London and a demand, sometimes in hysterical terms, came from every borough that something be done at once. The airship crews were, quite unfairly, cartooned as cowardly murderers of women and babies and threats of vengeance poured out; the citizens of Antwerp and of Ypres might have suggested that far worse had happened to them but that they and their fathers had no comfortable illusions about what war meant. The only response possible was to increase the Marine force, and another four guns were brought in before the next raids at the beginning of September.

Sir Percy Scott was sixty-two and had retired from the Royal Navy in 1909. For the last twenty years of his time he had been, by common consent, the top gunnery expert of the service. The Victorian Navy, never having been called upon to fight a fleet action, took very little interest in gunnery, ranking it as an accomplishment far below seamanship and smartness. It was Scott who, in the words of Fisher, "taught the Navy to hit the target", and his fame was equalled only by his unpopularity. Invention after invention came from his fertile brain: in the 1880s he produced the first practical gun-sight and it was followed by the sub-calibre aiming rifle, the electric director and many other devices of great ingenuity. During the siege of Ladysmith he had done much to make good the Army's weakness by dismounting the 4.7-inch guns of his ship HMS *Terrible*, mounting them on carriages of his own design and construction and sending them with blue-jacket gunners to take on the Boers' Schneider-Creusot "Long Toms". He made a fortune from his inventions and did not suffer fools, whether above or below him in rank; worse, from the Navy's standpoint, he was never slow to claim the credit for other men's work. Since his retirement he had been a very active director of the great Vickers company.

It was not difficult for Toby to put two and two together. His own contacts with the far more experienced French were known and he had been filling in his spare time with the armoured cars by applying his trained engineer's mind to the problem of modifying the existing guns such that they might have some chance of hitting an airship and destroying it. As the speed of a Zeppelin, especially against the wind, was less than that of a motor-car, the task did not seem hopeless.

The September raids took place on two consecutive nights and nearly a hundred bombs were dropped. This time thirty-two civilians were killed and over eighty injured. They were followed by a petition from the Lord Mayor in consequence of which, as Toby put it, "the Government got the wind up and got a move on". He was actually working on one of his designs on the afternoon of 11 September when the summons came. It said no more than that the new First Lord wished to see him at once at the Admiralty, but Toby knew what it meant. It was not work for which he felt any great enthusiasm: his inclinations were far more towards fighting the Germans and the battle of Loos was in the offing. However, it was useless to blink at the fact that his chances of employment there were not bright. The damage done to him at Aubers Ridge was not cleared up and, by some means, his left leg had suffered an injury that compelled him to wear a surgical boot. He had technical knowledge that few, if any, other men possessed, and his duty was clearly to accept whatever post he might be offered.

First Lord Balfour explained that Sir Percy had been appointed to the charge of the air defence of the capital and that their Lordships, knowing of Toby's experience of the organization of Paris, desired him to assist in the establishment of something of the same kind in London. Toby took to the old admiral and they began at once to discuss details. He knew exactly the composition and distribution of the defences of the French capital and it was his own suggestion that he should travel there to see his friends and ascertain what equipment he could beg or borrow. Balfour and Sir Percy cordially agreed and Toby was told to go without delay. The men of his armoured-car squadron could serve as the nucleus of the new force. The general idea was that, as Zeppelins moved so slowly, the guns should be as mobile as possible; they should not sit in fixed positions hoping that the Germans would fly over them at an altitude low enough for them to hit but should go out and hunt their tormentors as best they could. The French, as Toby knew, had just the gun that was needed.

He was not able to leave until the morning of the 16th; even then, the necessary documents had not arrived from the Admiralty, so Sir Percy took a sheet of headed writing-paper and produced a letter to the Minister of War (General Galliéni) in his own hand. Thus equipped, Toby set off for Paris. Sir Percy telegraphed the Naval authorities at Folkestone to give him every assistance, and by the same afternoon the car was speeding along the well-known road to Paris.

Next morning Toby sensibly, before presenting his credentials, paid a call on his friends at the Arsenal in order to find out exactly what was in the French armoury; there could be no harm in Galliéni knowing that Toby was well informed about what was available. There he was shown the latest thing in anti-aircraft guns, the "Canon-Automobile", one of which was just about to undergo final tests before being despatched to the front. Armed with this useful information, he called next on his friend General Clergerie. Clergerie was extremely cordial, observing that he was much relieved to find Toby still alive after his adventures with the mortars. On hearing of his new mission, he led him at once to General Galliéni. He too expressed pleasure at seeing Toby again and said that he would give him all the help he could; the existing guns, however, were already ear-marked for various destinations and only General Joffre himself could authorize the loan of one. He would, however, willingly go so far as to say that, provided Joffre had no objection, Toby might have what he pleased. Satisfied with this, Toby climbed once more into the car and motored to GHQ at Chantilly. He felt sufficiently confident of the help of the Commander-in-Chief of the French army to telephone to the Arsenal before leaving asking that the gun, together with all its bits and pieces, be got ready for the raid against his return. His confidence was not misplaced; Joffre agreed that he should have it, and, within half an hour of entering Chantilly, Toby was leaving it on his way back to Paris.

There he spent several tedious hours, checking every particle of equipment that went with his prize. Even when that was finished, he was not allowed to take it, for the tests were not yet complete. At dawn next day he was in the moat of the fort of Mont Valerien, where the test was carried out to everybody's satisfaction, and just before noon, with a team of French mechanics in charge, the gun and its caisson left on the 160-mile drive to Boulogne.

The "motor-cannon" was, in fact, an ordinary seventy-five-millimetre gun housed in an ingenious mounting which allowed both for a high angle of fire and for a 240-degree traverse; it incorporated a shield and the whole assembly was firmly bolted down on a platform at the rear of a De Dion lorry chassis. To bring the gun into action it was necessary only to lower a strut at each corner of the platform; there was a seat provided for the gunner which rotated with the weapon, and the breech, once the piece had been elevated, was low enough for the loaders to perform their duties from the ground. The "Seventy-five", though it had been in service for nearly twenty years, was a gun far in advance of its time: the breech mechanism was of a rotary nature, simpler and stronger by far than that of any comparable field gun; the rate of fire was very fast; and the muzzle velocity was greater than that of the British eighteen-pounder. A caisson, attached by a towing-bar, carried 200 shells. The big De Dion engine produced an output of 100 horse-power, so that, in spite of its solid tyres, the entire outfit thundered down the long, straight roads at a speed of more than fifty miles an hour, until the hills between Abbeville and Boulogne compelled it to adopt a more decorous pace. Toby drove it for part of the way in order to learn its idiosyncrasies, and was enchanted by its possibilities. As he admitted to himself, luck must have something to do with the chances of hitting an airship, but here at last was a weapon which was capable of performing such a feat and he intended to be sure that no Zeppelin would approach London from now on without, at least, being given something to dissuade its crew from the idea that their target was defenceless.

They reached Boulogne at tea-time and, while Toby was entertaining the Frenchmen to a belated luncheon, gun, caisson and Hudson were swung on board the waiting steamer. There was an irritating delay of some hours before they sailed, and it was not until early the next morning that they arrived at Newhaven and Toby was able to telegraph Sir Percy that he was on his way. Just after 11 a.m. he reached Sir Percy's London home and was ordered to take his capture straight to the Horse Guards Parade, for inspection by the First Lord and others. With commendable foresight Toby had arranged for a troop of his men to be there, and, before the dust had settled, they swarmed over the new weapon with rags and metal polish. At 2.30, Balfour and his entourage arrived to examine the gleaming equipage, the workings and possibilities of which Toby eagerly explained. The First Lord and Sir Percy congratulated him on his speed and enterprise, and when they had gone Toby borrowed a room and sat down to write his report. The document which he handed to Sir Percy the following day explained what he had done; Sir Percy, still groping in the dark, asked for as full an appreciation as Toby felt able to give of the arrangements made for the defence of Paris and for recommendations as to how the plan could be adapted for London. Toby submitted a detailed analysis of the defences of Paris and argued that, given that the metropolitan area of London is much larger than that of Paris, it would be best to concentrate on mobile, as opposed to fixed defences.

Sir Percy concurred with every word of Toby's recommendations and ordered him to re-form his armoured-car squadron into the Royal Navy Mobile Anti-Aircraft Brigade. Their headquarters was at the Talbot motor-works in Ladbroke Grove, and to begin with they had only the one motor-cannon. All the instructions had to be given by Toby personally, for none but he understood the mysteries of the height-finder, the range-finder and the optical sight. The place was well chosen, for his gunners, dressed in naval "fore and aft rig" with black buttons above the waist and in Navy-blue breeches with black leggings below, more closely resembled a party of chauffeurs than any regular military body. Perhaps their appearance was not deceptive, for these were all keen, mechanically-minded men who were thoroughly suited to this novel form of warfare.

Soon a routine was established. Training went on continuously from early morning until late afternoon, when all hands were allowed a three-hour break before the next parade, at 9 p.m. Then everybody mustered and waited for the raid which must come one night. Toby, who had been given very much of a free hand, came to the conclusion that the most likely target was the City and he explored it thoroughly for some convenient place from which his motor-cannon could make its presence most effectively felt. He settled on the Artillery Ground, just off Moorgate, and the authorities gave him the use of it whenever he wanted. They were not kept waiting long.

TOBY

On 13 October, after a hard day's training, the brigade was dismissed as usual for its rest at 6 p.m. Toby went back to his billet to have a meal and a sleep before "Quarters" at nine; he had not been there for more than an hour when his telephone began to ring. The Duty Officer at the Admiralty told him excitedly that some—he did not know how many—Zeppelins had just crossed the coast-line and were heading for London. If they kept their course and speed they should arrive at about nine o'clock. It seemed almost as if the enemy must have had information about the habits of the Mobile Brigade, for its men were dispersed to their billets and would not reassemble for another couple of hours. Toby rushed back to the Talbot works, collected up such of his men as he could find and put them to work loading up equipment and starting the engines of the vehicles. It was an agony of frustration as he waited for the early comers to dribble in; at 8.25 came a peremptory order over the telephone for the gun immediately to take up its position in the Artillery Ground. Toby had to admit with shame that, until more of his men came in, he was unable to comply. His torment was made worse by the knowledge that only his gun was equipped with proper high-explosive anti-aircraft shells and that even the guns of the Marines could fire only cannon shell, which stood far less chance of doing anything useful.

With every minute that passed a small party would wander in, smoking and chatting, only to be seized by an irate commanding officer and put instantly to work. As nine o'clock was striking they were ready to go, with one exception: the Chief Petty Officer, the most experienced gunner of them all, was late on parade. He appeared at four minutes past the hour and Toby, forgetting the convention that an officer does not curse a subordinate in front of his men, addressed him for a full minute. The time was not wasted, for a new sense of urgency suddenly appeared.

At exactly five minutes past the hour the procession left the Talbot works, passed Wormwood Scrubs, and trundled towards the City, gathering speed as it went. There were no air-raid warnings in 1915 and the population of London was blissfully unconscious of what was happening; the blazing headlights and the sirens of Toby's lorries, however, soon left no room for doubt that something was going on and that it would be wiser to keep out of the way. Omnibuses mounted the pavement as Toby's lorries tore down Oxford Street with the Hudson at their head and pedestrians flattened themselves against shop windows. As they thundered down the hill in Holborn, Toby glanced at his speedometer; it registered fifty-six miles per hour. Unknown to them a Zeppelin was following much the same course, rather more slowly.

As he looked up, Toby experienced another moment of horror;

the road was "up". Only a narrow passage was left and that was crammed with vehicles. There could be no question of stopping at that speed, so, with the racing driver's quick reaction, he did the only thing possible, put his foot hard down on the accelerator and charged the part of the carriageway that was under repair. It was blocked by a pole supported on two trestles, beyond which lay, for all he knew, some great trench. For the first time that night, fate, possibly feeling that something was owed to him, was kind to Toby. The pole was low down and the front tyres smashed it, sending the parts spinning high in the air; the steering wheel was momentarily wrenched from his hands but the ditch beyond it was not deep and the Hudson, after a brief shudder, flew on undamaged. As he went through, Toby was treated to the exhilarating might of a helmetless Metropolitan policeman apparently racing him towards the pole that marked the far end of the work; the officer made excellent time and succeeded in pushing it over just before the car would have hit it. The Hudson leapt into the air without pausing in its stride and the column tore on towards the Artillery Ground. Toby swung his car round so that its lights illuminated the gun position and his men went through their drills at the double. As the engines of the lorries fell silent, the sound of a Zeppelin's motor was clearly audible, and, before the wheels of the motor-cannon had stopped turning, Toby saw it. It was coming straight towards them from the north-west at a speed which he estimated at fifty miles per hour. The roar of its motors became louder and was punctuated by the explosions of bombs along Holborn and the Strand. The Artillery Ground was brilliantly lit and Toby made no attempt to have the lights put out or dimmed; the airship commander would certainly be under the impression that not a single anti-aircraft gun existed in London and nothing could have suited Toby better than that he should be helped to pursue his apparent purpose of dropping a bomb on them. The nearer he came, the better the chance of scoring a hit. Apart from that, light was essential if the men setting fuses and laying the gun were to do so with necessary speed.

There was no time to go through the routine of using instruments, for the enemy was nearly overhead. Toby made a quick calculation; he reckoned the altitude at between 7,000 and 8,000 feet, the range at 5,000 yards, and shot out his orders accordingly. As soon as the layer called out "Ready, sir", he gave the order to fire. The seventy-five gave its characteristic whip-like crack, and, during the interminable seconds while the shell was on its way, Toby looked at his watch. It was exactly 9.25. Twenty minutes, from Ladbroke Grove to Moorgate, including getting the gun into action and firing, he considered not too bad for a raw crew. The Zeppelin was heading directly for them when the shell burst; it was short, but obviously caused some consternation. Before another shell could be fired, the layer called out "Gun no longer bears, sir." Toby cursed fluently; this meant that the airship was directly overhead, and no gun can fire vertically. He made his calculation for the next shot, increasing the range to 6,500 and the altitude to 10,000 to allow for the rise which must take place after the fall of the bombs which were obviously coming. "They fell all right, I don't know how many of them, but they made a devil of a noise, and brought down several of the houses on the Moorgate Street side of the ground, with a roar of falling masonry which it was pleasant for me to hear; for, as I explained at once to the men, if he had hit the houses east of the gun, it meant that he had passed over us and, as he could not come back, we could therefore be sure of getting another shot at him; the imminent danger of his putting the gun out of action before we could fire again, which had existed, was past." A few leaden moments later there came another cry from the layer. "Gun bears, sir." "Fire." This time they saw the shell burst, above and quite close to the Zeppelin. An instant later it disappeared from view as if in a sudden fog-bank; the commander had dropped all his water ballast and was climbing as high and as fast as he could go. There would be no chance of a third shot, but, so far as that Zeppelin was concerned, the raid was over.

The brigade motored back to Ladbroke Grove at a more sedate pace, Toby's brain working furiously on the lessons to be learnt from this first encounter. He heard later that all the remaining bombs had been jettisoned with the water ballast which had caused the fog and all had fallen together in Petticoat Lane, where they had done little damage. The bombs, however, had been bigger and more effective than those dropped in the earlier raids and it was plain that a new dimension of warfare now existed. The gun had made a promising start, but there was still a long way to go before it could be asserted that London was effectively defended.

Chapter Nine

There could be no gainsaying the unwelcome fact that in 1915 there existed no effective defence against the Zeppelin. In March of the previous year the matter had come under discussion in Parliament, and Churchill, then First Lord of the Admiralty, had given the sanguine assurance that the danger was greatly overstated and that "any hostile aircraft, airship or aeroplane, capable of reaching our coast during the coming year would be promptly attacked, and in superior force, by a swarm of formidable hornets". It is true that the undertaking had now expired, but it had continued to stand up during its brief life only because it had never been seriously tested. There were no hornets in 1915; such aircraft as were available for home defence were more in the nature of bumble-bees. They carried a sting, but their flying performance was elementary and, as no means of pointing them towards their target existed, they could do little more than blunder hopefully around; hope was seldom realized. There had been a moment in June when it seemed that the bumble-bee was more formidable than it appeared. Lieutenant Warneford of the RNAS had destroyed an airship in Belgium by manoeuvring his aeroplane above it and dropping half a dozen small bombs into the gas-bag; it was a notable feat and Warneford richly deserved the immediate Victoria Cross which the King personally awarded to him. When he was killed in a flying accident only a week later, the nation grieved for him as it was to grieve for Edith Cavell. The euphoria which his exploit engendered was, however, of short duration.

Weather and mechanical failures were the only really inhibiting factors to the German airmen. One of the two Zeppelins which had carried out the May raid had been compelled to turn back when a propeller unaccountably broke and ruptured the envelope; the other, under command of a soldier, Major Linnarz, returned with stories of tracer bullets and incendiary shells but even worse than these imaginary terrors had been the numbing cold. When the time for the raid in October arrived, Kapitänleutnant Breithaupt of LZ 15, Toby's adversary during their strange duel, found nothing at all to trouble him. His ship cruised across a moon-lit London from the north-west and he was able to carry out the notorious raid on the theatres unmolested.

Toby duly made his report to Sir Percy and later went to see him at the Admiralty. The two men were in complete accord as to the first essential in producing a volume of fire which would hit, or at least deter, any future raiders. It was perfectly obvious that the only weapons worth using were those capable of firing high-explosive shells fused to burst in the air near to the target. It would be a complete waste of time to persevere with any others. Sir Percy, well aware that the Navy relied basically on its tested common shell but also possessed the high explosive lyddite, made immediate inquiries about stocks of the latter. The result was thoroughly discouraging; there was hardly enough lyddite for the needs of the Fleet and such tiny surplus as might remain would have to go to the War Office for the guns in France. No other high explosive was "authorized". The Explosives Committee was by no means defunct. He then turned to the subject of time-fuses to be used with high explosive, if such he could contrive to get. There were no time-fuses. Yes, the matter had been under consideration for a number of years but no satisfactory solution had been found. Sir Percy would, of course, understand that the danger attendant on the malfunctioning of a time-fuse, possibly causing the shell to explode while still in the gun-barrel, was of such seriousness that approval could be given to nothing until it had been tested over and over again. Sir Percy, repressing his rage as best he could, explained that, although the difficulties were undoubtedly great, the French seemed to have overcome them. This observation disconcerted the authorities but not quite in the fashion Sir Percy had expected. Keen questioning followed as to whether the French could give an absolute guarantee of the safety of their device. If they could not, its use by His Majesty's forces would never be approved. The Admiral went back to his office and wrote a scathing letter complaining at "Admiralty red-tapeism" and firmly stating that "if the Admiralty are to settle what guns are to be used for the defence of London, and how they are to be obtained, then they become responsible for the gunnery defence of London and I resign."

Toby was a member of Sir Percy's inner conclave and was sought after as the expert on time-fuses. His experience with the mortars and the invaluable instruction he had received from French experts had made him one of the most well-informed men in England on this neglected subject. The basic difficulty with all time-fuses is that they must ensure that the shell cannot explode until after the shell has left the gun-barrel. With black powder a premature explosion had not much mattered, but with high explosive it will shatter the weapon and its crew with it. Toby, who since his car-racing days had had great respect for the expertise of the engineers across the Channel, was entirely satisfied that they had found the answer and could point to the technical success of the Toby mortars as evidence that this was so.

Sir Percy asked him to produce a drawing and specification of such a fuse as they both knew to be needed. Toby asked only for paper and pencil together with the use of a room for a short time. Within the hour he produced working drawings of a fuse which he asserted to be absolutely safe; Sir Percy, the professional gunner, grasped the idea on the spot, expressed unqualified approval and took it to the Director of Naval Ordnance. Then, as Toby irreverently put it, the fun began. The Director flatly refused to put his hall-mark on the handiwork of an amateur and even expressed misgivings about the continued use of French high-explosive shells from French guns. The only course left to the innovators was to go cap in hand to Versailles and ask that more seventy-fives be lent or given to London. Until these arrived, batteries had to be made up from whatever guns could be found, suitable for their purpose or not. Naval three- and six-pounders, designed for use against swift torpedo craft nearly a generation before, together with a few more three-inch guns on Naval Vavasseur mountings were all that could be had. Even for these no carriage existed which would enable them to be moved rapidly from one site to another, nor could they be elevated to the degree needed to enable their shells to reach anywhere near to a target high in the sky. Sir Percy's old company, Vickers, set their people to work on a suitable piece of machinery for the three-pounder, which was their own product, and also on a platform which enabled them to travel and fire from the back of a Lancia lorry. The resources of the great Arsenal at Woolwich were obtained for a better mounting for the three-inch gun, which had the cachet of official approval.

It was all a very slow business, and by the middle of November there were only twenty-four guns available to defend the capital. The only shell in the least useful was the French one, but even that was far from perfect. It was still a field artillery projectile, made for the smashing of earthworks, and constituted a serious danger to people on the ground as its big fragments fell at frightening speed. Toby brought all his recently-acquired knowledge of shell design to bear upon its improvement. Ever since the first explosive shell had been fired from a gun it had been an article of faith amongst designers that the base must be strong and solid, in order to withstand the pressure exerted on it by the explosion of the propelling charge. The walls of the shell were thinner and tapered off towards the nose; the result was that, when the shell burst, the walls would fly to pieces while the heavy base remained intact and itself became a formidable missile when it descended. Toby and his team, selected almost entirely from his own command, worked hard on the problem and, after the inevitable false starts, came up with a completely new design. The base of the shell, instead of being flat, was in the shape of a dome; this provided the strength needed to withstand the explosion of the propellant and had the further advantage of disintegrating under the interior pressure at the same time as the walls when the charge exploded. Not only did it do away with the very dangerous chunk of falling metal but it increased noticeably the amount of steel shards directed at the marauding airships. Satisfied with this, Toby turned to the shape of the forward part of the shell and came up with a new, streamlined projectile which would have a greater range and would completely shatter itself into small pieces on explosion. It was, incidentally, a lot cheaper to manufacture than its predecessor. There remained one last subject for research: the time-fuse was a good one but if, through some imperfection in manufacture, it failed to burst the shell in the air there was still a serious danger that it would go off on hitting the ground. After more experiments a fuse was produced which withstood firing into solid concrete at 100 yards without exploding. Thanks to the persistence of Sir Percy and to the awe which his anger inspired, blessing was obtained and the new shells approved. They might not be the last word as Zeppelin-killers, but at least they removed a serious additional peril to those below.

During November, Sir Percy subdivided his command into two portions. The fixed guns and searchlights were placed under command of Commander Grenville Grey RNVR, while Toby was assigned to the Mobile Brigade with headquarters on the heights to the north of London at Kenwood. A third, smaller, mobile column armed only with the lighter guns operated further afield. Before the move took place there was one more public duty to be performed. The Lord Mayor's Show of 1915 was enriched by the presence of the Mobile Brigade in the procession, complete with five guns and a searchlight. Toby occupied a leading place on the original "Canon-Automobile" and stoically endured the drenching rain which, amongst other considerations, kept the crowds smaller than in happier days.

All through the winter the brigade was constantly being exercised by practice turn-outs. Positions from which it could operate were selected north, south and east of London and everybody came to know the sites intimately. Toby heartlessly turned them out over Christmas and was well pleased at seeing every one of the eight guns they then possessed moving out from barracks, complete in every detail, within eight minutes of the dummy warning being received. In four minutes over the hour the guns were all reported "in action" from stations as widespread as Aldwych, Higham Hill, Manor Park, Becton, Streatham and Clapham. Their efficiency was enough to make him recommend to Sir Percy that a trial should be made of changing their positions from one side of London to the other, on the supposition that an attack expected from one direction had developed elsewhere, so that the greatest advantage might be taken of such remarkable mobility. Sir Percy agreed and the test was carried out triumphantly.

The first weeks of 1916 brought a substantial increase in the number of guns protecting London. As the great batteries of huge modern weapons which all the resources of the Krupp and Skoda works had turned out were massing before Verdun, London mustered fifty pieces, ten of them Toby's mobile weapons. There were a further ninety-eight guns available, including a dozen Russian cannon, but all were unusable for want of mountings. The Explosives Committee assisted by promulgating an order forbidding the use of French high-explosive shells, because the country of origin had felt unable to provide a written guarantee of the safety of the time-fuses. All the seventy-fives, therefore, were for the time being reduced to the ridiculous shift of firing shrapnel. The chances of destroying an airship with this projectile were about the same as those of hitting a rocketing pheasant with a rifle.

At the end of the month Sir Percy Scott handed over his responsibilities to the Army, and Sir John French, sent home after muffing his last chance at Loos, became, in his capacity of Commander-in-Chief, Home Forces, responsible for the defence of London. The Mobile Anti-Aircraft Brigade thus, anomalously, came under the Army for operations whilst remaining subject to the Admiralty for all other purposes.

It was an unhappy time for Toby. His heart was with the Army in France, and as 1916 wore on he became increasingly aware of the great battle that would soon be fought in which his brother's Fourth Corps, now expanded into the Fourth Army, would have the lion's share. His friends in his present situation were few, and, though he continued to do a great deal more than his duty, Toby felt himself to be something like a shirker. Now in his fiftieth year, he had almost abandoned hope of being offered what he deemed suitable employment for a trained soldier; it remained only to do everything he could in the area of the work allotted to him. He was a powerful man and his vigour of mind and body were still at their peak; he must employ them both in bringing his command to the highest possible pitch of efficiency and to continue to improve the material at his disposal.

For Toby's little force—it never numbered more than about 200 men and officers—the watchword was still speed. He obtained permission during March to try out his scheme of moving guns from north to south during a dummy raid and the result was gratifying. On a March night such citizens as were abroad shortly after 10.30 were treated to the spectacle of three sections, each of two motor-cannons with all their equipment, tearing through central London to take up positions between Wandsworth and Grove Park in place of their earlier ones at Finchley and Becton. Toby travelled with the gun which had the longest journey to make, from the reservoirs at Tottenham to Streatham by way of the City; a condition of the leave given him for this evolution was that Captain Stansfield of the Royal Navy should sit beside him to make sure that he did not go too fast. Even with that inhibition, the whole brigade completed its journey and was "in action" on the new sites within thirty-five minutes of being given the order to move.

Sir John French, though pleased with the result, remained to be convinced that such speed and mobility could be maintained and set Toby a further test, this time taking the guns as far out as Great Dunmow and Maldon in Essex. This was a test far more severe than the crossing of London, for it obliged the gun-teams to move at their best speeds over distances of between twenty-five and fifty miles. Again the result was a triumph.

The unit's very success added to its difficulties. Lord French, as Sir John had now become, decided to take advantage of such unusual mobility and orders were given that sections should stand by to travel even greater distances at short notice. On the last day of March the entire brigade was turned out to its usual stations when a Zeppelin alert was received, but none came near them; the first days of April produced several alerts but no opportunity of getting a shot in at anything; and during the same period Toby was ordered to send guns to hearten the inhabitants of places as far away as Dundee, Edinburgh and Sunderland. The bulk of his command was transferred to North Walsham in Norfolk, a county which had been receiving a good deal of attention. He himself remained in London and was furnished with drafts of low-category men from the Army whom he was bidden to instruct in the mysteries of the seventy-five so that they might take over some of the fixed defences of the capital as the guns arrived. As a result of this dispersal there were only three guns available in the brigade when the next crop of raids came on three successive nights at the end of April. One searchlight was left and

Toby, being the last officer remaining, was compelled to command one of the guns himself. Again, he was denied his prey.

Life for the detachment at North Walsham was proving much more interesting. On 24 April they were seriously engaged throughout the night and a bomb from a Zeppelin put the searchlight out of action. It was swiftly repaired and both guns opened fire at a real target for the first time; the long hours of training paid a dividend, for the range was obtained with the second round and soon all four guns were firing as hard as they could go. The shells were seen to be bursting gratifyingly near the airship and a sudden yell proclaimed that No. 3 gun had scored a hit. It was not, however, a killing blow, for the Zeppelin, struck aft near the rudder, recovered its trim after some staggering. The gunners had behaved admirably under bombing and Toby, usually sparing with his praise, was not slow to say so in his report. Although the hit was confirmed by five different people, including the Coastguard, it was never acknowledged.

The improved mountings began to come in at about this time and with them more guns. The mounting which Sir Percy and Toby had devised for the three-inch weapon appeared from the workshops of the Southern Railway at Ashford and Toby was invited to display it on the Horse Guards Parade to see how it compared with the official Woolwich model, manned by the Royal Garrison Artillery. An unexpected spectator was the King. The *Daily Telegraph* of 20 May 1916 tells what he saw:

> The King paid a visit of inspection to the Horse Guards yesterday morning and witnessed part of a competition in progress on the parade ground between the anti-aircraft teams. Field Marshal Viscount French, Admiral Sir Percy Scott, Mr Balfour and a number of other naval and military officers witnessed the proceedings, as also did a crowd of spectators. The guns were of the new type and were drawn by motor-cars. The two guns were brought into position in front of the Admiralty, and the heavy weapons were brought into action with extraordinary celerity. At the finish of the inspection they were taken round the parade ground until a speed of 40 miles an hour was attained by the R N V R gun, which was magnificently handled and proved itself far superior to the Woolwich product.

Toby had never lacked for competitive instincts; one feels that the Woolwich men never had a chance. The carriage devised by Sir Percy and Toby was in the form of a trailer mounted on two wheels; the gun, weighing a ton, was swiftly lowered onto a circular platform once the wheels had been removed and was capable of an all-round traverse. The design remained basically unchanged for the next thirty years.

As more and more guns came in, together with all the equipment that experience had shown to be necessary, it at last became possible to organize the gun defence of London on something better than an *ad hoc* basis. It was to be built around the three-inch gun, and the French weapons, which Toby understood better than most men, came to be regarded as exotica. It was proposed that his brigade should be armed entirely with the motor-cannon and that the number of them should be increased to sixteen.

As the dreadful 1 July approached, Toby found excellent reasons for returning to France, ostensibly to compare notes with his friends at the School of Anti-Aircraft Gunnery near Paris. He was initiated into the mystery of the Le Brocq electro-magnetic system of sighting guns for use against aeroplanes, an appliance which few other men in uniform would have understood, and made it his business to demonstrate it at Fourth Army Headquarters a few days before the battle. The demonstration can have been of no more than academic interest, as the device was too complicated to be adopted at the time, but it gave him an excuse to stay with Sir Henry and possibly to see something of the battle, even from the outside. In this he was disappointed, for he could not delay his return, and, naturally, he did not know exactly when the battle would begin. The preliminary bombardment began as he was climbing into the Hudson and he was back in London when the finest army ever to leave Britain rose up from its trenches and marched in ordered lines towards the German guns. All the way back Toby could hear the roar of artillery, diminishing with every mile, and even in the capital a murmur borne on the wind brought the muted voice of the British guns, speaking as never before. His own task seemed so petty by comparison, but it was the only task he had, or seemed likely to have. Toby had not abandoned hope of more pugnacious employment; his damaged foot gave no trouble now, so long as he continued to wear his special boot, and even that was inconspicuous. For the time being, however, he must go back to his dry-land sailors and wait, filling in time with such ploys as trying to lure Zeppelins over a certain spot by making it look like a factory.

Early in August the entire brigade was ordered to the Norfolk coast, the contingents from the northern towns having come home. The orders were given at 6.30 p.m. The brigade, twelve guns, three lights and a score of vehicles, left Kenwood for the last time at 3.30 a.m., tore along towards their destination, and moved into the tented camp prepared for them at North Walsham at 1 p.m. Toby called it "a very successful march of 150 miles".

Chapter Ten

The east coast of England was the centre of activity for the Zeppelins during the summer of 1916 and the main focus of interest was a lightship some eight miles off shore known as the Happisburgh. Toby soon learnt to pronounce it in the proper Norfolk fashion as "Hazeboro". It had been ascertained beyond doubt by the British Intelligence Service—an organization of the highest efficiency—that the Zeppelins used it as a seamark before setting off overland to London, and, as they now operated from bases in Jutland, it was ideally situated for their purpose. The fact that it was suffered to remain on station was by no means attributable to carelessness: the ship was in constant telephone communication with the installations ashore and served as a distant early-warning system of greater utility to its own country than to its foes.

The brigade did not linger at North Walsham but was deployed in a number of positions along the coast, with its headquarters at the pleasant village of Bacton. They had not been long in that position when a new scare was announced from the Horse Guards. Bacton is no great distance by air from Sandringham, where Queen Alexandra, the Queen Mother, was in residence. On a number of occasions airships had passed over, a natural enough thing to happen on their way to London, but an interpretation far more sinister was placed upon it by Lord French's staff. The presence of the airships could mean only that the Kaiser, whom everybody knew to be capable of any enormity, was diverting substantial forces for the questionable military purpose of murdering an aunt whom he was known to detest nearly as much as she loathed him. Toby received peremptory orders to advert such a flagitious enterprise; without delay, he personally took two of the motor-cannons and a searchlight through the narrow Norfolk lanes at great speed and reported himself to Her Majesty. The Queen Mother took a more robust view of the matter, for she laughed heartily and assured Toby that to believe that an attempt was to be made to blow her up was beyond her. Nevertheless Toby had his orders and Queen Alexandra, of all people, would not seek to come between a man and his duty. With the aid of an equerry and with some cunning he disposed his force; the two guns and the light were posted at the points of an equilateral triangle, well away from the house, so that an enemy might conclude that Her Majesty was to be found in the middle. Whether by accident or in consequence of this display of guile, a Zeppelin did make an attack on Sandringham in the early hours of 3 September and its bombs missed the house by a good margin. The police at King's Lynn telephoned to McKenzie Ashton, the RNVR officer left in command of the detachment, at 3.25 a.m. to say that a raider was just leaving their borough (where it had dropped a few random bombs) and was "steering direct for Sandringham". It is impossible to improve upon Toby's own account of what happened next.

> This customer evidently knew where he was, and had taken his bearing very carefully, for he passed right over the house, providentially without being able to identify it. He doubtless expected that the searchlight would be switched on and that he would, by that means, be advised when he had reached his objective. He was, however, mistaken in that supposition as, in accordance with my order, he was allowed to pass right over and clear of the house before any move was made or searchlight shown. Once past and clear of the house, however, the searchlight was switched on and rapid fire at once opened.... Lieutenant Ashton's report claims that the second round hit the airship, which he considered was, in any case, certainly damaged by the burst of the shell. In spite of every endeavour, however, I have been unable to obtain any definite proof of this hit, though the subsequent action of the airship points to the probability of some damage having been done to it. On fire being opened the target rose instantly and made off on its homeward course, at the same moment dropping five bombs together, which all fell within a radius of 50 yards. These seriously damaged a group of cottages and their occupants, which were actually within 2,000 yards of the gun in action and well within the triangle of our three posts. They, in the dark, were doubtless mistaken by the enemy for Sandringham House.

He does not mention whether the occupants were sensible of the compliment paid them. Toby was furious with the petty officer in charge of the gun for missing the easiest target they were ever likely to get and he told him so. Then he went on to pay his respects to Queen Alexandra and to Princess Victoria, who was there also. The Queen Mother was "dreadfully anxious as to the injuries of the inhabitants of the damaged houses in the village, all of whom were personally known to her". In addition, "she laughed heartily at any suggestion that she might be nervous of anything they might try to do to herself, all her anxiety being concentrated on what suffering might be inflicted upon her poor villagers, for whose safety she showed the liveliest concern".

Shortly after the setting-up of the air defence of Sandringham, but not on account of it, Toby received the first recognition of all that he had done since that remote day when the RAC drivers had disembarked in France. He was made a Commander of the Order of St Michael and St George (CMG), but the award did not give him the pleasure that it might have done at some more fortunate date. The terrible battle on the Somme was still going on and decorations for taking pot-shots at airships in England could not then weigh very heartily. Apart from, very properly, heading his minutes henceforth as those of "Commander A. Rawlinson, CMG, RNVR" he makes no mention of the award. It seems entirely in character.

The night of 2–3 September was an eventful one, quite apart from the dastardly attack on Queen Alexandra. The remaining guns, two motor-cannons, and a couple of three-pounders with their attendant searchlights were waiting on the lonely coast between Bacton and Mundesley when, as the darkness fell, a motor-cycle despatch-rider arrived with a message relayed from the Horse Guards enjoining the utmost vigilance. Within minutes all the equipment was fully manned and the men waited as they scanned the cloudy sky. Round about ten o'clock, a dozen bombs were heard whistling down some miles to the south, and a few minutes later there were explosions to the north and engines could be heard out to sea. The cloud closed in and it began to rain; in Norfolk low cloud always seems to be lower than anywhere else in England and its rain has a quality of unusual wetness. For an instant, half an hour later, there was a blink in the clouds and a Zeppelin appeared for as long as it takes for a man to draw a breath. The searchlights reflected uselessly from the cloud-bottoms and the guns stayed silent; the throbbing died away to the south-west, to be followed soon by the crack of twenty-three more bombs a good distance away. Another sixty were heard in the next hour, nine of them out at sea, but still there was nothing to be seen but the endless cloud. A further twenty bombs landed in the sea before Bacton church clock announced to the straining ears of the gunners that midnight had come. There was not a breath of wind and sound carried for miles. An hour more and the watchers of Mundesley saw something: a Zeppelin, away to the north-west and steering east-by-south. It was not a promising target but, as Toby had dinned into them, it was better to try than not to. The lights were switched on and the little three-pounders sent half a dozen shells in the general direction of the cloud which might be hiding their enemy. The gunners drew what satisfaction they could from seeing the Zeppelin rise and head for Denmark.

So it went on through the night, men with glasses glimpsing an airship for a moment as the clouds broke but never for long enough to take a deliberate aim; more galling was the certainty that the things were there and within range, for the beat of the engines was unmistakable. The news over the telephone at about 3.30 that one of them had been shot down by aeroplanes near London was cheering, but it was not enough. An hour later came the "All Clear" and the men, except for the sentries, went morosely back to their tents.

Toby made his routine report and pondered long. Zeppelins, four in all, had passed near his guns, probably all in range and certainly using the well-worn path over the Happisburgh lightship. Had it not been for the cloud, there would have been a very decent chance of scoring hits; but his men had not been able to see the target. So what was to be done next time? Sight was not the only sense a man carried with him; he could hear also, and, when he heard a sound, he looked in the direction from which that sound came. Why? Because, being blessed with a pair of ears, he turns his head so that the sound shall be heard equally by each of them. Was there a moral to be drawn from this? Toby began to think that perhaps there was. The germ of an idea was beginning to form in his mind and it called for certain experiments. Within a day or so strange articles were delivered to Bacton on the orders of Commander Rawlinson: a long pole with a pivot on its centre, two doctors' stethoscopes, a compass card, sundry pieces of wood and the trumpets of two gramophones.

Toby knew no more about the physics of sound than the next man, but, as we know, he possessed ingenuity and a gift for improvisation. He needed both. With the aid of a couple of fatigue-men, he began to assemble his contraption. First, the pole was set up horizontally, swinging freely around its pivot and with an upright at the centre; there was affixed the compass-card, properly oriented to show true north. Also in the middle, an indicator arm was fastened at right-angles to the pole and over the card, so that, as the pole moved, the arm gave the true bearing at which it was pivoted. So far, so good. Then, to the bafflement of the fatigue-men, Toby firmly placed the big, wooden trumpets at the extremities of the pole, both pointing in the same direction and at a right-angle measured as accurately as had been that at which the indicator arm was set. Lastly, the business end of a stethoscope was clamped to each gramophone-trumpet and the ear-pieces led to the middle of the pole.

> It only remained then to fix a man's head to the pole, insert the ends of the stethoscope pipes in his ears, and to tell him to listen, and to turn his head, and the pole with it, in the direction of the sound which he heard. The practical effect of this manoeuvre was that the man found he could not only hear sounds at an immense distance but he was able to turn directly towards them with the greatest confidence. At the same time, the indicator on the compass-card recorded the exact bearing of the sound to which he was listening, and the angle could then be immediately telephoned to headquarters.

Though it was, and remains, unaware of the fact, Bacton had just witnessed the beginning of a whole new art of sound-ranging, henceforth to be one of the gunner's most useful tools until, within recent years, something more sophisticated displaced it.

Men, of course, varied considerably in their aptitude for the use of the new gadget and Toby cerebrated again. What sort of man would be most likely to have unusually acute hearing? The answer was obvious. Toby, like many men, had a dread of blindness, though he did not bother himself in the least about the possibility of death or wounds. There must be many blind men, men blind from birth, who would be captivated by the opportunity not merely of doing something useful for their country but also of finding work which they could do better than their sighted brothers. A message eventually went out inviting those so afflicted to come and man these machines and show the way to bring down or drive off Zeppelins. A number responded and did most valuable work, though none actually served under the man who had started it all. Something of him, however, shines through his own last comments on his invention: "I can only hope that those who were so greatly privileged as to be present on these occasions were capable of appreciating the exquisite beauty and pathos of that wonderful scene, when it was the blind men who showed the way and the men who saw followed."

A few days after Christmas, the Mobile Anti-Aircraft Brigade received orders to move to Essex. The weight of future attacks was to come not from Jutland-based airships but from the new and formidable Gotha aeroplanes of the England Squadron, operating from aerodromes in Belgium. Their natural line of approach would be along the estuary of the Thames, and the brigade was to dispute their passage. The brigade's new line of operations was to extend along the marshy coast of Essex from Shoeburyness to the Blackwater.

Toby drove immediately to inspect his new area and settled on the pleasant little town of Burnham-on-Crouch for his headquarters. Only the four motor-cannons and one of the British three-inch guns followed him, for it was considered wisest to leave the little three-pounders and the other three-inch in their original positions for the time being. The committee of the Royal Corinthian Yacht Club was unsparing with its hospitality, and the clubhouse, little used in winter, became the brigade's officers' mess. Two of the French guns drove to a position on the north bank of the Crouch at the point where the river meets the sea; the three-inch and a searchlight went to "a most interesting old farm on the very edge of the marsh", four miles to the north; and the remaining section dug itself in around a ruined chapel at St Peter's, the eastward extremity of the southern bank of the Blackwater. It was even colder than Norfolk; the winds from Siberia encounter no obstacle between the steppes and the Thames estuary, and on many occasions the thermometer registered $-20°F$. The damp and the fogs easily beat those to which Bacton had been subject, and after a few weeks Toby felt obliged to make representations about bringing his command onto the higher ground some ten miles further inland. The point was taken and the brigade moved back from the dreadful marshes to a line between Burnham and Stansgate Abbey. There they endured the first four months of 1917 with many alarms but no action.

By that time, however, the days of the Mobile brigade were numbered. With the change in the pattern of air-raids, it was no longer as useful as it had been, and as a first step towards its disbandment, it was reduced to a single battery. Then Toby received a message from Lord French stating that, if he would be willing to transfer back to the Army, he would be appointed to a command in the military anti-aircraft defences of London, with Army rank and seniority equivalent to that which he held under the Admiralty. The command offered to him would take over the French guns, in which he alone was expert, and he could bring any of his officers and men who wanted to come.

Toby felt himself to have no choice. Again, it was not the kind of employment on which his heart was set, but there was no getting away from the fact that his present command was going to be disbanded. If he were to refuse this, no other work fit for a soldier would be offered him. He accepted, and at the beginning of May the last parade of the Royal Naval Anti-Aircraft Brigade was held in the main street of Burnham-on-Crouch. Toby, with yet another commission, this time as a lieutenant-colonel of the Royal Garrison Artillery (RGA), reported himself to the War Office.

Chapter Eleven

Toby assumed his new responsibilities at a particularly unpropitious moment, for in May 1917 the German air attacks on England began to take up a pattern much more formidable than anything that had gone before. The Zeppelin losses in recent months had persuaded the High Command that their day was past and, with one exception to be related in due course, their activities were now reduced to carrying out sporadic raids on outlying places mostly in the north. In their wake came the bombing aeroplane.

The events of later wars have tended to cause the weight and efficiency of the German air assault of 1917–18 to be overlooked. The main offensive weapon was the Gotha GIV, which with the exception of the pre-war experimental machines of Igor Sikorsky in Russia was by far the biggest aircraft that the world had yet seen. The fuselage was more than forty feet long, the wing-span seventy-eight feet, and it was powered by two Mercedes engines with a total output of more than 500 horse-power. It could climb to more than 14,000 feet, and this, together with the three cunningly placed machine-guns which it carried, went far to making it invulnerable against fighters. The fact that its top speed was no more than about eighty mph did not greatly matter; more to the point was the fact that it carried half a ton of bombs, which could be directed with fair accuracy by means of the Goerz optical sight. By May 1917 several dozen of these machines were organized in four wings, operating from airfields just across the Channel in occupied Belgium. Their only task was to "strafe England".

On his return to London, Toby found that the gunnery system there had been radically altered, but, when he presented himself at the Horse Guards and matters were explained to him, he felt himself unable to enthuse over the new dispensation. With his naval brigade he had been largely independent and had dealt directly with Sir Frederick Shaw, Lord French's Chief of Staff. He and Shaw understood each other perfectly and worked together in harmony. His new immediate chief was a man of different quality. Colonel Simon and Toby disliked each other on sight; this was a pity, for each in his way was a better man than the other considered him to be. Simon was a Sapper and an excellent, hard-working officer. His main weakness, at any rate in Toby's eyes, was a rigid adherence to regulations, coupled with a passion for pettifogging detail. He would delegate nothing unless it were quite unavoidable, with the result that much of his precious time was taken up with matters of trifling importance. If the two men had been confronted with Alexander's problem, Toby would have followed the example of the Macedonian; Simon, one feels, would have spent many hours making drawings and doing sums and, when he had finished, the Knot would have been untied and laid out for inspection with the ends neatly flemished down. He began by making it crystal clear to Toby that the old days were over and that henceforth he was just one of several sub-unit commanders with no right of direct access to any authority higher than himself. He added encouragingly that the command which Toby was about to take over was far and away the worst-disciplined, worst-trained and worst-equipped in the entire London Air Defence Area.

Simon explained the organization. The fixed defences, all Army save for a small RNVR force which had somehow survived at the centre, were divided into three districts or "sub-commands", one each for the north, east and west of London. Each was commanded by a lieutenant-colonel answerable to Colonel Simon, who came directly under the Horse Guards. The Western Sub-Command, Toby's, comprised nineteen gun-stations and thirty-six searchlights, from two miles beyond Watford on the north side to three miles south of Bromley at the other extreme. His headquarters was in some huts in Putney Heath, immediately on top of the subterraneous reservoirs of the Metropolitan Water Board. His guns were mostly French seventy-fives, four of them motor-cannons from his old brigade, but there were also three British three-inch guns; no more of the latter type were to be had, for the submarine campaign was at its height and the Navy demanded every gun it could get for the arming of merchant ships. The seventy-fives, of course, were permitted only to fire shrapnel. When Toby began to say something on this vexed subject, he was informed that for the last month or so they had not been allowed to fire anything at all. Lord French had been experimenting by keeping all the guns quiet so that the fighter aircraft borrowed from France might have a better chance; that order was about to be rescinded. The searchlights were a mixed lot but not too bad. The men were another matter: the two companies of Royal Engineers (RE) who operated the lights were quite good, but the gunners were not exactly the pick of the Royal Regiment. The best of them were those who had served in France and whose partially-healed wounds disqualified them from going back to the battle. The remainder included a good proportion of deaf, dumb, myopic and plain imbecile. The officers, Simon said, he hardly knew, as they came and went with monotonous regularity. Some, he believed, were quite good.

With these cheering words ringing in his ears, Toby went to see things for himself. It was soon obvious that Simon had not exaggerated; after taking one quick look at his command, he went to visit Lieutenant-Colonel Lloyd of the Northern Sub-Command, by repute the best run of the three. Lloyd and his adjutant were men nearer to Toby's heart and they went to much trouble to initiate him into the ways of the London Air Defence Area. (The title was not formally adopted until July but it was in current use.) Toby had "the good fortune to be actually present at the headquarters of the North Sub-Command on the occasion of the first day raid by aeroplane squadrons in formation", he learnt much from it, in particular the necessity for the same people to perform the same tasks time and time again until they became second nature. He went thoughtfully back to his office over the reservoirs.

One of his first tasks was to make a few changes around there. By some stroke of genius, the officers and the operations room, with all the elaborate telephone network centred in it, were on one side of the water board's ring fence; his own hut and the quarters for the men were outside. His first action was to vacate the comfortable hut and have a tent pitched for his own use alongside the officer. Next, having ascertained that the offices of the two companies of RGA and two of RE which made up his unit were eight miles apart, he had them move to join his headquarters at Putney Heath. Then he turned to his personnel; some of the officers were completely useless in any capacity and obviously had to go. The stout Adjutant of the old Mobile Brigade, Lieutenant Fillimore, was brought back in his old capacity. Having thus ensured that there was somebody reliable left behind at headquarters, Toby set out on a tour of the West Sub-Command.

The extent of it appalled him, fifty-five stations being dispersed over an area of 500 square miles and kept in touch only by telephone. Toby made calculations: how far would he need to travel to visit three stations each day? When the figure reached 1,000 miles he gave it up and fell back on rule of thumb; he devoted every afternoon to visiting, but, even when he gave up his command eight months later, "there was still, I know, one infernal searchlight station which I never did visit".

The quality of his officers, in particular, shocked him; the only ones whom he reckoned to earn their pay were a middle-aged company commander who had served in South Africa as a Regular and a few who had learnt real soldiering with the BEF before their wounds had sent them home for good. The Sappers alone pleased him.

> The personnel of the engineer companies contained a high proportion of very intelligent men. The capacity of their NCOs [non-commissioned officers] also was far in advance of the average of those of the RGA. The results of this were that in many cases the condition and efficiency of the searchlight stations, which were under the command of NCOs of the RE, compared most favourably with the conditions obtaining at many of the gun-stations manned by the RGA. This fact became of great importance during raids, as, in the first place, the searchlight stations vastly out-numbered the gun-stations, and, secondly, the stations of the advanced lights, being situated farther out, always obtained the first information of the actual attack.

Without timely intelligence of the direction, numbers and height of the raiders, which the directing staff could relay to the gun-sites by telephone, the whole elaborate system became useless.

Toby, his moustache growing again and Army ways once more ousting those of the Senior Service, laid down a programme of hard training for his unpromising force; there were now settled drills for every type of gun and light and those who used them were made to go through the prescribed movements over and over again, wherever possible under his own eye. Now and then the RFC could be persuaded to fly an aeroplane or two over the capital so that the men on the height-finders and other instruments could get much needed practice without the distraction of bombs bursting around them. The pilots, understandably, had no great enthusiasm for the task, for there was a real risk that some dim-witted gunner might fire at them and, remote though the chances were, they might be hit. Apart from such aid as this afforded, the only possible training was in an unending series of dreary tactical exercises without aircraft. The gunners improved, but still the standard could not be called high. After the raid of 13 June, the commander of the Third German Squadron, Hauptmann Brandenburg, wrote in his report that "the gunfire was not particularly strong and was badly directed". There is no reason to contradict him.

In spite of the indifferent results, much thought had gone into the planning of the gunnery defences since Sir Percy's day and refinements were continual. Each sub-command had its operations room, a large chamber with telephone booths lined along the walls. In the middle was a vast table covered with a map of the whole country divided into several hundred numbered squares each of which was sub-divided in turn into four quarters identified by letters. The telephones were of two kinds, inward for messages received and outward for messages to the stations. Each box was connected to three gun-sites, which were themselves in direct communication with their own searchlights. There were other boxes connecting with the Horse Guards and the two neighbouring sub-commands. Each box, in theory, contained its own regular operator, whose job it was to move in the moment a warning was given and to stay there until he was dismissed, possibly many hours later. As a message came in he recorded it on a form, and handed it to an orderly, by whom it was taken to one of the duty officers. He acted as a filter, relaying only the most recent and important of the tidings to the commanding officer at the table. On this officer fell the burden of deciding and ordering what guns were to fire and of giving them their detailed orders. In daylight the gun-commanders were allowed some discretion as to firing on their own initiative, but by night all firing was strictly controlled from above. In order that the messages that it passed should be accurate, each station was furnished with a glass table, lit by electricity from below, on which was a properly oriented map, squared identically with that on the operations-room table.

In July, Major-General E. B. Ashmore, a gunner officer turned pilot, was brought from France to command the London Air Defence Area and he had ideas of his own about what might be done. Under Ashmore, the first balloon barrage appeared, a far more elaborate affair than that familiar in the next war, trailing a heavy wire apron similar to that employed by the Royal Navy to discourage U-boats from passing the Dover Straits. Its unpredictable habit of breaking loose and trailing destruction as it went mitigated both its usefulness and its popularity. Ashmore's greatest contribution, however, was to obtain the use of six squadrons of good, modern aircraft to intercept the raiders from a ring of makeshift aerodromes around the city. These were the real defenders. As the summer wore on and the great battles of Messines and Ypres thinned the ranks of the fighting men in France and Flanders, a steady trickle of the best Gunners and Sappers left the London Air Defence Area and crossed the narrow seas. The quality of those left fell even lower than before, the replacements being men who were, for the most part, quite unsuited to any form of military activity. Inevitably the burden fell even heavier on the better men who were left.

The Gothas continued to come over in waves during July and August—Southend, Margate, Ramsgate, Sheerness and Chatham all taking heavy punishment from them. In addition there were well-founded rumours of another and even more terrifying aeroplane being prepared to thicken them up. The R 39, the *Riesenflugzeug* or Giant 'Plane, was indeed being made ready for the purpose. It was a weapon ahead of its time: the wing-span of 140 feet was considerably greater than that of the Second War Lancaster and only about three feet less than that of the US Superfortress; it carried a crew of 7, 2 tons of bombs, six machine-guns, and, with four engines of a total of 1,000 horse-power, could climb to the unheard-of altitude of 20,000 feet. Its speed was much the same as that of the Gotha. Three of the Giants came over with double that number of the smaller aircraft during the great raid of 29 September, the fourth consecutive night that London had been bombed. The occasion was fixed for ever in Toby's mind because the heaviest raid of all took place during the period when he had been forbidden to fire high explosives from his seventy-fives and was restricted to using shrapnel.

Even under such an interdict, West Sub-Command fired 1,370 rounds that night, the barrels becoming red-hot and every gunner realizing when it was over that his hands had been badly burned. The raiders drew off as the last shells were being slammed into the breeches amidst clouds of steam as men poured bucket after bucket of water over the crimson metal. Fourteen more civilians had been killed, and eighty-seven injured, to swell the total of dead in all the raids so far to something over 600. All the ammunition for the seventy-fives was at Woolwich, "and it will therefore be appreciated that the task of replenishing my widely-scattered gun-stations, so that they might be in a position to meet an even more serious attack the next night, was as difficult as it was urgent and indispensable. My day was therefore spent in using every effort to obtain the supply of the necessary quantity of motor lorries to proceed to Woolwich, there to collect the ammunition and to subsequently immediately distribute it amongst the gun-stations in the various districts". The double split infinitive underlines Toby's agitation. It was not without cause, for the distribution was not completed until 6.24 p.m. and the next attack came in just one hour and six minutes later.

This was, perhaps, for the defenders, the worst raid of them all. Only the absolute minimum number of men needed to work the guns remained on strength, the rest having gone to France, and there were no reserves of any kind. Add to that that the majority were of poor physique to begin with, that many were quite untrained and that most of them had been in action throughout the previous night as well as getting in the ammunition during the day, and the wonder is that any barrage at all greeted the Germans on 30 September. Nevertheless, it did. Three squadrons approached from the east, the most southerly of them flying north-west over Chatham and Greenwich towards the West End; the central squadron came along the river, the third over Islington and all three concentrated on the same target. The battle lasted twice as long as that of the night before, and for about ninety minutes West Sub-Command fired with an intensity never before reached. Some of the seventy-fives shot away over 500 rounds, guns having at times to be left to cool down before they could safely be reloaded, despite all the hissing water poured over them. When a message reached headquarters from one green crew that a round had jammed in the gun, Toby ordered them to "jam another in behind it and fire it out". Such drastic surgery appeared to work, though it would have horrified Colonel Simon.

The Gothas, unaccompanied this time by Giants, were driven away after having done very little damage, and some of the credit must surely go to the tireless cripples of West Sub-Command. Toby was well pleased with his men and was not slow to tell them so, though he knew that the attack on the aerodrome and the aircraft factory at Hendon, plainly a main target on this occasion, had been saved not by guns nor by intercepting aircraft but by a good, old-fashioned London fog, which had put in a most timely appearance.

Unaccountable rumours were now going about that some remarkable thing had been done to the half-forgotten Zeppelins and that it was going to give them back their old invulnerability. Nobody knew quite what it was, but the warning was out to expect them again on the next succession of moonless nights. September dragged on and once more the wind brought to London the distant rumble of the guns in Flanders. To those with the experience to understand, it betokened yet a further thinning of the British ranks, with what compensations no one yet knew. More and more of the fitter men found themselves on the way to Folkestone and the waiting transports, some of them for the third or fourth time. The drafts that come to take their places were of a quality lower even than anything that had gone before October came, and with it news from Broodseinde and Passchendaele Ridge; there was little enough to show for the terrible sacrifices the Army had made since July.

The raids by aeroplanes continued and it would be tedious to recount the details of each one, though they kept Toby busy enough for him to be a stranger to any such emotion. Still the Zeppelins did not come, though the rumours of their improvement in performance and handling were stronger than ever. On the night of 19 October they arrived, information coming in that a number of them had crossed the coast at 8 p.m. Less than half an hour later they were reported to be to the north-east of London at distances varying between fifty and ninety miles. Then followed a long silence. At 10.30, on orders from the Horse Guards, searchlights began to sweep the sky over the darkened capital, but they found nothing. Toby was, for once, thoroughly uneasy. He did not at all care for the idea of giving free navigational beacons to the enemy and, being a man never slow to speak his mind, he got on the telephone to Simon. His scheme, surprisingly, met with immediate approval.

All the lights were doused in succession and men waited and wondered what was happening. An element was taking a hand which only Toby, so far, had understood. The gentle breeze of sundown was freshening and it was blowing from the north-west; on the ground it was still only about ten mph, but at an altitude of 15,000 feet or more it was sure to be much stronger. The Zeppelins, safe in the upper strata from any attack, would drift gently over London and could drop their bombs with impunity. Once they had passed over the city, however, there would be no turning back and they had only the one chance of carrying out their mission. Toby, with memories of his own flying days, reasoned that the navigators high above would have great difficulty in estimating the wind speed, and without that information their own speed over the ground, and consequently their position, would be a matter of conjecture. Once a couple of lights were uncovered, however, it would be the simplest thing in the world to mark the change of bearings and work out the necessary sums. Toby, in common with the other commanders, spoke personally and urgently to each station. Not a glimmer of light was to be shown without his specific order. The next few hours he readily admitted to be amongst the worst in his life, and it is fair to suppose that many other people were of the same mind. Somewhere, perhaps directly above their heads, was an unascertained number of airships, each heavily laden with death and destruction, and the defenders were powerless to do anything about it. By 11 p.m. all reports indicated that there were probably seven of the intruders, all met up together and ready for the float over central London for which they had come.

The first bomb fell a few minutes later, a plain invitation to the men below to show a light; no light came. The wind was increasing now, a fresh breeze blowing along the ground, and there was just the shadow of a chance that they might float right over the capital in ignorance of their power. "The succeeding minutes were charged with such an anguish of anxiety, and the horror of the awful tragedy which appeared likely to be enacted at any moment was so great as to cause me an absolute spasm of nervous agony. This I found it almost impossible to control, and it threatened every moment to render me physically sick from apprehension." It probably did exactly that to many with hearts less stout and stomachs less strong. Another single bomb fell, this time in Piccadilly Circus; Swan and Edgars collapsed in roaring ruin, but still no light was shown. This was the moment of truth; if all the many bombs poised overhead were to be dropped now the heart of London would be torn out. One more bomb came down, but it took a moment for news to arrive of where it had landed. The report emanated from the site at Grove Park. Toby could have thrown up his hat. The Zeppelins were now to the south-east and there could be no going back against that wind. The last Zeppelin raid was over and London might echo the words of Queen Elizabeth: "Deus afflavit, et dissipati sunt" ("God blew and they were scattered"). Only the good west wind had saved London from a destruction the extent of which may be deduced from the fact that the three bombs dropped had killed forty-three, injured forty-nine and done structural damage to the tune of £50,000 by 1917 values. The number of bombs not dropped was certainly nearer 200 than 100.

Providence stood England's friend that night and its work was not yet completed. None of the seven Zeppelins reached Germany again. French gunners destroyed one near Lunéville, another was forced down by Allied aircraft in western France, and two came to grief in the High Alps near Gap. The exact fates of the remainder are uncertain, but they were widely believed to have been carried by the same wind far out over the Mediterranean and, their fuel exhausted, to have been lost with all hands. It was a fitting envoi to the bombing airship, the reign of which was now over.

After another raid by aeroplanes on 1 November there came a lull and during the next few weeks there was an opportunity to get on with the uphill work of instilling at least some discipline and training into the new intake. There was an attack on the night of 6 December which lasted for only half an hour and a much heavier one came in twelve days later. Toby's gunners were kept continuously firing for nearly three hours. When it was over, he wrote in his report that "Generally, in view of the inexperience, want of training and indifferent physique of the personnel they can be said to have acquitted themselves fairly well." General Ashmore was energetic and capable but Toby was rapidly becoming disenchanted, particularly with his immediate superior. He tried hard to be fair about it. "I much fear and deeply regret that my way of getting things done was frequently not his way, and I became well aware that he would vastly prefer to have some other less independent and more amenable officer in my place, who would be more after the regulation pattern and less likely to give unintentional offence through a lack of observation of all and every formality."

The end came over a business that was really rather piffling. Toby, having been required to submit some names for promotion, included that of an officer whom he reckoned to have spent quite enough time in an office and to need to get out on to a gun-site in winter. Simon disagreed and Toby did not attempt to bridle his tongue. When Simon invited his resignation as a result, he wrote it out immediately; Toby did not really expect to go, for he quite thought that Ashmore would overrule Simon. He miscalculated and his request to be relieved of his command was accepted. Perhaps it is not all that surprising. He had no heartache at leaving, though for a time he regretted his action as perhaps giving the impression that he was shirking his responsibilities. Before he was relieved, however, two more sizable raids occurred and during them there were incidents that confirmed to him that this was no longer any place for him. At the height of a barrage one loading number, instead of putting a shell in the breech, shoved in his hand instead. Toby thought him mentally deficient, but it may be that he outwitted the rest by thus getting his discharge. A deaf ammunition number, at about the same moment, passed up two rounds of the wrong kind of shell, and large numbers of pedestrians insisted on claiming a right of way through the gun-site during the battle.

It was on 16 February 1918 that Toby finally took his leave; he went home to his house in Putney and greatly enjoyed the next air-raid, basking in a happy sunlight of irresponsibility. "Joy of all joys on earth, I was no longer responsible. The deaf, the blind and the mentally deficient could now commit every kind of possible and impossible enormity, but I could go to sleep."

As usual, a time-limit was set to his euphoria. It was near to March 1918 and all well-informed men knew what was almost certain to happen in France before that month was out. Toby, at fifty-one, was resolved not to be left out of things any more and wanted only to get back into the real war, anyhow and by any means. His old un-friend Lord Kitchener being long dead, Toby's thoughts turned again to the War Office.

He went there by appointment, for the new Chief of the Imperial General Staff (CIGS), Sir Henry Wilson, was an old acquaintance. Toby made a mental note of their conversation which ran something like this.

"Well, Toby, what are you going to do now?"

"I hope, sir, I may be able to be of service somewhere."

"Would you go to Persia?"

"Certainly, sir."

"When could you leave?"

"What time does the train start?"

Chapter Twelve

The Near and the Middle East had been the bane of statesmen in many countries for a long time past. The area supposedly was the heartland of the human race and, contrary to all presumptive evidence, it contained the site of the Garden of Eden, but, despite these attractions, it had seldom spelt other than trouble to men in London, Paris, Vienna and St Petersburg. The Ottoman Empire sprawled disreputably over great swathes of it, brought up short only by the forbidding mountain range that indicates the frontier between Mesopotamia and Persia. The endless quarrel between Turk and Muscovite had landed Britain and France in their last European war, Plevna had introduced a new name into the classic sieges of history, and an enfeebled Persia presented an easy victim for either of the contending parties. For Britain there were two relatively new problems. Asia Minor, Persia and Afghanistan lead inevitably to the teeming cities of the sub-continent of India. It was true, as the Duke of Wellington had said, that a man with a house in London and an estate in Scotland does not need to own the post-houses of the Great North Road, but he still would not wish to see them closed to him. The Grand Design of Napoleon Bonaparte in that direction had been frustrated by Lord Nelson and Sir Ralph Abercromby, but the possibility remained that, in other hands, the adventure might be repeated and with greater success. The Kaiser's much-advertised Berlin to Baghdad railway had pointed up the danger, which was not entirely averted when, in 1917, the further terminus fell into British hands. The other consideration was oil. Since Churchill had turned the Royal Navy over from Welsh steam coal to Persian oil, the security of the Gulf and the adjacent littoral had become a major concern to Britain.

The greater events which had taken place elsewhere had tended to keep the eyes of most people focused nearer home. After the Dardanelles disaster there had been little interest in the Caucasus and north Persia, except for a brief moment in 1916 when John Buchan's exciting novel *Greenmantle*, which recounted with advantages the story of the storming of Erzerum by the Cossacks of General Yudenich, first appeared. As the author had also compiled a strictly factual account of the same incident for Nelson's history of the war, it could be taken that it was not impossibly far fetched, and, indeed, it was not. At about the same time as the British–Indian garrison of Kut was roasting to death, an entire battalion of Cossacks was wiped out by the murderous cold of a Caucasian blizzard. The ancient city of Trebizond fell to Cossacks in April, and shortly afterwards they destroyed the Turkish Third Army of Vehip Pasha at Erzincan. This, however, passed almost unnoticed in England.

War between Russia and Turkey had, however, continued incessantly, and the neutrality of Persia had been entirely ignored. Yudenich's subordinate General Baratov had bravely and competently taken on far superior Turkish forces along the road between Khanikin and Kermanshah. At the end of 1915 he had been chased out of Hamadan and his army took up an impregnable position along the mountain ridge athwart the road to Kasvin, with its centre on the Sultan's Pass. From that eminence he defied all attempts to budge him.

With the arrival of Toby's old school-fellow Sir Stanley Maude, new life was breathed into the languishing British army in the Middle East. Early in 1917, Maude broke the Turkish Sixth Army to the west of Kut and went on to seize Baghdad itself. The spectacle of a British general seated, metaphorically speaking, on the throne of Harun al-Rashid was one of the odder consequences of Kaiser Wilhelm II's wanton attack on his European neighbours. Sad to say, Maude did not live long after his army's victory. In November he died suddenly. Officially it was put down to cholera, but there were many who believed that he was the victim of the traditional Eastern method of disposing of enemies, by poison.

General Marshall, on whom fell Maude's cloak, was a worthy successor. Early in December he marched out of Baghdad and took Khanikin, just inside the Mesopotamian border, whence he put himself into direct communication with Baratov. A line of sorts existed from the Persian Gulf to the shores of the Caspian. At the end of March 1918, Marshall struck hard at the Turkish army on the Euphrates and won a substantial victory at Khan Bagdadi, on the road to Aleppo. 5,000 men were taken prisoner and many guns fell into his hands. In the same month revolutionary Russia, having virtually surrendered to Imperial Germany, signed the Treaty of Brest-

Litovsk. The army of Baratov ceased to be an Allied force and northern Persia, from Khanikin to the Caspian at Enzeli, lay open to invasion. The urgent need of troops on the Western Front consequent upon the great German offensive which began on 21 March had sadly weakened the armies of both Allenby in Palestine and Marshall in Mesopotamia. The Turks had been beaten, it is true, but they still had substantial resources and the Anatolian peasant, as many British soldiers knew, was an enemy to be taken very seriously indeed. There was real danger to Afghanistan, where a friendly shah was faced by a powerful pro-Turkish, pro-Islamic party; if Afghanistan were to go under, nothing stood in the way of an invasion of India. It would need not operation orders but only march-tables.

The political situation was as obscure as only a political situation can be. Imperial Russia had proved a most faithful ally, giving freely of her blood and treasure regardless of the cost to herself. Little enough was known of the men who had supplanted Nicholas II and that little was not encouraging to the Allies. Plainly the remnant of the Russian armies would no longer fight the Germans and Austrians; would they instead turn on their former friends? Nobody knew. There is an admirable military aphorism which asserts that to do nothing is to do something definitely wrong. Sir Henry Wilson, at the moment when strong and seemingly irresistible German armies stood at the gates of Amiens, had to do something. If what he decided to do seems now to have been an exercise in futility, in fairness one should reflect a moment and ponder whether, at that time, he should have been expected to know that within a year, contrary to every expectation, the war would be over and the Allies everywhere victorious. By far the more likely prospect before him was that of a Germany freed from maintaining more than a police force in the East, a Germany whose armies were, to all outward appearances, as strong and as numerous as ever. Turkey, with no war worth mentioning left to fight near home, could easily entrain some of her excellent divisions to give the *coup de grâce* in France. The future potential of the United States, no matter how great, could avail nothing at all if these things were to happen. No one should presume to criticize the CIGS on this occasion for not being aware that the dead armies of 1916 and 1917 had hit their enemies so hard that, in the final extremity, it was to be the Germans who would give way.

Wilson was no expert in Eastern affairs, though he had manifested more interest in and understanding of them than had his predecessor, Sir William Robertson. At least he knew that across the root of the Caucasus between the Black Sea and the Caspian lay three quasi-states which might be willing and able to produce scratch forces of some kind to stand in the way of any eastward drive by

Turkey. The ancient kingdom of Georgia, with its capital at Tiflis, had inhabitants reputedly descended from the Golden Horde of Genghis Khan, and had lost its separate identity only a little over a century before. Adjoining Georgia to the east lay Armenia. If any people had cause to hate the Turk and to cherish thoughts of bloody vengeance, surely it was the much-persecuted Armenians. Had not Gladstone at least made loud and well-disposed noises on their behalf at the end of the last century? Beyond Armenia was Azerbaijan, rich with cotton, rice and oil; Baku was one of the oldest oil-fields in Europe. Would the Azerbaijanis tamely allow all this wealth to pass into alien hands? These questions had to be answered and they could be dealt with only by trial and error. It was, of course, a counsel of despair, but it can be fairly argued that desperate needs demand desperate remedies. Wilson came to the conclusion that the effort must be made and a military mission sent to teach the Armenians and the rest to defend themselves.

In point of fact, Wilson had already acted before the German attack began. It was in January 1918 that Major-General Dunsterville was given orders to present himself at Baghdad and be ready to head a military mission to Tiflis. Dunsterville had, till this time, been commanding a brigade on the North-West Frontier of India, his only claim to recognition being that he had attended the same school as Rudyard Kipling, who had taken him as the model for his central figure in "Stalky and Co". Kipling must have commanded a wider readership than one would have expected, for a Baku newspaper dated 16 July 1918 makes mention of the fact. More to the point, Dunsterville was one of the few senior army officers to speak fluent Russian. He shared one characteristic with Toby: the ability to be entirely serious without being solemn.

He soon found himself in need of this admirable quality, for the situation with which he was confronted was a daunting one. The Russian forces were disappearing at a great rate, partly by being called home as complete units but even more by straightforward desertion. Attempts to persuade individuals to enlist as a kind of British foreign legion had proved a complete failure. Despite the fact that they had been, on the whole, victorious and that their generals were amongst the best officers in the Czar's service and had cared for their men in a fashion unknown elsewhere, the Russian peasant soldiers had had enough of war. It is hard to blame them, for news of the fate of their families was scanty and the spirit of revolution is heady. The result, however, was that a vacuum of 450 miles existed on the British right. To fill it, Dunsterville was allotted 200 men, every one hand-picked from other theatres of war, including France, and many of them were tough and resourceful characters from

Canada, Australia and New Zealand. They did not arrive *en bloc* and it took the whole of February and March for the little force to assemble. In the meantime, the Caucasus and northern Persia showed every sign of breaking up into factions run by self-appointed warlords and committees, all of them well armed with discarded Russian and captured Turkish weapons. Nobody could even guess where their loyalties, if any, would lie. Everything centred on the long road from Baghdad to Enzeli, 600 miles long; the road had been made long ago by a Russian company, under a concession granted by the Persian government, and Enzeli was still, theoretically, a Russian concession port.

The road was, of course, Dunsterville's first subject for study. From Baghdad to Khanikin was just short of 100 miles with a fairly good surface over hard clay; the next 240 miles, to Hamadan, were described as "very doubtful, difficult in good weather and impassable in bad". The remaining 267 to Enzelli by way of Kasvin were over a stretch that had once been good but now suffered from long neglect. Snow in the mountains was commonplace and from time to time it was severe enough to block the passes completely. The expedition was, inevitably, to be carried all the way in motor vehicles, and the first party, which set off late in January, comprised twelve officers, two clerks, four touring cars and thirty-six Ford vans. Their way ran through the country of the tough and savage Kurds, whose ancient tradition of highway robbery rivalled that of the Pathans. The last seventy miles lay through the dominions of Mirza Kuchik Khan, who enjoyed a reputation for xenophobia and bloodthirstiness all his own. It took the party eight days to make Kermanshah, after many adventures; these, however, were occasioned entirely by the severity of the weather, for the snow had driven the Kurds to seek shelter in the valleys below. There Dunsterville found an ally in the person of Colonel Bicherakov CB, DSO, whose Cossacks had evinced a loyalty to him that no revolution could entirely dispel. With guides and escorts provided by him, Dunsterville and a small advanced party arrived at Hamadan early in February, the commander and a couple of others finishing the journey on ponies in a snowstorm. After a short rest, the party, now increased to forty-one vehicles and strengthened by an armoured car, pressed on to Kasvin, where Dunsterville was informed that Kuchik Khan was working with the Bolsheviks and had sworn a mighty oath never to let the British pass through his domain. Dunsterville, who had had much experience of hill tribesmen, would not allow himself to be deterred and set off to cover the last twenty miles through the country of the Jangalis, as Kuchik's people were called.

Kuchik was not, at bottom, a bad man; like so many others he had drunk deep of the platitudes of revolution and he had appointed a committee, many of whose members were men far worse than he. He had, however, an army of sorts, led by a German officer named von Passchen, with plenty of weapons. Kuchik's philosophy was simple and direct: he was a Persian, and the Persians do not love the Russians. In the euphoria produced by great clouds of swelling words, the hatchet had temporarily been buried, for the Russians were leaving Persia, presumably never to return. The road was choked with their straggling columns and Kuchik was doing a thriving trade buying their arms and ammunition at knock-down prices against the day when they might come in useful. When the last Russian had sailed from Enzeli, he, Kuchik, would be undisputed lord of a large, rich tract of territory, his power mitigated only by an allegiance to his overlord the Shah, which would sit lightly on him. As for the British, he wanted nothing to do with them, for, given the slightest encouragement, they could play King Stork to the Czar's King Log, and that was no part of Kuchik's plan. One observer, seeing him lavishly draped in Mauser automatic pistols and wicked-looking knives, remarked that he expected to see the chorus of "The Maid of the Mountains" appear at any moment and burst into song.

In an atmosphere of undisguised hostility Dunsterville set off, the armoured car leading with the gunner's fingers wrapped firmly round the pistol-grip of his Lewis. There were no fighting men apart from the drivers and each had his rifle and bandolier ready to hand. As they drove over the saddle and down into the forest, parties of banditti appeared and gesticulated menacingly. Dunsterville, however, had been right in his appreciation: the Jangalis, for all their formidable appearance, were not in the same class as the Pathans. A few shots were fired from a discreet distance but nothing more alarming took place, and on 17 February the column drove to the waters of the Caspian. There were about a couple of thousand Russian troops in Enzeli, but their demeanour was quite friendly.

It was not, however, with the Russians that Dunsterville had to contend. His first charge was to find out what shipping was available to take his party on to Baku, as the next step towards Tiflis, and this brought him into contact with the local Bolshevik committee. They were quite firm about it: there were no ships available to take him and his vehicles to Baku or, indeed, to anywhere else. Furthermore, it was strongly rumoured that the Ford vans contained large quantities of gold. With only a handful of men and in the midst of a large, inimical population plainly bent on loot and murder, he could achieve nothing. Even if he were able, by some stratagem, to get his party embarked, there were three Bolshevik gun-boats lying off the port and in touch with it by wireless. Against these he could offer no defence, so, making the best of a bad job, he came to terms with the committee and drove back. Resht was controlled by a heavily armed mob and was clearly no place in which to linger; Kasvin was in no better case, so, very sensibly, he returned to Hamadan. The convoy negotiated the Sultan Bulaq Pass in deep snow and arrived at the town on 25 February. The prospect of raising a Georgian–Armenian–Azerbaijani army looked as bleak as anything could be.

Dunsterforce, as it was now officially called, remained at Hamadan until the beginning of June. The town, known in the great days of the Achaemanian Empire as Ecbatana, had little to show for its past, but it did have a great quantity of spies. There were German spies and Turkish spies, Bolshevik spies and spies of Kuchik, spies of the rudimentary but growing Pan-Islamic movement, and spies of various aspiring Persian factions. When they could find no one else upon whom to spy, they spied upon each other, and all of them spied upon the British, against whom, now and then, various groups made common cause. Happily, they were not very efficient, and Dunsterville, who had his own agents amongst the staff of the Posts and Telegraph office, intercepted many messages.

General Baratov was also in Hamadan, but he was no longer the fierce Turk-eater of earlier years; his army was now utterly without discipline and wanted only to go home. Baratov could do little about this without money and the new government in Russia was sending him none. He had been reduced to issuing his own paper currency and was trying desperately hard to persuade the British authorities to back it. A Georgian himself, with his home in Tiflis, he had done his best to help in raising the still-born foreign legion and had thus made himself very unpopular with the Bolsheviks, whom, as a loyal officer of the Czar, he held in abhorrence. Dunsterville, though personally sympathetic, could do nothing to help him. Unable to return home, he was eventually invited by the British Government to pay a protracted visit to India, which he duly did.

The winter weather continued and, before long, famine added to the existing problems. For several weeks Dunsterville's little group was distracted from all other occupation by the need to obtain and distribute food over a large area; they got little enough thanks for their pains. When the snow lessened, reinforcements began to arrive. A group of officers came in at the beginning of April, followed by a platoon of the First Battalion, the Fourth Hampshire Regiment, who arrived just in time to prevent a serious attack on the British Legation. Apart from Bicherakov's Cossacks, they were the only fighting soldiers in the force.

As the winter weather dragged on, it became apparent that nothing could be achieved in Georgia and the Tiflis enterprise was written off. Instead, Dunsterville was ordered to make for the oil port of Baku. The Turks were believed, with reason, to have designs on the oilfields and it was plain that the power which held Baku commanded the whole of the Caspian shores, together with their important produce. Dunsterville's command was still tied down by the necessity of keeping some form of organized society in existence in a disintegrating Persia and it was not until 1 June that he felt himself able to move out again along the same old road. This was the locality to which Toby was consigned and the state of affairs that he would find there.

Chapter Thirteen

Toby's travels had never before taken him to Persia, but, all the same, it did not come to him as entirely foreign. His father had been largely responsible for the training of the Persian army back in the 1830s; after that he had served with Nott and Pollock during the march through Afghanistan with the Army of Retribution following on the military disaster known as the First Afghan War. When that had been satisfactorily concluded by the blowing up of the great bazaar at Kabul, Henry Rawlinson had moved back to Persia. Enzeli had been his wash-pot and over Ecbatana he had cast his shoe, but his greatest work had been around the rock-face at Behistun, where he had spent years in deciphering the cuneiform inscription of Darius Hystaspes and so lifting the veil on a wealth of information about the distant past. "The Arabian Nights"—the expurgated version—had been reading both required and popular in the Rawlinson nursery, along with the book on Herodotus written by Uncle George, the canon. Darius, Xerxes, Alexander, the Ptolemies and Harun al-Rashid had been names as familiar as those of Hereward the Wake and Tom Brown, but Toby had served long enough in India to cherish no illusions about the gorgeousness of the East and his father's adventures at the time of the siege of Herat had bred in him an instinctive suspicion, which was not dispelled by a change of management in Petersburg, of Russian aims in that quarter.

Wilson was not the most reliable of prophets. Although he had been to Russia in 1916, the outbreak of revolution had taken him completely by surprise. Unlike Sir Douglas Haig, he had been surprised again when the German blow fell on the Fifth Army front on 21 March, for his appreciation had been that it would come a month later and much further north. Toby, however, knew none of these things as he was passed down to a pompous staff colonel who would give him all the details he needed to have. The colonel annoyed Toby from the start by announcing with much dignity that he was sending him to Persia, in a manner that implied the decision to be his alone and doubtless of some surprise to his listener. After some unrewarding conversation he furnished Toby with two envelopes, both sealed; one contained his orders, the other a list of the kit with which he would do well to equip himself. Toby read the second one first; it assured him that officers designated for service with this particular expedition must expect to undergo every sort of climatic rigour from blizzards at sub-zero temperature to scorching tropical heat. Then followed the inventory. It contained very many items, from snow-shoes and fur-lined sleeping-bags to sand-fly nets and spine-pads. Toby read it with increasing scepticism: he had seen lists like this before and all experience had taught him that, as they were compiled by the London military outfitters, most of the articles set out were either unnecessary, useless, or obtainable locally at a fraction of the price demanded at home. He cheered up, however, on finding a note at the end which informed him that, on presentation of these orders, a cashier would provide him with a draft for £5 to defray the cost of his equipment.

Toby reasoned with himself for a moment. The object of having all these elaborate trappings, for the transport of which he would need a private pantechnicon, was to protect his important person from the elements. That, he argued, could be equally well done from within and he persuaded himself that the reasoning was sound. He drew the £5 with a resolution to convert it forthwith into food and drink, of which he stood in far more need than of yak-skin gloves or mosquito-boots. Over the meal thus provided he studied the contents of the other packet.

After perusing it once and then unhurriedly re-reading it, he could find no information that was not already readily available to any man who troubled to inform himself about the state of affairs in the Middle East. From the point of view of the British Army, the war there seemed to be dying away. Allenby's seizure of Jerusalem the previous Christmas had put an end to the Ottoman supremacy in Arabia and southern Palestine, but little had happened since then. The death-grapple on the Western Front which had begun on 21 March had demanded that every British soldier whose presence elsewhere was not indispensable should come at once to France. The army in Palestine had been milked hard of fighting men and was in no case to produce any more oriental epics; in any event, men's taste for these had fallen off since the brave days of the Gallipoli landings. In Mesopotamia, General Maude's successor, Marshall, had his hands full and there were no more Baghdads to be taken; his task now was to plug the gaps left by the disappearing Russians as best he could and with no help from home. Georgia was, it seemed, in the process of converting itself into some sort of ragged republic, and there remained a faint hope that Imperial Russia, in spite of the dreadful mauling her armies had received and of the even more dreadful events of recent months, might still recognize who her enemies were and be capable of yet another rally. Presumably Toby's efforts were to be directed to that end. Since he was to be unhampered by any companions, Toby made his own arrangements for the discomfiture of whatever enemies might present themselves. The Colt machine-guns came out of their wrappings and two more of the products of Hartford, Connecticut, were added, in the form of a pair of ·45-inch automatic pistols. With these as the nucleus of his kit, he set off on his longest journey yet.

After a short stop at the château of Flixecourt, in the Somme valley, where Sir Henry Rawlinson was establishing his new headquarters, Toby continued to Marseilles, where he joined a convoy bound for Alexandria. One of the ships, the Orient liner *Omrah*, which Toby had originally been booked to travel on, was torpedoed on the first night after leaving port and sunk. The destroyers succeeded in saving all its passengers and crew and brought them safely to Malta, where the convoy broke its journey in order to take on coal and redistribute the shipwrecked passengers. Toby managed to get ashore and took himself at once to Government House, for Lady Methuen, the wife of the Governor, was his cousin. Unfortunately both she and the Governor were away, but an invitation to dinner was some sort of compensation, though Toby was not feeling at all well. Like everybody else, he had been inoculated at Marseilles rather comprehensively, "against smallpox, enteric, typhoid and cholera for a start and I don't know how many other things incidentally". His left arm began to swell in alarming proportions and by the time the convoy began to thread its way through the elaborate mine-fields off Alexandria it had reached the stage when he could no longer pull the sleeve of his jacket over it. His head felt as though it were bursting and the usual symptoms of a bad bout of fever were on him. An old friend, Fred Stern, was on the staff at Cairo and to him Toby made his way in search of medical attention. Stern, after taking one look at him, carried him off to his own house and put him instantly to bed. By the time the doctor had arrived, the arm was "terribly swollen right up to and into the shoulder, a horrible colour and quite dead to the touch, and more like a bit of pretty hot metal or the branch of a tree with some tiny little fingers at the end than an arm of flesh and blood". Through the fever-clouds, Toby clearly caught the word "amputation"; this brought him at once to the surface "as I'd had surgeons threatening to cut limbs off me before and thus far had always been able successfully to resist their anxiety to operate". Stern was fully persuaded that when his friend left the house it would be feet first, but both he and the doctor yielded to the faint but clear instructions to leave the arm where its maker had put it. For three days they massaged and poulticed it; at the end of that time Toby got wind of the fact that a ship would be at Suez on the following day and, intent on catching it, left the house unsteadily with his jacket over his arm. During the railway journey from Cairo to Suez by way of Ismailia he was able to take his mind off his own predicament when he caught sight of the Australian Light Horse training in the desert. All the old Lancer in him came to the top as he watched these splendid troops through the window of the crawling train. "It was in every way excellent, better than anything of the kind I had ever seen before and covering a much greater distance and at a much faster rate than I had hitherto thought possible while the general control of the advance and the individual horsemanship was a revelation indeed."

Noon at Suez was as hot as it always is; Toby, still unattached to anybody, managed to get an Egyptian cab to take him to the office of the Embarkation Staff Officer, who, when eventually he appeared, after a protracted luncheon, allotted Toby a cabin in the P & O liner *Kashgar*, which was due to sail in two days' time. The arm was, by then, very painful indeed, as even Toby admitted.

On 5 June, after a voyage that had been hell, Toby reported himself to Sir George MacMunn, the Inspector-General of Communications at Basra, and, in the morning, he paid a visit to the officers' shop and set himself up with sensible kit.

The next day, he left for Baghdad by a form of transport novel even to a man of his wide experience. The muddy waters of the Tigris were made muddier yet by the stern-wheelers of the Irrawaddy Flotilla which had been borrowed for the occasion. They were, inevitably, crammed above capacity with troops, who slept as best they could where they could and were innocent of any form of protection against the insect life that plagues Mesopotamia. Toby was no more protected than they, and by the time the minarets of Baghdad drew into sight, he had been comprehensively bitten. The torment went on for eight days and nights more, with scant compensation. However, Toby's immediate prospects were brighter than those of most people, for Wilson had furnished him with a letter of introduction to the Commander-in-Chief, whose hospitality it was reasonable to suppose he would enjoy. As at Malta, however, Toby's luck was out. The Chief was away and a staff officer informed him that he was required to leave almost at once to take a convoy of 500 cars some-where into the wilds. Having no invitation to remain, Toby withdrew to the nearest hotel; the temperature he observed to be standing at 115°F in the courtyard, and, wretched though he was feeling, he set out to make his arrangements.

He did not get far with them. Within an hour of leaving the hotel, he had been picked up by a car and whipped into hospital, uncon-scious. A brief examination sufficed to justify the hospital authorities in sending a cable to the War Office that Colonel Rawlinson was seriously ill. The War Office dutifully passed on the information to Flixecourt, where Sir Henry drew the obvious and reasonable infer-ence that his young brother was not much longer for this world. Not so Mrs Rawlinson. "Thanks to some special gift that God has given her, and of which, without the least understanding it, I have had conclusive evidence on subsequent similar occasions, [she] entirely refused even to consider the possible accuracy of such a statement and maintained stoutly that, though I might be looking dead, yet in fact I wasn't, which was actually the true state of the case." Though one hears little of her, there can be no doubt that an unusual degree of understanding existed between husband and wife.

Toby was out for a count of twenty-four hours; when he came round he was kept tied down in bed for the next three days on a diet of milk and castor-oil in equal proportions. This unattractive combi-nation proved effective and he was allowed to sit up in a chair on the fourth day, after which he was removed to a convalescent home on the bank of the Tigris. There the thermometer on the verandah established new records, 113°F at 8 a.m., and 130°F at 5.30 p.m. Nobody cared to take a noon reading. His cure seems to have been completed by a tactless young doctor who observed, unfeelingly, that Toby would never be any good in that climate, as he was too old and ought to be sent home at once. "If that same gentleman had repeated that same remark to me a little later on, when I was a bit stronger, it would have afforded me the very greatest satisfaction to demonstrate his error to him without delay in a thoroughly effective manner." The therapeutic effect of sheer rage might make an interest-ing study.

His normal equanimity returned when, on the second day at the home, a message arrived that General Marshall had returned and would be glad to receive Toby as his guest. Telephone wires buzzed, and within the hour an aide-de-camp had arrived and Toby was on his way in state to the great rooms, cool terraces and fountain-sprink-led courtyards of the Commander-in-Chief's residence. There he passed the next three days, exchanging news of Fourth Army for that of more local interest while he enjoyed "electric fans, ice, a first-class

123

cook and servants, a launch on the river and cars for the city." The only disappointment was to find that his father's old house had been pulled down long ago.

For the next three days he wandered rather unsteadily around the ancient city of the caliphs buying the kit which he lacked and which experience showed that he would be likely to need. A tent, a Primus stove, hurricane lamps, saddlery and as much tinned food as funds would permit went to join his private armoury. On the evening of 25 June all was ready for his departure, and, after watching the finals of the Army Boxing Championship with his host, he entrained in the miniature Decauville railway for the base-camp of Dunsterforce at Ruz, sixty miles to the north-east. It was fifty-seven days since he had left London and the new adventure could at last be said to have begun.

He reached Ruz in the early hours of the following morning; after a satisfying breakfast he was provided with two Ford vans and was bidden to do his best to catch up with the convoy which he ought to have been commanding, then ten days' journey ahead. By 9.30 packing was complete and the chase had begun. Toby and his party passed through Khanakin at noon, the road becoming rougher with every mile and with the high mountains of Persia which were their goal looming distantly ahead. In the course of the first day alone, it was necessary to mend seven punctures. As the light of day began to thicken, the two vans entered a narrow valley running sharply uphill for some ten miles with a swift stream at its side. When the valley ended, a sheer cliff rose in face of them to a height which Toby estimated at about 2,000 feet. They were at the foot of the Takht-i-Gehri, the ancient pass of the pilgrims and the only place negotiable for vehicles in some hundreds of miles either side. Of a road there was no trace. However, a sturdy British corporal presented himself and explained matters. He was, it appeared, in charge of the military post on that side of the mountain and under his direction Toby was just able to descry, hundreds of feet above their heads, a narrow ledge in a cleft in the rocks which seemed to rise perpendicularly towards the sky. That, the corporal gravely explained, was the road. The only piece of encouragement was that the corporal was in touch by telephone with another post at the top, and, after much turning of handles and swearing, he was able to give a firm assurance that no other vehicle would be permitted on the road in either direction until their arrival at the summit had been confirmed to him. This was some comfort, as the track was so narrow in places that there was barely room for one car on it at a time. What would have happened had two met does not bear thinking about. The two vans set off, Toby fervently hoping that his faith in the skilful workmen of Detroit had not been misplaced; even he had never before seen such a road as this.

For a time they growled up in bottom gear without the zig-zags presenting too much difficulty, for the road had a fairly decent surface. After a while, however, this petered out and they found their wheels turning over the naked rock worn smooth by the feet of pilgrims beyond counting who had used this same way to travel from Persia and the lands of Central Asia in order to win the right to wear the coveted green turban and bear, for the rest of their lives, the title of Hadji. On Toby's left rose the vertical wall of cliff; on the right was a descent, equally sheer, into a bottomless abyss. The gradient became fiercer and with it the nervous tension that gripped the passengers; inevitably the moment came when, with radiators boiling, the small Fords gave up the ghost. Toby and his drivers emerged from their seats intent on the obvious and essential task of chocking the back wheels with something before the force of gravity proved stronger than their hand-brakes, There was no question of walking round to the back, for each van was hard up against the cliff on its near side and there was no space worth speaking of between the off-side wheels and the void. Fortunately the vehicles of 1918 were built with a good ground clearance and, loss of dignity apart, there was no great difficulty in crawling beneath them from one end to the other. This done, the wheels were secured with rocks and the whole party applied itself to heaving on each van in order to assist the small engine, and so, by fits and starts, they arrived at the summit of the pass just as the night closed in upon them. It was hardly the treatment for a convalescent, but Toby was past thinking about such things. He dined with the brigadier in command of the camp there, at a table set on a platform of rock on the edge of the precipice they had just climbed. The scene was memorable, for as a great moon rose there was nothing visible but empty air beneath which lay a quivering haze of heat. To the side the great hills stood out in sharp relief and the tinkle of falling water came faintly to them from the depths below. That night Toby slept well.

In the morning they were off again as soon as there was light enough to see, well content that in only twelve hours' driving they had covered a hundred miles and climbed 4,000 feet. For a dozen miles they continued to climb, though less dramatically, over a stony track, from time to time removing the boulders which constantly cascaded down from the mountains on either side. Then began an easy descent for another twenty-five miles into a marshy plain, cultivated in places and sprinkled sparsely with villages. This was bandit country, the home of the Bakhtiari brigands, but the journey was enlivened by nothing more than their becoming bogged at a couple of stream-crossings, and they crossed the last ridge, at an altitude of 6,500 feet, at sunset to find themselves looking down on the ancient and famous city of Kirmanshah. It was then that some of the second van's wheel spokes broke (stout hickory spokes went into the making of the artillery wheels that were then in general use on all motor vehicles). Lacking the necessary spare wheel, Toby could only leave the victims with one of his precious machine-guns and drove on alone to the city, having prudently removed the more useful and valuable articles before quitting the benighted van. No harm came, for there was a well-equipped transport depot at Kirmanshah and a suitable wheel was quickly found. As Toby pitched his tent, he calculated that another 120 miles lay behind them and he was well content.

The ASC officer in charge of the depot was next morning able to augment Toby's convoy with eighteen Ford lorries, made up by "cannibalizing" twenty-five which for mechanical reasons had dropped out from the original column. Both Henry Ford and the ASC came in for some deserved praise. The enlarged convoy then set off along a decent road, which, soon after leaving Kirmanshah, passed below the great rock of Behistun. Toby was determined to stop and see this, especially as the opportunity would probably never come his way again. "This was the lodestone which retained my father in those parts for 12 long years, and on its surface is the famous cuneiform inscription which had remained unread and undecipherable for 2,500 years till he determined he would persevere until he achieved the success which was his at last, when, after 12 years continuous study, he gave the long-lost language back to the world, with alphabet, grammar, dictionary complete and so laid bare to history the records of Darius, the King of Kings."

Toby had, of course, been brought up on the story of how his father had achieved this feat, but only now did he fully realize the magnitude of it. It took him a hard climb up a hundred feet of sharp rocks before he found a place from which the great work could be seen, and he marvelled at what he saw. Upwards of thirty panels of drawings and writings, deeply carved by master-craftsmen into the diamond-hard quartz, were as fresh as on the day when the last workman had been paid off. It seemed apparent that, when the carving was finished, the face of the cliff had been cut away below, leaving the panels inaccessible to any who might come later with inimical intentions. There stood the great king, his prisoners bound and kneeling before him with their hands tied behind their backs, with the official history of the events commemorated deeply incised beneath. Toby remarked that Darius "looked a hell of a swell, with his hair and his square beard all beautifully and elaborately crimped in the fashion of that day."

One other piece of ancient work proved to be less durable. Close by the foot of the rock runs a stream, crossed by a hump-backed bridge of brick. The angle of it made it necessary for the lorries, each weighing something like five tons, to charge it at full-tilt in order to get over. The moment came, as Toby's convoy so mistreated it, that the old bridge cried "Enough", and as one of them began its charge somebody realized that the crown had disappeared. Fording it with the remainder took so long that they made only eighty-five miles that day, an average of less than six miles an hour, and they passed the night by the side of the road with the Primus stoves roaring merrily. They drove off for the last leg of the journey at 5.30 in the morning with the prospect before them of another climb of several thousand feet, over the Asadabad Pass, and every vessel capable of holding water was filled up for that purpose. The crossing was formidable enough, but after the Takht-i-Gehri it seemed child's play and was notable only for the splendid view from the top.

They came to Hamadan early in the afternoon with all their lorries in good running order. There Toby met the man who was to be his new chief, Dunsterville himself. At the General's suggestion Toby pitched his tent in the garden of the house which served as headquarters and residence and, when that was finished, walked over to the Mess, where the two men took stock of each other.

Chapter Fourteen

"I must admit that I was astonished to find that his bedding appeared to be used chiefly as a wrapping for assorted weapons of war. I seem to remember that a machine-gun, or a portion of one, peeped from beneath his pillow. I instantly realised that I was confronted with a personality that was not of a usual type and one that was likely to impress itself upon others." It is unnecessary to say which of the two was the writer of this appreciation. It was reciprocated by Toby thus:

> Never in the course of a very varied career have I met any personality so instantly claiming or so permanently retaining my respect and sympathy. Possessed of an exceptional sense of humour, no difficulties were ever so great, nor situations so hopeless, that he could not, and did not, see and appreciate the brighter side of every event, however tragic. Himself possessed of the inestimable gift of courage in the face of adversity, he knew how to communicate to others, less gifted than himself, that confidence in themselves to which is due the measure of success achieved by the force under his command in the face of the apparently impossible task with which they found themselves confronted.

Either man could have stood as a pattern for all that was best in the breed produced by that now derided institution, the English public school. The situation in which they were placed was one bound to inculcate in any man a strong sense of the ridiculous, even had he been unlucky enough to be denied it at his birth.

Toby moved on the last 140 miles to Kasvin without incident, having been brought up to date with the events that had taken place since the last news had reached him. Kuchik Khan had, for the moment, been cut down to size. He had established himself across the line of advance to the sea in a position, centred on the bridge at Menjil, which should have been impregnable. He was strong in machine-guns, possessed a certain amount of artillery, and, by all the rules, it should have been impossible to drive him from such a stronghold without the employment of resources far exceeding those available to the allies. In spite of this, Bicherakov had advanced upon him at the head of his 1,000 Cossacks, with a squadron of Fourteenth Hussars for solidarity, and the Jangalis had fled. The battle of Menjil Bridge, if such it can be called, had taken place on 12 June and the discomfiture of the Jangalis had been completed by the appearance of a pair of British aeroplanes, which had teased them by diving and swooping on them as they ran, though they did not fire a single shot. On 18 June, two companies of the First Battalion, the Fourth Hampshire Regiment, with the same two armoured cars, brushed aside ambushes and strode to the sea marshes at Resht. Two companies of the First Battalion, the Second Gurkha Rifles, went with them and a little kukri-work on their part dispersed all opposition. Dunsterville himself re-entered Enzeli on 27 June.

Equally encouraging was the fact that Dunsterforce was now on the way to becoming a serious military body, for an entire infantry brigade—the Thirty-Ninth, part of the Fourteenth Division—was on its way from various places to provide the solid flesh that the skeleton organization so badly needed. Four good New Army battalions—the Seventh Battalions of the Gloucesters and the North Staffords plus the Ninth of the Royal Warwicks and the Worcesters—would make a very great difference to what the force could do. For the moment, however, there was no security anywhere and Kuchik was scotched, not killed. Bicherakov, on smelling the sea, had announced his conversion to Bolshevism, a word which at that time and place could mean anything one wished. The word had got around with great speed and he had been offered command of something called the Red Field Army, away beyond Baku. He had accepted and left, accompanied by the British staff officers who had been with him all along and also by Commander Locker-Lampson's armoured-car squadron. The garrison of Resht consisted of a Hampshire sergeant and a dozen men. On the other side of the hill, a Turkish army of about 12,000—half of them regulars—was advancing from Tiflis towards Baku, though they were making heavy weather of it. The railway line on which they depended was in bad shape, its rolling stock worn out, and fuel was short; to complicate matters even further, the Germans in Tiflis, because of a private arrangement with Lenin, were doing all they could, without emerging into the open, to slow the Turks down and, if possible, stop them from getting there at all. There was a ramshackle Bolshevik government in Baku, which had no more appetite for seeing the Azerbaijanis' valuable oil-wells fall into Turkish hands than for seeing them fall into those of their own late allies. Even so, it was long odds that the Turkish force would appear before Baku sooner or later, for the compelling reason that there was nobody to stop them. Much turned on the Yeldakh Bridge over the Kura River: destroy that and the Turk would at least be delayed for a long time. Dunsterville had hopes that the task would be carried out by Bicherakov's new army, said to be 10,000 strong, whose interests in this respect chimed in with those of the Allies.

Such, in general terms, was the situation as Dunsterville expounded it to Toby on 7 July: to rescue a community of 80,000 Armenian Christians and others who for the past twelve months had been surrounded by two Turkish divisions. In the event, however, the Christians managed to extricate themselves from their predicament, and Toby was found other work. The two armoured cars had proved a potent weapon at Menjil Bridge but no more were to be expected and the original pair had left with Bicherakov. Could Toby, with his well-known mechanical aptitude, but with precious little in the way of materials, produce something thhat would at least look like an armoured car? The Jangalis might easily become troublesome again at any moment, and, being uncomplicated souls, the sight of an armoured car would probably cause them as much consternation as before and they would be unlikely to wait long enough to find out whether or not the armour were real. Toby said he would do what he could; the idea had, in fact, been his own. Within a matter of hours he had sketched out his design. A Ford chassis, various items from a dump of old Russian vehicles, and, for the rest, thin planking, paint and suchlike were utilized in producing what was probably the only dummy armoured car ever employed by the British service. It had a daunting air and, as Toby and Dunsterville both knew, shadow counted for at least as much as substance in the Persia of 1918.

Whatever its technical deficiencies, Toby's machine led the next convoy to Enzeli, its creator travelling by the driver's side and traversing his gun as the spirit moved him whilst they made their passage through some very "ambushy" country; the fact that nothing happened was ascribed to the publicity attendant upon the gunnery trials which had ostentatiously taken place the day before they left. Toby found nothing about the port which commended it to him. The temperature reached a new record of 138°F, a damp heat pervaded everything and it was obviously the home of every breed of venomous bug known to science. Later in life and after mature consideration, Toby wrote that it was the hottest and unhealthiest place he had ever been.

He was not, however, fated to remain there for long, as much had been happening during the past fortnight. The Bolshevik government in Baku had been thrown out on 27 July following a local *coup d'état*, its place being taken by a body styling itself the Central Caspian Dictatorship. Nobody, probably not even the dictators, was entirely clear as to what was their policy, but the general feeling was that any change could hardly be for the worse. At the end of the first week in August, a small party of British troops disembarked in the town by invitation and it began to look as if the place might be held against the Turks after all. There was one complication. Large quantities of arms and equipment supplied some time ago by the allies for the use of the Czar's armies had never got beyond Baku, and now lay scattered about the wharves and quays of Baku, unsorted and unguarded. However, the Thirty-Ninth Brigade had now arrived at Kazian, to all intents and purposes a part of the port of Enzeli, and when they landed at Baku all this could be taken in hand.

Other matters, however, were more pressing. The first small party of Hampshire Territorials had landed at Baku on 4 August just as a Turkish attack was beginning. Though their number was paltry, such was their soldierly bearing that the inhabitants were, for the moment, fired with military ardour and turned out with arms in their hands to beat back their assailants. It promised well but was not to be repeated. As the British battalions arrived they were shipped to Baku, a trip of about eighteen hours from Enzeli, and were deployed into some sort of covering position. Four battalions, however, cannot defend a front of 21,000 yards undug, unwired, and without support from either artillery or machine-guns, to say nothing of reserves. The task of organizing the local people into units and of trying to shame them into fighting fell mainly upon a small band of British officers. By comparison with their duties, the labours of Hercules were no more exacting than a child's crossword puzzle. Two sentences from the report of Colonel Keyworth to Dunsterville sum up the whole situation: "The one idea of the Baku army is to retire and rest from those parts of the front occupied by us. . . . They either cannot or will not understand the difficulties we have and insist on looking on us as universal providers." To this disagreeable prospect Toby had to look forward as his latest command, an iron tank more or less in the shape of a ship, bore him and some seventy British soldiers towards Baku. On 17 August they lurched into the great harbour of Baku, in which, according to Toby, all the fleets of the world could lie comfortably in any weather.

On reporting himself to British Headquarters, Toby was

informed that he was being "lent" to the Central Caspian Dictatorship in order that he might "enumerate and organize" the ordnance resources of the new republic, most of which were still lying about the harbour in a splendid confusion. He was first to visit the Minister of War, an Armenian general named Bogratouni. In him Toby found for the first time an Armenian with whom he could do business, for Bogratouni, despite the unpromising earlier syllables of his name, was a soldier and a gentleman. He was still recovering from grievous wounds received in the service of the Czar and it was plain that the feelings Toby came to bear towards him were returned. Bogratouni explained the situation. The Baku army had so far been managing to hold its own against the Turkish–Islamic army, though things were now much more difficult, as, since mid-July, reinforcements had been coming steadily in by the railway from Tiflis and the attempts to halt them had proved vain. It had been hoped that Bicherakov, with his new Red Army, would have been able to destroy the vital bridge, but his Bolsheviks had displayed no stomach for a fight and as soon as the Turks had began to move forward in earnest had precipitately retreated into the northern sector of the peninsula on which Beku stands. Even there they might have stood fast and prevented the city from being overwhelmed, but Bicherakov was withdrawing into Russia proper and was already away up the Caspian coast heading northwards. The few guns in use by the defenders were museum pieces and Toby's task was to be the sorting out of the mass of artillery equipment which had been so unceremoniously dumped on the quayside, the rendering serviceable of as much of it as possible, and the delivery of it to such units of the Baku army as could be persuaded to use it. There were, Bogratouni explained, about 80,000 Tartars in the peninsula who were, in effect, stropping their knives against the day the Turks would break in and give them the chance to employ them in disembowelling the feeble Armenians. In case this were not enough, Baku had been the site of one of the biggest prisoner-of-war cages on the Russian front and anything up to 30,000 ex-prisoners, mostly Austrian, were at large and ready to be of service to their allies the moment the chance came their way. There was no disguising the fact that Baku was indefensible. The moment the Turks made a serious effort, they could walk through the many gaps, some of them a mile or two wide, where there was not a solitary soldier of any kind to dispute their passage. He could provide neither labour nor money with which to hire it, but food, which would probably be more acceptable than wages, was available.

It was a state of affairs that might have induced many a man to throw up his hands in despair; the word, however, was one that did not figure in Toby's vocabulary. On taking leave of the Minister, armed with a commission giving him sweeping powers but little else, he began by furnishing himself with a staff, a Russian officer as aide-de-camp and a Russian barrister ("who smelled of drink") as his secretary. Then he went to inspect the facilities available for the execution of his task. The manufacturing capacity of the town was non-existent, but, quite apart from the stack of munitions unloaded from the Bolshevik ships, there was obviously a great quantity of stores lying about in the most unlikely places and the first job was to concentrate in some spot where a little order might be brought to its checking and issue. He selected the customs house on the sea-front; it had its own piers, the railway line extended to it and there were existing trolley-lines leading to the wharves. This seemed a reasonable enough start, especially as the place was, for the moment, out of range of the Turkish guns and surrounded by a solid wall behind which some sort of last stand might be made should it become necessary.

The next thing needful was a labour force; rumour of what was afoot had already got round and the force assembled outside the gate without waiting for any invitation. There were Russians and Armenians, Kurds and Tartars, Turcomen, Mongols, Persians and Daghistanis, all impelled to press their services in consequence of the one factor that united them, an utter starvation. Toby enlisted as many of the half-starved men as he reckoned himself able to feed, on the understanding that they would barter work for bread, a suggestion that these unfortunates accepted with rapture, and, as soon as his lorries had been able to collect food enough to provide a meal, work began. The ragged ordnance corps applied themselves to it with a will and before very long some fifty good, modern guns, French, German and British, had gone to replace the relics in the city defences. There were the latest 5·9-inch howitzers from Krupps, a battery of the very newest French 105-millimetre guns, and a couple of 4·5 howitzers fresh from Coventry, all of which were hastily serviced and hauled out before Toby turned his attention to lighter weapons. He unearthed more ammunition than the British forces disposed in the whole of Mesopotamia, over 100,000 shells of all calibres and many millions of rounds of small-arms ammunition from the United States—quantities such as overflowed the customs-house and spilt out onto the wharves. There would have been even more, he learned, but for the fact that certain of the Baku commanders were conducting a thriving business by selling to the enemy all they could lay their hands on. In a few days he was able to report to Bogratouni that eighty-six guns were in position, fully equipped with sights and everything else needed to bring them into action.

Whenever time permitted, Toby went personally to acquaint

Dunsterville of his progress. This meant going either to his head-quarter ship, SS *President Kruger*, or to British Headquarters in the Hôtel de l'Europe, where the staff was hard at work in the vast empty rooms whose gilt, plush and mahogany spoke of happier days. Inevitably he made as many journeys as he could to the front line. What he saw and heard was not reassuring. The Baku troops, soldiers only in name, conscripted, undersized and underfed factory hands in fact, obviously would not stand for a moment against any serious attack. The height of their military prowess was to fire off their rifles at the clouds and dash back to the town in a formed body whenever the Turks displayed the least sign of animation. On about the only occasion when an advance was suggested, the troops, through their spokesman, pointed out that an invitation to move to a place towards which the enemy was also walking was positively laughable and quite out of the question. It was plain beyond argument that Baku must fall, and fall soon, unless the situation could, by some stroke, be altered for the better.

Toby had such a stroke in mind, and in his meticulous way he made his plan before submitting it to his chief. In essence, the plan was for a dash for the railway bridge by a small mechanized force, which, after its purpose had been accomplished, would have to make its getaway as best it could. The plan contained all the essentials of the commando raid of the next generation. Six light cars crewed by sixteen officers and men and with a machine-gun apiece would be embarked in one of the transports and sail as if returning to Enzeli. In fact, they would land at a small port some miles to the south and drive across the open steppe the 150 miles to the place where the bridge straddled the Koma River. Each car would carry a number of gun-cotton charges and each man was to be carefully instructed as to what he must do, with the aid of a large-scale plan of the bridge, supplied by Bogratouni. German uniforms were to be carried (Toby having been kitted out with the complete regalia of a German staff officer) and, so disguised, they should be able to pass the guard of forty second-line Turkish soldiers who defended the structure. As neither of the two rivers, Aras and Kours, which lay between them and their prey, was bridged or boasted a ferry, inflatable bags were made from leather, complete with nipples for attachment to ordinary tyre pumps. Good maps were procured and Toby expounded the scheme to Dunsterville. The chief saw little hope of the raiders' ever getting back, for Toby's observations about reaching friendly Kurdish tribes on the Persian frontier 200 or 300 miles away sounded optimistic, but the case was a desperate one and he gave his consent. It was on 31 August that Toby was told to go ahead and he began to pick and train his team. On that same day the Turks made a serious attack, which was repelled, but by 13 September, when Toby had his team fully prepared and ready to go, it was clearly too late to stop Baku from falling to the Turks, and that soon. Toby was bitterly disappointed, but there was no alternative but to drop his scheme.

Though there was no place for him with the fighting troops, Toby's business with Baku was by no means finished. Great quantities of guns and ammunition could not be allowed tamely to fall into enemy hands, quite apart from the fact that the Allies could put any salvage to good use. He was left very much to his own devices as to what line he should take, for Dunsterville had far more important matters in the forefront of his mind. With his usual length of vision, Toby had already put certain contingency plans into operation concurrent with the planning of the raid and the arming of the Baku troops. For some days in early September the Turkish shells had been creeping closer and closer to the wharves and at any moment a chance salvo might have landed around the customs house and blown Baku sky-high. To minimize the risk, Toby had commandeered a number of harbour hulks and a 200-ton steamer named the *Armenian*. Under the hammer and sickle and manned by a Bolshevik crew, she was daily employed in ferrying guns and ammunition to the hulks while the best of the stuff was stowed in her hold. All of this was watched with unconcealed interest by the Tartars, who were growing more bold every day and whose increasing satisfaction was matched by the undisguised terror of the Armenian women. As fighters their menfolk were beneath contempt, but many of the women had behaved like heroines, carrying ammunition to the lines and doing work that should have been done by their husbands. They had, after all, far more to lose, and it was not necessary to reach back into the mists of tribal memories to know what their fate would be when Turk and Tartar joined hands. Toby pitied them with all his heart but was powerless to help them in their appalling plight.

On 12 September an Armenian officer deserted from the Turks and made his way through the lines to General Bogratouni, with whom he was acquainted. He brought reliable news that the attack would come in at dawn on the 14th. It was obvious that the end was very near. Toby made his preparations: charges were placed in the hulks so that they could be blown up at a moment's notice, the *Armenian* was brought alongside the wharf, and all available hands were put to work loading her with the best of the guns which happened to be under repair, together with the most valuable of the spare parts and many truck-loads of small-arms ammunition. Toby's fighting troops consisted of two drivers and his batman: staunch and stout-hearted men but insufficient to repel the rush of the mob which was seeking sanctuary in the ship. Dunsterville found time to allot him four more men and explained that, as soon as it was dark, three lights would be displayed at the *President Kruger*'s mast-head to rally stragglers, and that, as soon as she was on the point of casting off, the lights would be lowered and the *Armenian* was to follow as best she could. Toby's reinforcements, with the bayonets fixed, forced a passage through the mob; bands of looting, blood-maddened Tartars were everywhere, and screams of women from the invaded Armenian houses were punctuated by the crack of rifle and pistol shots. The Turks were already in the upper part of the town. Toby managed to get his car loaded, together with his machine-guns and the breech-blocks of nineteen of the best cannon, especially the Krupp howitzers, which he had been assiduously collecting. The *Armenian* was then warped out about ten feet from the wharf and remained connected only by a single gang-plank. Down this marched a commissar of the Dictatorship to inform Toby with some relish that the gun-boats had orders to blow him out of the water if he attempted to sail. Toby, to whom such a situation was meat and drink, bundled him into the cabin, informed him that, should that unhappy event occur, he too would go up, and gave orders for him to be shot if he attempted to escape. On returning to the deck he learnt that a second commissar had presented himself at the foot of the gang-plank and that he too desired immediate audience. Toby recognized him at once as a red-hot Bolshevik whose obvious intention it was to stir up the Russian crew of the *Armenian* against the British. As the only way to prevent him from haranguing the sailors from where he stood was to invite him aboard, Toby agreed to receive him in the diminutive cabin, himself politely ushering him to the door. This he opened with one hand whilst, with the other, he grabbed the astonished official by the scruff and pushed him inside to join his colleague. To his batman, standing with his bayonet fixed, he gave the brief order, "If there's any trouble with either of these blighters, shoot them both, as I shall now draw the men on board and get under way, if I can."

His threat was no bluff, for the little ship stood in deadly danger. She was unarmed, and the gun-boats, antiquated though they were, could have sunk her with the greatest of ease and with no danger to themselves. Toby went ashore to bring in the last of his picket and backed the car perilously onto the deck, its Colt being kept trained on the pier from which at any moment Turkish troops might debouch onto the quay. Only the menacing demeanour of a few British soldiers and of Toby himself with "my automatic still in my hand, where it had been the greater part of the evening and appeared likely to remain all night", kept the mob from swarming aboard and probably capsizing them where they lay. Driver Morris was set to stand guard over the plank while Toby himself went with a knife to cut the lines that held them to the wharf; as he did so his strong sense of the grotesque overcame everything for a moment. As he looked up, he saw Morris, floodlit by a nest of electric lights overhead, standing in the middle of the plank with knees slightly bent, rifle and bayonet firmly held in the "on guard" position and with an expression on his face that recalled Horatius. Toby burst out laughing and called, "He only needs the Union Jack behind him and a band to play 'Rule Britannia' to make a matchless poster of the British Army." An enterprising, or very desperate, Kurd took advantage of the momentary comic interlude to make a dash for the quay, only to impale himself on Morris's bayonet. The Kurd "reeled back on to the deck, where he proceeded to writhe about and emit a series of bloodcurdling groans. This was the very best thing which could possibly have happened, as the effect produced on the over-strained nerves of the crowd of Bolshevik riff-raff on board the ship was to the last degree gratifying, and in reality had much to do with our eventual success in over-awing such a crowd—all armed and openly our enemies, and numbering ninety-six to our picket of four men, two drivers and one batman." In mid-September 1918 the British had few friends in Baku: the Bolsheviks hated them for obvious reasons, the Armenians felt that they were abandoning them, the Dictators were furious because four battalions only had arrived, instead of the great army which they had persuaded themselves was coming, and any others regarded them as a most promising source of loot.

As Toby cut the last rope, the *Armenian* drifted gently away from the wharf, but it was far from certain whether the crew would get her under way. Most of them had congregated on the forward end of the deck and were muttering darkly amongst themselves. Toby's first concern was to have his car lashed firmly down to some convenient cleats and his machine-guns swung to cover the deck. That done, he sought out the captain, while some ostentatious arrangements were made by the drivers to drag six cases of dynamite alongside the bridge. They made a useful chest-high barricade in front of the wheel and nobody aboard was ignorant of what the cases contained. The captain, perspiring freely, watched wordlessly as Toby placed a detonator and length of fuse in each of the cases, the ends being collected together so that a touch from a cigarette end was all that would be needed to send the ship and all aboard her to Kingdom Come. There was the additional advantage that any chance shot from the crew might produce the same result. The mutterings forward died away and Toby let out the deflated commissars so that they might join the crew. The captain, it was clear, would obey orders so long as his life depended on it, but would seize any chance to get the intruders off his ship.

TOBY

It was just after 11 p.m. The soldier who had been posted to watch the *Kruger*'s lights sang out that they had been lowered. Toby jabbed his pistol into the captain's spine and told him to raise steam. Very grudgingly he gave the order down the speaking-tube and the engines began to turn. The *Armenian* moved slowly into the crowded anchorage. Toby's intention was to wait in the fairway until the *Kruger* was clear and then to follow her out to the open sea; the crew, however, foiled him in his enterprise, for they let the anchor go willingly enough but, as soon as Toby called out "Enough chain", one of them knocked the pin out of the shackle and anchor, cable and all rattled onto the bed of Baku harbour. The muttering forward began again, more hopefully now as the little steamer started to drift aimlessly. The game was in their hands if they had had the courage to take risks: Toby would most certainly have blown them up at sea rather than risk losing all their precious cargo and spend possibly years in a Turkish prison, but it is doubtful whether he would have done so when, by igniting the fuse, he would inevitably have blown up a large part of Baku with them. However, the Bolsheviks hesitated and the captain deemed it wisest to keep way on his command, at any rate for the time being. In the blackness of the night they waited, the engine running slowly and the single screw giving just enough revolutions to keep them in their place. A darkened hospital ship crept past, crammed with British wounded, and seemed to Toby to be heading in the wrong direction. He ignored her and continued anxiously to await the arrival of the SS *Kruger*; half an hour dragged slowly by and still she had not come. Toby knew perfectly well that in the fifteen miles between them and the guard-ships lay a complexity of shoals and sandbanks on one or other of which the captain would certainly run them if the navigation had to be left to him. Almost worse was the fact that tobacco was out of the question.

Around midnight he could stand it no longer and he commanded the captain to move very gingerly towards the *Kruger*'s old berth; as they approached it, Toby's worst fears were realized. The *Kruger* had gone, and somehow they had missed her. "In despair I raised what voice I had left in what, I fear, was a somewhat quavering hail of '*Kruger*, ahoy', and to our inexpressible relief was answered from another berth on the far side of the pier: 'What ship's that?'." He identified himself and was told that the *Kruger* was on her way out and he was to follow her. As the slow and unhandy *Armenian* swung round, the *Kruger* slid past at all of ten knots, "only giving me time for one plaintive prayer as she passed of 'Show a light over your stern' ". The *Kruger* obligingly complied and the *Armenian* took station in her wake, falling steadily further and further behind with every minute. As the light drew further and further ahead, the speed of the *Armenian* gradually dropped; it could hardly have been fortuitous. Luckily for Toby and his party, they had one friend on board. Mr Dana was an American engineer employed at the oil-wells; he had come aboard at the last minute, he was fluent in Russian, he was armed and he was an extremely brave man. At Toby's request, he went down to the engine-room to find out what was happening and to put it to rights; it called for courage to go alone amongst nearly a hundred panicky Bolsheviks who could have murdered him with impunity in any one of a dozen different ways and would have done so with relish. It was not too helpful to be assured by Toby that he and all his men would be with him at the first shot; however, down Dana went and a few minutes later he returned to the bridge and nodded cheerfully to Toby. The *Armenian* began to pick up speed; exactly what had happened in the engine-room is uncertain, but it did the trick for the time being.

All the same, their troubles were really only just beginning. Though they contrived to keep the *Kruger*'s stern-light in their vision for a dozen miles or so, as soon as they reached the guard-ships and she commenced her turn to lay a course between them it suddenly went out. Shots and whistles came from the blackness ahead, but Toby, his eyes strained beyond anything he had thought possible, could make out nothing. The only certainty was that no big gun had fired and, as no searchlight came to sweep over the black waters, there still seemed some chance of creeping past unobserved. This, of course, was the captain's opportunity. He flatly refused to go any further. Toby did the only thing possible: he formed his four men in a square round the captain with orders to allow nobody to approach. He himself returned his pistol to the unfortunate seaman's already contused spine and "swore to him by every oath I could think of in Russian that if the ship did not keep a straight course, or if any signal was made, I would myself shoot him on the spot and take the ship out in spite of him". Toby had not been a Naval officer for nothing, even though neither seamanship nor navigation had loomed very large in his education for that service. All this was bellowed at the top of his voice; a Bolshevik sailor who sought to calm his nerves, rather thoughtlessly in the circumstances, by lighting a cigarette was instantly felled by his neighbours. The *Armenian* moved forward into the darkness.

There had never been any real chance of her moving between the guard-ships unobserved, for a good part of her length was painted white and showed up like a rabbit's tail against a thunder-cloud. The nearer gun-boat began by sounding two blasts on her whistle; Toby grabbed the cord of their own instrument from the captain and politely whistled back twice also. The gun-boat thereupon blew three blasts; Toby, entirely oblivious of what it all meant, answered with five. This, apparently, was not in the code-book, for the gun-boat replied with a shot; the explosion of a shell within a foot of their heads and within a pace of the nearest case of dynamite was too much for the captain; he made a dive to get away, leaving the wheel to spin and the ship to go where she pleased. Toby moved even more quickly, grabbing him by the collar as he passed and flinging him down on his back; once more the big Colt was jammed into him, though now, for a change, under his chin, and he was roughly bidden to get up and lay her on course again. It seemed better to comply, for during the scuffle, while Toby's batman was steering the ship, three more shells struck the *Armenian* in the poop; common shell, Toby noted, thankfully. There was nothing he did not know about the difference between that and high explosive and, while it was bad enough being shelled by anything at point-blank range, it was not likely to send up the dynamite without a direct hit. Then came some relief as their course took them between the two guard-ships, neither of which dared fire for fear of hitting the other. The captain was now gibbering with terror and it seemed as if he might, with the force of utter desperation, be going to start something as he struggled. A rush of armed Bolshevik sailors at that moment would have meant the end and Toby decided that he had no choice but to shoot the captain then and there, to ensure the safety of the rest of them. He applied the pistol to the nape of his neck and quietly asked his batman to move out of the way as he was about to make a nasty mess. The captain had denied all knowledge of English and his limited intercourse with Toby had had to be carried out in such Russian as the latter could command. On hearing what was said, however, the miserable man fainted and made no further trouble. It was quite a relief to everybody that he learnt so swiftly.

All this time the *Armenian* was drawing further away from the moored guard-ships, and, although four or five more shells hit her, they did little material damage. Toby knew that the danger would be over once they were out of range, for there were something like 200 other ships in Baku roads, many of them far more important than the insignificant *Armenian* seemed, and if either of the guard-ships were to leave the harbour mouth there would be a general exodus. They steamed away as fast as they could for the open sea, wiping their brows and congratulating themselves that this floating ammunition-wagon had escaped extinction. It seemed beyond belief that shells could have burst so close without touching it off, but the fact remained that it had so happened. Had the gun-boats thought it worth firing high explosive at them, the *Armenian* would, for certain, have gone up in spectacular fashion.

As soon as they were clear and on the way to the open sea, the next peril presented itself. Onto the bridge marched an outstandingly offensive Bolshevik sailor and addressed Toby "in a tone of voice which I was by no means prepared to admit him to use". The tenor of his speech was that he had been delegated by the "committee" to inform Toby that the ship would not be allowed to proceed any further. Democracy in action was something outside Toby's experience and he dealt with it in a way that many would now envy him. The two terse words "Down him" were sufficient to have the delegate flat on his back "with a good British bayonet scratching at his chest" and Toby's batman looking hopefully towards him for the next order. The two of them booted the politician to his feet and informed him that the ship was going to Enzeli, like it or not. If the crew carried out their duties they would be paid 100 roubles each on arrival; if they did not want to accept the offer, Toby and his men would fight them at once. This was duly passed on from a position of little ease over the top of the dynamite boxes, with Toby's man thoughtfully running the point of his bayonet up and down the politician's spinal column. He grasped the point that, if his comrades elected for battle, his expectation of life was not great, and turned his powers of oratory towards persuading them to accept the bargain. They did so at once.

The remainder of the voyage passed without much excitement. Toby took the ship well out to sea, for there was no knowing where the Bolshevik seagoing naval ships might be, and it was not until the morning of 16 September that the Elburz mountains loomed out of the morning mist and it was possible to make out the entrance to the harbour of Enzeli. Toby was, very properly, determined to enter harbour in the nautical equivalent of marching to attention. There was nothing that could be done about covering the shell-holes, but the small Union Jack from his car was hoisted to the mast-head over the Bolshevik flag and his troops were paraded on the battered upper deck as soldiers should be. So the *Armenian* steamed into port, ninety-six armed Bolsheviks obeying the orders of ten Englishmen and an American citizen. Dunsterville, who was beginning to give them up for lost, was delighted.

The taking of Baku was the last victory, if such it can be called, of the Turkish army. Two days after the *Armenian* berthed, and far away to the south-west, Allenby's guns proclaimed the opening of the battle of Megiddo and, along with other troops of the Empire, the Australian horsemen whom Toby had so admired in the desert moved in for the kill. On the first day of October their commander entered Damascus and on the last day Turkey asked for an armistice. With the benefit of later knowledge, one cannot help wondering whether the expedition to Baku was a wise move, but that had hardly been Toby's responsibility. As there was no more work for him in Persia and reports were coming in that his brother's Fourth Army was through the Hindenburg Line, his only anxiety was to get back to France before it was all over. He was not allowed to leave, however, without some memento of his time with Dunsterforce. On arrival at Baghdad, General Marshall told him that, on Dunsterville's strong recommendation, he had been awarded an immediate DSO, and two of his men, Morris and Parsons, the Military Medal.

Chapter Fifteen

The King's enemies were now, one by one, hauling down their flags. The Bulgarians had gone down at last by the end of September, and Franchet d'Esperey's men were in full cry for the Danube. Austria and Italy were no longer at war by the middle of the month which followed and only the oldest and most powerful foeman remained in the field. Though the Allies were now everywhere victorious along the Western Front, the war was far from over and much hard fighting remained before Germany, too, was to ask for terms. Toby was determined that, come what may, he would be there at the end as he had been at the beginning, and he had useful friends. Even so, there were still one or two troublesome officials to be met on the way. The town major of Kut he found wanting in energy. "He was inclined to, first of all, remain in bed until much later in the morning, and then at his leisure to arrange for a boat to leave next day." Toby had him out of that as he had had the chickens out at Melun, and a steamer was pronounced ready to leave within the hour. Early on the 13th he was in Basra, where he transhipped, and before the day was out he was on his way to Suez, having covered well over 1,000 miles in nine days. The remainder of the journey, however, was a slow one, by way of Taranto and Rome, from which city he cabled Sir Henry to have a car waiting for him in Paris.

It took fifty-six hours to reach Paris, even by the train *de luxe*. The car was there with the driver patiently waiting, and, in reply to Toby's inquiries, he told him that Fourth Army Headquarters was located in a captured German military train at Le Cateau. Toby, who had had very little sleep on the way to Paris, reckoned that he could spare a few hours for it now and took a hotel room, to which he retired after breakfast. Hardly had his head sunk into the unwontedly soft pillow than he was rudely awakened by the sound of gunfire. Improbable though a battle seemed, he thought he had better find out what was afoot and marched out into the corridor in his pyjamas. "There I found all the world gone mad." From the teeming streets below rose the roar of cheering and the unmistakable word "L'Armistice". Every gun was being fired as fast as it could be loaded, and every factory hooter was making all the din of which it was capable, while towers reeled under the brazen din of great bells. Toby, having digested the message, went back to bed. There was no longer any point in hurrying and he could do with some sleep. Anyway, he had been in London on Mafeking Night and nothing could surpass that.

He rose late in the afternoon and went to join the crowd. There was very little "mafficking" about what he encountered. The younger element, not surprisingly, was celebrating its deliverance from a prospect of wounds and death, as youth always has done, but this was only a small, noisy minority. There were far too many black veils, wheel-chairs and crutches for this to be Carnival. "Amongst the hundreds to whom I spoke that day I could see the little twitchings of the muscles and note the little catch in the speech which told of feelings far deeper than any that could be expressed by mere exhibitions of joy and gaiety The whole atmosphere, in fact, could best be described as filled with a deep and sincere feeling of relief and a thankfulness far too deep to be expressed by outward signs, but which found its true reflection in the reverent masses who were to be seen kneeling in every church throughout the day and night." To this day the generation of Frenchmen who would never return home remains unnumbered.

The next morning, early, he was speeding down the old familiar road to Le Cateau by way of Noyon, Ham and St Quentin, where every village held some memory of the hectic days of 1914. As they drove, he pondered to himself that, having travelled over half the world and seen six different fronts, he was now back where he had started. Inevitably the brothers had enough to talk about to keep them up for most of the night, the last hours of which Toby passed in a newly-made dug-out alongside the train, in the snow. He did not care, although a mild bout of fever was on him. When he spoke it was much worse, but he was not going to allow so small a thing to spoil his return. A closed car took him through Cambrai and Arras to Boulogne, where arrangements had been made to whisk him straight to London—"too ill, however, to go and find my wife who did not know I was coming and afraid that my state would frighten her. So I slept at my club and sent the faithful Morris to find her in the morning; after which I was in good hands and, getting the nursing and care which were sadly needed, I was fit for duty again in a very short time." Though for most people the prospect of a long, unexciting peace had its attractions, it was not so for Toby, and, as soon as he had got his strength back, he was looking for further adventures. After all, he was barely fifty-two and the war had left a great deal of unfinished business in its wake.

Germany apart, the most pressing problems were to be found on the frontiers of Bolshevik Russia, both in the north, where a British and Allied force still languished around Archangel as a hang-over from the days of the first convoys to Russia, and in the south, where the frontiers marched with those of the Ottoman Empire. Sir George Milne, the former commander of the neglected British Army in Salonika, had moved his headquarters to Constantinople in mid-December, with two divisions under his command; the Twenty-Seventh was centred around Tiflis and the Twenty-Eighth based on Constantinople, but both were rapidly shrinking in size as the result of demobilization. The Greeks, hitherto little engaged but with a keen eye on the fruits of victory, had strongly established themselves in Anatolia, and Smyrna seemed to be firmly in their hands. The unconditional surrender of Turkey had been followed by an armistice of which the most important clause for immediate purposes was the one which required the handing-over of the bulk of the heavy weapons of the army. The man charged by the Turkish government with the supervision of this duty was Mustafa Kemal Pasha, who had won much-deserved fame at Gallipoli and was well respected by his former enemies. It did seem, however, that the weapons were coming in very slowly, and a good proportion of those that did arrive seemed suspiciously antique. Milne and his staff were hardening to the conclusion that Kemal's heart was not in the task allotted to him. The Russian homeland did not appear to pose any immediate problem, as General Wrangel, with Allied blessing, was still fully operational in the Crimea. The first essential was to find out exactly what was going on in Turkey-in-Asia.

Baku had been retaken without a struggle, a sad anti-climax after the terrible events of only a few months before; Batum, on the Black Sea coast, was held by a British garrison, and the railway forming the sides of the triangle Tiflis—Batum—Baku was British-controlled. In a vast area of land where civil disorder, revolution, counter-revolution and a prospect of starvation and disease were the governing factors, a British presence was felt to be necessary not so much to hold down Turkey as to ensure the evacuation of her armies and of the substantial German Military Missions which still abounded. Sir George Milne, a taciturn Scot in the Haig mould, asserted with truth that "Little is known in Great Britain of the amount of hard work done by the British troops in 1919 and early 1920, at a time when the

British Flag was held in honour from Merv to Smyrna, when Batum was a model port and when it was possible to go by a railway managed by British officers from Constantinople to Egypt." Probably even less is known about it today.

The first Rawlinson to become involved in the great tidying-up was Sir Henry, who was designated to see to the evacuation of the British contingent from Archangel. It was natural that he should breakfast with Sir George Milne during one of the latter's visits to London and it was no less natural that an unemployed Toby should share it with them. Inevitably, when the two generals had done with exchanging their news, Toby's recent adventures cropped up and Sir George was more than mildly interested. A man who knew the country, whose resourcefulness had been proved over and over again and who would not clamour to be sent home within a week of his arrival in the East could well be exactly what he was seeking. He wasted no time in asking Toby whether he would care to go back there and, "on my gladly assenting", the bargain was struck. Toby was to be appointed a Special Service Officer attached to the Intelligence Branch of the General Staff in Constantinople, with responsibility for travelling into those places to which no British force had penetrated and there to find out exactly what the Turks were up to. Hopefully he unearthed the machine-guns and wiped off the mineral jelly in which they had been packed away.

As he worked he pondered upon what he was likely to find. Such Bolsheviks as had come his way had been contemptible creatures whether judged as soldiers or as men; the Turk was another matter. From men who had been with Allenby during the last stages he had heard reports of dreadful atrocities committed against the civilian population, atrocities such as no British soldier had seen since Masséna had pulled back from Torres Vedras. The manner in which prisoners taken at Kut had been maltreated and starved, contrasting bitterly with the princely treatment meted out to and accepted by their commander, General Townshend, had made the adjective "unspeakable" a necessary prefix to their very name and it had always excited suspicion that so few Australians had been taken prisoner during the first rush after the Gallipoli landing. Nevertheless, there was no strong anti-Turkish feeling amongst the soldiers. By and large, the Turk had fought well and fairly clean. His courage had never been in question and there was no need to rub his nose in the evidence of the darker side of his nature. However, it was highly probable that an oriental race such as the Turks, once disembarrassed of great territories that had done no more than render its empire vulnerable, would become stronger rather than weaker. No doubt there were many more war-lords after the style of Kuchik Khan, and, should these take their courage in both hands, there could be serious trouble ahead. Somehow it did not seem likely that a man of Kemal's antecedents and known record could be accepting defeat quite so submissively. Before long, the British and French armies must inevitably go home; they were already too weak to impose their will but too many just to show the flag—always an awkward position. That left the Greeks, whose plans nobody knew. So long as Venizelos remained at the head of affairs they would not be likely to do anything rash, but, if he were to go, what then?

Having thought out the situation, Toby settled down to wait until his formal orders should arrive. Christmas passed and January dragged out its dismal length but still the War Office remained silent. It was not until well into February 1919 that the heavy sealed envelope arrived and Toby was once more an employed officer with a specific function to perform. The long wait, irksome though it had been, was beneficial to his wasted body and it was a far more robust Toby who finally left Victoria on 15 February than the skeletal figure which had detrained there three months earlier.

He managed a single night in Paris with the Rothschilds and in the morning he was introduced to the doubtful pleasures of rail travel in a Europe whose overmastering interest was demobilization. Ancient rolling stock, preserved during the war by miracles of botching and makeshifts, was now approaching the time when it could no longer be relied upon to function at all, and all of it was crowded beyond capacity by vast numbers of troops, no longer in formed bodies, whose discipline had been thrown to the winds. Eventually, however, after enduring much discomfort, Toby reached his destination and presented himself to Sir George Milne in Constantinople. The Commander-in-Chief had himself been doing some travelling and had only just returned from an extensive tour of his bailiwick which had taken him to Baku and across the Caspian to Krasnovodsk. As a result he was able to tell Toby exactly what was expected of him. It was apparent that the Sultan's government, docile and well-conducted as it appeared, was not the centre of power in post-armistice Turkey. The bazaars were quite insistent on two things and the bazaars were seldom wrong. The Greeks, with the active aid of Mr Lloyd George, were planning for a new Greek Empire in and around Anatolia. Why else were they buying up enormous quantities of second-line transport for which the British army had no further use? The country Turks were certainly not going to accept such a situation lying down, and Mustafa Kemal, in concert with a number of tribal chieftains, was making a new army out of the ruins of the old and was equipping it with the heavy weapons that, in conformity with the conditions of the armistice, ought to have been handed over. The once-powerful British army could no longer impose its will upon anybody, as the daily loss through demobilization bled it white, and the young, recently-enlisted Regulars who came in driblets to replace them were mere boys. The Indian element of the old force was in even worse case, and, with the departure of most of the experienced officers who had led it in war, discipline was breaking down. In any event, the political masters seemed to be absurdly biased in favour of the Greeks, whose military value was not proven. Toby was to furnish himself with two cars and the necessary drivers and others; as soon as this had been done, he was to hold himself ready to travel to any part of the Caucasus in order to find out exactly what was happening away from the railways and the main-road network—"a most congenial task". He was allowed a couple of days for sight-seeing while his party and vehicles were being got together.

On 5 March he embarked his cars and his men on board ship and sailed along the Pontine coast for Batum. The ship's first port of call was Samsun, where, unknown to all but his own adherents, Mustafa Kemal was planning resistance to a new Greek influx and working for the creation of a new Turkey. There was a small British garrison in the place, which gave comfort to the Greeks, who were in great fear of the Turkish troops nearby; these, in theory, were preparing shortly to return to civilian life, but did not appear to be doing so with any alacrity. Toby, having no business in Samsun, continued his voyage, and next day the 10,000-foot-high mountains, snow-clad almost to the foot, proclaimed that they were nearing Batum. The city, just inside Georgia, was the main base for the British forces on the Black Sea, in addition to being the terminus of the oil pipeline from Baku and connected by rail to Moscow. Again Toby had no opportunity to linger, for General Cory, Milne's Chief of Staff, had arrived just ahead of him in a destroyer and offered him a place in the Czar's private train, which was waiting to take him to Tiflis and far beyond. The train was as luxuriously appointed as the troop-crowded train by which Toby had travelled from Paris to Constantinople had not been.

At Tiflis Toby took himself off to the Advanced Headquarters of the British forces in the area. Tiflis he thought a very fine town, the inhabitants being true Georgians for the most part, and strikingly dressed in the national costume of high black boots, black frock-coat with small breast-pockets each holding six cartridges, and tight around the waist, a silver chain-belt from which depended a silver-handled dirk. With the ensemble crowned by an Astrakhan fur cap worn jauntily over one ear, they seemed fine, manly fellows.

It was in Tiflis that there came into existence the new unit of the

British army officially designated "Colonel Rawlinson's Establish-ment". It comprehended two Ford cars, two horses and fourteen men with specified duties varying from interpreter to mess-waiter. Toby was able to select them for himself from a sizable body of volunteers and he was well satisfied with their quality, "really tough fellows who could go anywhere and do anything without expecting three meals a day and a bed at night, which were about the only things they could be quite certain they would not get". All of them were mature men who had served through the Macedonian campaign and who were looking for excitement, though without the vague aspirations of those to whom it was only a hopeful word. The interpreter was a genuine interpreter; the rest were simply cheerful, tough customers who made no attempt to comply with descriptions such as cook, clerk or farrier. With such, much may be done, and Toby was able to give over a few days to indoctrination; for a start, they were going to have a good look round and report what appeared to be going on, but very soon they would venture much further afield, into some of the wildest country in the Caucasus, where they must be prepared to stay for some time in anarchic conditions, acting as a report centre. All had a pretty fair idea of what that meant.

Their first assignment from General Beach, the Chief of Intelli-gence, was to acquire reliable information about the actual state of affairs existing on the frontier between the new Socialist Republic of Georgia and its eastern neighbour, the equally new Tartar Republic of Azerbaijan, whose capital was at Baku. Little sign of activity was found in that direction, and the same was the case when, on General Beach's instructions, Toby took a cast to the north, to just inside Russia. However, within twenty-four hours of this second trip, a cable reached him direct from Sir George Milne in Constantinople. The next journey was to be to Kars, where the famous siege had gone on and on in the 1870s as every Victorian schoolboy remembered. This was a compliment to Toby's energy and sound judgement, for there was a battalion of the Rifle Brigade in the town and other sources of information were available to the Commander-in-Chief. The Turks, so the cable said, were about to give trouble and Milne wanted to know all about it. Kars is about 170 miles to the south-west of Tiflis, and, as a perfectly good railway existed, Toby was to go by train. He, being a disciplined man, complied with the order but took the precaution of loading his two vans complete with the machine-guns and most of his command into suitable wagons. Over the whole assembly Toby proudly but quite irregularly flew his small Union Jack.

The politics of Kars were complicated, as was inevitable in the Middle East between the Turkish surrender and the treaties. The

Imperial Russian Province was populated by a majority of Armenians, "the master-rogues of the East", as they have been called. Hardly less in numbers and vastly more formidable in everything other than commerce were the Tartars, closely akin to the Turks. The province had been occupied by the Turkish army since early in the war and, in theory, it had been evacuated by them after the armistice; theory and practice did not match up. Woodrow Wilson, whose Far East ended somewhere about Cape Cod, was well pleased with his new word "self-determination", which appeared to embody the quintessence of Benthamite justice; and the environs of Kars were to have the melancholy distinction of being the first places in which its workings were to be observed. The New Armenian Christian Republic was to reflect the will of the President of the United States and that of God, in that order. The fact that every Tartar, armed *cap-à-pie* and accustomed to killing, would instantly annihilate every Armenian bold enough to take any part in the new dispensation was a tiresome irrelevance, but it did not alter the fact that in every village in the province the Tartars were banding themselves together and training seriously under German and Turkish instructors; there was apparently no shortage of modern weapons and ammunition. The small British force was to be the policeman, enforcing a system of government in the making of which it had had no voice and of which it did not approve, against people whom it rather liked. Doubtless there were some who admired the Armenians, for the law of averages eschews complete unanimity of thought. The fact that Kars was, in late March, pretty well snowed up made things no easier for them. Had it not been for the happy chance that the train had picked up a party of railwaymen and a Russian snow-plough on the way, Toby and his party might well have never reached the place.

Toby spent a couple of days in Kars gathering information; it was as certain as that night follows day that the Turks were giving military support to the Tartars and so he reported by cable to Constantinople. What was needed, however, was much more exact news, and Toby concluded that it was not in Kars itself that he would find it. The obvious first place to examine was the great camp at Sarikamish, the scene of the terrible and still rather mysterious battle of January 1915 where the Russians had roundly defeated Enver Pasha's Turkish army. The casualties, mostly dead, ran into many tens of thousands, but no details had, or have, ever emerged. As the train was being got ready for the journey, Toby noticed things that excited his suspicions. A party of Tartars took a locomotive from a siding and ran it to the points from which a short line led to the boiler-filling pump, the only place where a supply of unfrozen water for the trains could be got. As soon as their locomotive had passed the points, all began to push and shove until it was derailed and access to the water effectively cut off; then they moved busily to another locomotive, with the obvious intention of employing it in the same way to block the main line to Alexandropol and Tiflis. Toby had no mind to stand and watch this being done. Before the Tartars had got under way, he was standing over the points, "with my pistol drawn and very much in the mood to use it". The wreckers melted away and the train moved off, with Toby on the foot-plate keeping the throttle open.

At Alexandropol (confusingly called Gumri by the Turks and now known as Leninakhan) the engine-driver disappeared, apparently unnerved by having had to watch Toby fingering his big Colt throughout the entire length of the journey. Another was found and the train once more took up its journey back through Kara Province. Tartar bands, in rough military formation, were to be seen everywhere, marching purposefully towards the Armenian frontier, where many thousands of President Wilson's protégés were huddled together in the bend of a river and were already under intermittent Moslem sniper fire. This was the kind of information Toby sought; General Milne had been at Kars a few days previously and was known to be in Batum, on his way back to Constantinople, and Toby decided that he must catch him there before he sailed away. He had the train driven as fast as possible to Tiflis, where he left it in order to race to Batum in one of the Fords. He succeeded with an hour to spare, and within ten minutes, Milne had cabled orders for the reinforcement of the Riflemen at Kars. His orders were promptly obeyed and the Tartars were denied the annihilation of the Armenians to which they had been so much looking forward. Milne, having given Toby the best luncheon he had enjoyed for a long time, laid his next burden upon him. He was to go back to Tiflis and collect his party, to reach the frontier by some other means, and, in any event, to meet the Commander-in-Chief again at Kars on 27 April, exactly three weeks thence. By that time, said Milne, "the situation could not fail to have developed further throughout all the Turkish frontier country", and he was not a man given to exaggeration. Toby drove back to the Georgian capital and, in conjunction with General Beach, made a plan. Colonel Rawlinson's Establishment would sail from Batum to Trebizond, a hundred miles along the Pontine coast, land there and then drive 200 miles inland to the headquarters of the Turkish Ninth Army at Erzerum. Having made their number there, the party would get on as best they could for another 200 miles, crossing the old Russo-Turkish frontier somewhere and keeping the appointment in Kars on the 27th. The only information about the road journey was that it was likely to be "extremely difficult, with many high passes, all under deep snow". That, too, was no exaggeration.

Toby and his hardy band once more loaded themselves into a train and set off on their adventures with light hearts. Though he would never see fifty again, Toby had all the zest of a boy subaltern going out with his first tiny independent command, to seek their fortune in an unknown and savage land where hardship was the only certainty and death in half a hundred forms a real possibility; if he ever contemplated it at all, Toby saw the prospect as simply an additional spice, flavouring the last escapades of an English gentleman born out of time and condemned to live in a world rapidly growing humdrum. Before long, however, he was to acquire a companion in his travels who would remain at his side for as long as life endured; it came about as follows.

The engine which drew them from Tiflis to Batum was worn out and short of fuel; at the fourth breakdown in the first hundred miles Toby decided that he must get out and stretch his legs, and went to examine the nearby ruins of the magnificent summer palace of the Grand Dukes of Imperial Russia, who had served as Viceroys of the Caucasus in time past. "During our halt there I observed amongst the ruins a great black shape which, although a skeleton only and in the last extremities of starvation, I could see at a glance was in reality a magnificent hound, evidently one of the Imperial breed of bear-hounds which have for generations been exclusively bred for the Imperial family in the Caucasus." Toby and George had met. The latter was, not surprisingly, very shy, but Toby was so captivated by the sight of him that he sacrificed his last sirloin of beef, with which he cunningly enticed the great hound into the train and then shut the door on him. Within a very short space of time George (thus called because he was a Georgian) had made himself entirely at home and was contentedly working his way through the remainder of Toby's stock of provender. The two were delighted with each other: "a more faithful and intelligent friend and companion one could never hope to find", wrote Toby years later; "from that time, with the exception of my short visit to London in August and the six months which he spent in quarantine in 1922, he had never left me, and lies beside me while I write here, at home, in England to-day".

They travelled side by side through the rich valleys that sprawl in the hinterland of Batum, where they were delayed for a week while the credentials that the party would need in the interior were obtained from Constantinople. The Sultan, in the limbo of the palace where he was immured, did not count for much any longer, but he was still Caliph and Commander of the Faithful and a visit to a Turkish army without his "firman" (they were on their way to the

Turkish Ninth Army) would have been a waste of effort. Eventually the paper arrived, complete with the great seal of authenticity, and the six boxy little Ford vans were embarked for Trebizond. On arrival there, port officials blandly informed Toby that to disembark the vans was quite impossible, as there was neither harbour nor pier and the small drifter that bore them carried neither crane nor derrick. To most men these difficulties would have been fatal rather than technical, but Toby was not to be so easily thwarted. An inspection of the facilities available revealed only two artifacts that might prove useful: a leaky, derelict iron oil-barge drawn up on the beach and a diminutive Turkish steamer, which boasted an equally diminutive hand-crane. Toby made a calculation, empirical rather than professional, and reckoned that if the vans could be winched onto the barge it might, with a bit of luck, not completely disappear under the unfriendly waters of the Black Sea before it could be beached. There was, indeed, a risk, but it was unthinkable that they should do nothing. And so the arrangements were made: the barge was pumped out and the larger holes plugged with whatever the workmen could find for the purpose, and the Turkish captain agreed to co-operate on the strict understanding that he would not be blamed for failure. The drifter was edged alongside the Turk, the oil-barge was poled alongside, and one van was wrapped around in hawsers and lifted jerkily from the deck by strong arms; slowly and gingerly the barge was worked under the crane and the van lowered onto its unwilling deck. It began, perceptibly, to settle down in the water. Six times the operation was repeated, and, as the last van reached the platform, water began to lap gently over the top. The crew shoved at the poles with cracking muscles and the entire crazy structure inched towards the beach, sinking as it went. Fate once again was kind to Toby, for the barge hit the beach with water over the tyres of its burden, some pocket of air keeping them just afloat for just long enough. The rest was easy, for a pile of railway tracks made an efficient ramp and all six came safely ashore, to the astonishment of the assembled populace. Toby wrote severely that "it is a good instance of what may be done if only people will try".

Soon they were ready for departure. Toby's first main concern was to get his little convoy over the Zigana Pass, 6,500 feet above sea-level, probably covered in snow and exposed to all the freezing winds that blow. The pass lies only fifty miles from the sea, so it was reasonable to suppose that they would traverse it in the course of the first day's journey. In fact it took them a day and a half, with a freezing night in the foothills into the bargain. A hair-raising descent through a world of rocks, precipices and melting snow took them down to the rushing River Kharshut, where they turned to the east through warm valleys of cherry-blossom towards the ancient city of Baiburt, where a Turkish garrison was stationed. Through his interpreter Toby learned that what had happened so far was a pleasant Sunday afternoon drive by contrast with what lay ahead and the Turkish officer spoke eloquently of the terrors of the Khop Pass. A company of infantry was working on it, shovelling away all the snow it could, but the summit was 2,000 feet higher than that of Zigana and the storms there were matter of legend. The wind at Baiburt was enough to blow away one of their two tents; imagination recoiled from exercising itself about what must be the state of affairs at the top. Toby slept, wrapped in every fur he possessed, sheep-skins and all, while George did sentry duty.

In the morning a message came back from the Turkish working parties. The road at the top had been carried away in places by a recent avalanche and the snow lay deep, moist and uneven. The company commander, with commendable foresight, had arranged that in the last extremity oxen from the other side would haul the vans over the pass. There was nothing for it but to get under way, and soon it became apparent, even to Toby, that this time they might have bitten off more than they could chew. The gradient was fierce; the wind had blown away much of the loose snow and left a sheet of ice. There was only one thing to be done, and that at once. The vans were stopped from their glissades, the wheels were chocked and the ropes were got out; as many cross-poles as possible were inserted, and a company of tough, uncomplaining Turkish infantry bent itself to the task of heaving the vans to the summit one at a time. As this involved heaving each one a distance of some miles, it was not a small feat, but eventually all six reached the top and Toby surveyed the scene. Though the view was one of sheer fantasy, taking in the Euphrates Valley in one direction and mountains of up to 10,000–12,000 feet, he did not linger over it. The wind and the glare were of a quality unknown to Englishmen and the temperature was so low that "on several occasions the whole of my party have lost the skin off their faces from exposure to this truly icy blast". The oxen were yoked in pairs to the vans, spans of six to twelve as occasion demanded, and they set away down through the snow like some survivors of the Great Trek who had lost their way. Twisting and turning by unending zig-zags, the experienced oxen brought them down to the next valley, where they spent the night huddled amongst some ancient ruins. By tea-time next day they were in Erzerum itself, with a fine mansion placed at their disposal by the Army Commander. It had formerly housed an American school. Erzerum was a most interesting place: at some time, probably about the end of the eighteenth century, a regular star-fortress had been constructed after the fashion of Vauban or Cohorn; as the increasing range of guns had made this useless, a series of works had been created around the lip of the saucer in which the city stands, but it was plain that to man them all and to keep an adequate reserve would have demanded a garrison so huge that it could not be fed. So Erzerum, while splendid to look at, had declined into being an indefensible fortress but a most agreeable garrison town. Part of that garrison, of about platoon strength, was detailed to guard Toby and his men, firman or no firman.

The Governor was courteous enough, as Turkish officers usually are, and took him on a conducted tour of the arsenals, store-houses and defence works; in addition he made available to Toby files from which he might deduce, if he could, how swiftly demobilization was proceeding, in conformity with armistice terms. Toby was little the wiser after perusing the files, and, in any event, he had a rendezvous with Sir George Milne in Kars, 130 miles away, in three days' time. He left to keep it with only two of the vans, having a shrewd suspicion that Milne would send him straight back to continue the work. After the Khop Pass the journey, though bad enough, was hardly deserving of record.

His three days in Kars included one of forced rest. Milne was kindness itself—he was known to his army as "Uncle George", a distinction rarely bestowed on general officers and achieved only when their soldiers thoroughly approve of them—and avuncularly produced whisky, an almost forgotten beverage, and English newspapers, which Toby devoured with equal relish after being so long out of touch with home. All the same, the fever was on him again, and the next day he passed in the unaccustomed luxury of a bed with sheets, in a room with a roaring fire. One day of this was enough, for as soon as his temperature was down he and the dog George were back in their van *en route* for Erzerum once more to finish off the business of trying to find out whether the Turkish army was really demobilizing or whether it was all a charade. The journey was horrible, for, with the onset of spring, snow was disappearing and the pestilential marshland was revealing itself as the haunt of every germ known to medical science, taking no account of those awaiting discovery.

Toby found that the Ninth Army had been downgraded and was now known as Fifteenth Corps; its new commander, Kiazim Pasha, had just assumed command. Kiazim was a thorough professional who had been Chief of Staff to von der Goltz in Mesopotamia, and Toby found much in him which he could like and admire. Since he was an out-and-out Kemal man, it was impossible for him to be entirely candid with the representative of those whom he could hardly deem to be friends, but "I have always found him as straightforward as his orders permitted him to be". As these words were written after Toby had suffered much at Kiazim's hands, it demonstrates a very forgiving nature on the part of the writer.

The month of May was devoted to carrying out a kind of census of the Turkish Eastern Armies and their equipment. It was an impossible task for an organization as tiny as that at Toby's disposal. He knew that there were divisions away to the east of Erzerum, but no information about their strength, their armament or their state of training could be obtained without a personal visit and the deep snow made this impossible. The Turks indeed answered all his questions about them, but there was no reason to suppose that they were being entirely frank with him. Erzerum itself excited suspicion, for it contained more than 500 artillery weapons and nearly a quarter of a million shells, but all that were shown to him were museum pieces. As his orders from Milne were to render the guns unserviceable and to reduce the number of rifles from over 100,000 to 15,000, he had the breech-blocks taken from the guns and the bolts from as many rifles as necessary; next, he had to find some means of getting those vital parts out of the country, and the Turks, not surprisingly, put themselves to minimal trouble to facilitate this. All Toby could do was to cable to Constantinople pleading for the railway to be repaired in order that he could finish his job and asking that he be sent a staff sufficient to see that it was done. Until this happened, Colonel Rawlinson's Establishment and its unauthorized accretion were cut off in Erzerum, cold, hungry and reduced to a diet of eggs and black bread. Scurvy, the result of a total absence of fruit and vegetables, made an ominous appearance amongst his men. The only cheerful spirit was George, now grown into a magnificent animal, "with a particular antipathy for all things Turkish".

On the first day of June, the weather having made travel less of a burden than before and because strange rumours were circulating in the vacuum of the old fortress, Toby decided that he must go back to Trebizond in order to compare notes with General Beach. He was as sure as a man can be that the Turks were hiding their better guns away, and as the sun came out and he was not pressed for time he decided to have a look around. This time he was in luck. In a nameless valley a few miles from the port he stumbled upon an artillery park containing forty excellent modern field pieces and an abundance of ammunition for them. The Turkish authorities protested their innocence and promised heavy and condign punishment to be visited upon the careless subordinate who had overlooked their existence. It was pretty certain that more were about the place if only the men and the means were available for finding them. With the evidence forced upon him, Kiazim could not refuse to permit Toby's people to verify the truth or otherwise of his returns of the Erzerum artillery and a satisfactory number of guns which did not figure in these uncandid documents were unearthed and sent back to Constantinople. At about this time a new Inspector-General of the Turkish Eastern Armies arrived in Erzerum. His name was Mustafa Kemal Pasha.

Chapter Sixteen

Toby had heard a good deal about Kemal, most of it to his credit. As the commander of the Turkish troops at Maidos in 1915, it had been he and he alone who, by a tempestuous counter-attack, had brought down the British assault on Sari Bair and ended Sir Ian Hamilton's chances of setting his foot in Constantinople. Such a man deserved the respect of a brother soldier and a reputation for an exalted patriotism did nothing to modify it. To Kemal, whose horizons both geographical and mental ended at the Turkish frontier, Toby was just another interfering British officer, but it was wiser for the moment to keep him sweet. The two men met on several occasions during the month of June and Kemal made no secret of his aspirations, nor did he attempt to conceal the fact that he intended to convene at Erzerum during the following month a conference of his principal supporters. Before June was out, however, Kemal fell from grace. His master the Sultan, at the behest of the Allies, summoned him to return to Constantinople. On his refusal to go he was instantly dismissed from the army and left free to devote the whole of his time to the pursuit of his political ends. To Toby this was a matter for regret. With Kemal's departure, Kiazim Pasha returned to the saddle.

The situation in eastern Anatolia was becoming progressively worse. Unaccountable " accidents" to the railway line were making communications with the capital less and less reliable, and a White Russian colonel who had served under the Grand Duke Nicholas during the Russian advance on Erzerum in 1916–17, a splendid victory for the Imperial army and one still under-appreciated by the West, was sent to help Colonel Rawlinson's Establishment. His local knowledge proved invaluable and, thanks to him, great stores of arms and ammunition were uncovered. Many of these were of Russian origin, buried by loyal troops during the Revolution, but the Turks were well aware of their existence and studiously omitted them from their returns.

Probing eastwards again, as far as Kars, Toby found the state of affairs there confused and ugly. Nobody knew what was happening or what the Allies were proposing to do. To every Turk it seemed expedient to cut the throat of every Armenian in reach while the going remained good. The Armenian view was that, as President Wilson was giving the country to them, they must somehow disarm the Tartar Moslem population and the Allies must help them before they left or, better still, do the job themselves. Toby came to the conclusion that he would be most usefully employed and conforming to the spirit of his orders if he continued his eastward journey in order to find out for himself what was happening on the marches of Armenia.

When his cars arrived he began again, crossing the plain and heading through the Aras Valley, from where could be seen the great, snow-capped peak of Ararat, 170 miles away. This was the country of the Kurds, a race whose misfortune it has always been to dwell around the places where the frontiers of greater nations meet. Despite the fact that their people have no common allegiance in the political sense, the Kurds have a strong corporate sense of nationhood. Neither Turk nor Armenian, nor Persian nor Iraqi, least of all Armenian, the Kurd remained a Kurd. His problems never having loomed large at Princeton University, he figured not at all in Woodrow Wilson's rearrangement of mankind in the Middle East. Selfsufficient in the way of mountain-folk and formidable in battle, the Kurds had long resigned themselves to the fact that they had no friends and must manage as best they could by their own exertions.

Toby found them admirable, "physically the finest men it has ever been my privilege to meet. They are to this ancient and inaccessible country what the Bedouin Arab is to the desert—that is to say they have been in occupation of the land since prehistoric times." He added that, "though they are brigands by descent, as well as by inclination and training, once their confidence is gained their word can be relied on; they are, however, both wary and suspicious". They had reason to be both. As he well knew, it was a risky business to seek them out in their homeland, for the small party was completely at their mercy, but Toby placed reliance both on the well-known tradition of Kurdish hospitality and also on the fact that it was common knowledge that there were still substantial British forces within striking distance. As things turned out, he had the time of his life.

Hussein Bey was a magnificent figure of a man, overtopping Toby's six feet by half a head; his splendid furs, which he wore without apparent discomfort on a hot summer day, were garnished with silver-mounted pistols, daggers with ivory hilts, boxes, gold chains and purses to an extent that called to his new friend's mind the window of a London pawnbroker's shop. A ride in the car at the best speed it could manage won his horseman's heart, and, when he found that Toby, who despite his lack of recent practice was an alumnus of the Indian Cavalry School at Saughor, had nothing to learn about equitation either, he treated him as a man and a brother. His last reserve melted when he found Toby to be no admirer of the Armenians, at the mention of whom Hussein invariably spat. The climax of the visit was his challenge to Toby to race him down the pass, the little Ford against six picked Kurdish horsemen. Toby accepted with alacrity. Part of the bargain was that Hussein should be his passenger, and Toby could not but agree. A look at the course made him wonder whether he had been wise, for, although he had twenty years of motor-racing experience behind him, including all the early Gordon Bennett road races, the worst roads he had encountered in Europe were as nothing to this.

The contestants drew up in line, in width about thrice what the road would take in its widest part, and at a signal they roared off. The first furlong was flat and easy, but then came a sharp turn to the right under a steep wall of rock with the road descending at a frightening gradient along a ledge in the cliff with the river roaring far below. Fortunately for Toby, the road did not go straight and the horsemen left it to take a short cut. This gave the car a chance to work up to its maximum speed alone, so that it became a race as to who should first reach the entrance to the ledge. The horsemen arrived first in a flurry of dust and small stones, but such was their speed that two of them collided with the rock face and dropped out. For some time Toby had to follow the four survivors, Hussein yelling encouragement all the while, for there was no room to pass them. Skidding and sliding, they kept close company, the chieftain nearly losing his seat during a mad swerve past a foundered steed and being saved only by Toby's swift action in grabbing his coat-tail—which escape appeared only to increase his exhilaration. Another horse disappeared—"though I never saw it, having enough to do to mind my own job"—and only two were left. The road became progressively worse, with the surface as loose as could be imagined, but the horses, although obviously "done", remained obstinately in front, being still ten yards ahead at the last zig-zag. As Toby put on a final burst of speed, a bang announced that a back tyre had blown clean off, but there was no stopping now. An instant later the other back tyre followed suit, and the last fifty yards were covered on the rims. The result was judged a dead heat, as the skidding car and the exhausted horses arrived together to receive the plaudits of every Kurd for miles around. After much mutual back-slapping (during which Toby noted approvingly that the Kurds' first care was for their horses) he was carried triumphantly off by Hussein for an orgy of curdled milk. It was not what he would have chosen, but it was a small price to pay for making such sturdy friends. As soon as the necessary repairs had been effected, the party was on its way again to find out what other mysteries Kurdistan might hold. Before taking leave, Toby promised that at the first opportunity he would explain to his chief the feelings of Hussein's people about the future, which did not include an enthusiastic acceptance of Armenian domination.

As he progressed throughout the eastern marches of Anatolia, it became plain that Hussein's point of view was shared by all the Kurdish tribes. Omar Aga, lord of all the land between the south side of the Aras River and distant Ararat, spoke feelingly of his intentions should he be placed under Armenian suzerainty, and proudly paraded his army, complete with German drill-master, to show that he meant what he said. Eyeeb Pasha, in the Olti country, with an army that looked even better than Omar's, felt the same. Toby secured his place in Eyeeb's esteem by riding with his cavalry and joining in a game of the kind of polo without rules known as *djerrid*. With an admiration for the Kurds that matched his economy of enthusiasm for the Armenians, Toby drove back to his former camp at Zivin, his tour of inspection complete.

When he reached Sarikamish, his anti-American bias, which had been steadily growing, reached a fresh intensity on learning that his car, which had been left behind there, had been ambushed by them and the corporal shot. Fortunately his wound was not serious and the driver had got him onto a train for Kars and hospital, but the car had been thoroughly looted. Obviously the Armenians were now on the rampage, as every one of the Moslem Agas had prophesied they would be, secure in the knowledge that they possessed the only artillery outside the regular national armies and confident that the Allies would not stand idly by and watch them being routed. Toby, whatever his personal inclinations, had to content himself by sending with his right hand a furious telegram to the Armenian Commander-in-Chief assuring him that he would be held personally responsible for the "undisciplined and barbarous actions of his troops" while, with his left, he despatched another to Kiazim requesting that the weapons which the armistice terms had allotted to the Armenians be transferred across the frontier and that working parties of Turkish soldiers be furnished for the purpose. At least, he thought to himself, this would compel the Turks to come out into the open and declare whether or not they intended to comply with the conditions they had accepted. He was perfectly well aware that Kemal was, at that very moment, holding his conference in Erzerum, and in all probability planning the overthrow of the Sultan and the foundation of a Turkish republic. It came, therefore, as no great surprise when Kiazim's reply amounted to a politely wrapped-up refusal. Swallowing his feelings and carrying out his manifest duty, Toby sent one further telegram. Kiazim must realize that his action amounted to a deliberate breach of the armistice, granted to the Turkish Government at its own request, and Turkey must not complain if hostilities were now renewed. As both men knew, this was a *brutum fulmen*, for, in July 1919 and with anxieties stretching from Archangel to Smyrna, the last thing the Allies wanted, even if it were within their reduced power, was a war in support of President Wilson's brainchild. Toby, feeling that he must at least talk to Kiazim as man to man before making the report that could activate the volcano, went to Erzerum. The meeting was polite, as was to be expected, but Kiazim was quite firm; he realized that his action was illegal and dangerous, but in the troubled state of the country he could do no other. Toby thanked him with equal courtesy and requested the use of the Turkish wires to enable him to report direct to Sir George Milne. Kiazim agreed and the message was sent, preceded by the ominous words, used only for the gravest purposes, "Clear the line." He also, again with Kiazim's help, employed the Turkish services to summon all his own officers at their various positions on the frontier to rejoin him at once.

Next day he had a meeting with Kemal himself. It was still cordial, and he obtained a promise that he should be the first to know of what decisions the conference might take. Armed with this, Toby returned to Zivin, where reports continued to come in of atrocities committed by the Armenian troops on the defenceless villages that lay within their reach. The telegraph was kept busy with further messages, this time to Beach at Tiflis to the effect that "in the interests of humanity the Armenians should not be left in independent command of the Moslem population as, their troops being without discipline and not under effective control, atrocities were being constantly committed for which we should, with justice, eventually be held to be morally responsible". As a result, a small body of British troops was quickly sent by rail from Tiflis to Sarikamish with orders to keep the Armenians under control. In this thankless enterprise they were entirely successful, but the evidence of the Armenian capacity for murderous revenge when no danger was present was plain for them to see.

Toby had left Eyeeb on the point of receiving an attack from the Armenians himself and thought it expedient to go and see what was happening thereabouts in order to complete his information. He need not have given himself the trouble, for Eyeeb's Kurds were in victorious pursuit and on the way to Sarikamish themselves. When he got back to Zivin it was to find that the train full of munitions which had provoked his brush with Kiazim had been looted in his absence by "brigands". As, however, the brigands had arrived with a convoy of empty GS wagons drawn by mules, facilities possessed only by regular armies, Toby drew his own conclusions as to their identity. It was, without doubt, Kiazim's way of getting his own back, and Toby saw no object in making accusations that he would never be able to substantiate. Kiazim did have the grace to express regret that Toby had suffered such a loss.

On 5 August, Toby's orders from Milne arrived, in cipher via Tiflis. Colonel Rawlinson was to gather his Establishment together and get it out of Turkey at once. He had a last interview with Mustafa Kemal before leaving. It was an opportune moment, for the conference had just risen and Kemal kept his promise to tell Toby of what it had decided. In a four-hour interview, the future President told him of the National Pact, which had come into existence only hours before, and of all his plans and hopes for the future. It was impossible to feel unfriendly to such a palpably honourable man and to such honest, patriotic emotions. The two men parted with "every civility, both appreciating the gravity of the developments which the future certainly held in store". Two days later Toby was in Tiflis, the Establishment was disbanded, and, having left in the hands of General Beach a copy of the Pact with which Kemal had supplied him, he was in the train for Batum. There he was fortunate in obtaining a passage to Constantinople in an American destroyer. On arrival at GHQ he had a long interview with Milne and was able to give him much news, fresh to Constantinople, of the birth of the Nationalist Party and of its intentions. Milne decided at once that this was of such importance that Toby must go home and make his report direct to the War Office. In the morning Toby set out, accompanied by a King's Messenger, and ten days later he was in London.

The CIGS was still his old comrade Sir Henry Wilson and their acquaintance was of long-enough standing for Toby to feel entirely free to speak his mind without any constraint. Wilson, for his part, had considerable faith in Toby's judgement and listened intently to all that he had to say; the news of Kemal's emergence as leader of a Nationalist Party of obvious and growing strength was a fresh factor in the affairs of the Middle East and did not at all chime in with Lloyd George's vision of a reborn Greek empire where the old Turkish Empire had been. There was no gainsaying the existence of the National Pact now that Toby was able to produce a copy furnished by the author himself, and, unless Toby had been completely gulled,

Mustafa Kemal was a great deal more than either a disgruntled ex-officer or a windbag politician. These were very serious matters, and, at the end of a three-and-a-half-hour talk, Wilson decided that Toby must repeat his story direct to the Secretary of State for Foreign Affairs, Lord Curzon. In the meantime Wilson, on his own initiative, postponed the already planned and announced withdrawal of British forces from Batum. Once they had gone, no sanction would exist to deter the Nationalists in any way, and the armistice conditions could and would be cast to the winds.

Toby looked forward with little relish to his interview with Lord Curzon. He had been a junior officer in India during the early days of the titanic quarrel between Curzon as Viceroy and Kitchener as Commander-in-Chief and was well aware of the disdain with which Curzon regarded soldiers and anything to do with them. The fact that the Army had, only a year ago, won the greatest series of victories in its long history had done nothing to mitigate this long-matured judgement, and, as Toby knew, any opinion expressed by a man of military background must, almost by definition, be not merely wrong but stupid, as viewed by Lord Curzon. He received Toby with the effortless superiority of a Balliol man, asked him many questions but plainly was unimpressed by his forecast that Kemal was a man of stature who might well bring into existence a Turkish Republic, compact and modern, vastly different from the old, sprawling and faintly disreputable Ottoman Empire. Turks simply did not behave like that. Toby, feeling angry and frustrated, went back to the War Office. Quite apart from matters of high policy, there was his own future to be discussed; his pre-war occupation was gone and his private means were minimal. His brother, Sir Henry, was asking that he come to Archangel to join him, but plainly that was neither an attractive theatre nor one likely to endure for much longer. When Wilson invited him to go back in his old capacity whence he had come, he jumped at it. This was work that he thoroughly understood and, almost more to the point, he would be able to join up with George again. He was, however, bidden to visit the Foreign Office once more before leaving for Constantinople and did so without enthusiasm. Lord Curzon, having taken thought, had work for him. Let Toby seek another interview with Kemal in the course of which he must point out the absurdity of the demands made in the National Pact and ascertain what were the lowest terms for which the man would settle. On no account must Toby even infer that he was his Lordship's emissary; he must clearly understand that no such honour was vouchsafed him and that he remained no more than he had been, a temporary Army officer charged with duty of reporting upon the observance or otherwise by the Turks of the conditions of the

Armistice. He need expect no written instructions nor any emoluments beyond the ordinary pay of his rank.

It was on 2 November that he landed at Constantinople and presented himself once more to Sir George Milne, who had been kept in deliberate ignorance of Toby's new quasi-diplomatic activities. All Milne could do was to ask him to raise a new Establishment and pick up the old job where he had left off. George was then collected from the friends who had been caring for him and he, together with the two Colt machine-guns, formed its nucleus. As there was no shortage of stores and Milne had given him a free hand to draw whatever he wanted, Toby decided to have more of an eye to comfort this time. His old batman, Private Leadbeater of the ASC, who could double when required as driver, machine-gunner or almost anything else, was the other founder-member of the new Establishment, but a glance at the volunteers who presented themselves for inspection demonstrated more clearly than anything else could have done that the Army a year after the Armistice was not of its old quality. Only one man seemed worth his salt and the others were simply the best job lot available. However, four of the well-tried boxy Fords were drawn, and two service Lewis guns brought up to five the total number of automatic weapons held. Gum-boots and furs of every kind abounded and the most useful catch of all was big tarpaulins, cunningly furnished with tabs, eyelets and pockets so that each car could be completely enveloped to form a kind of igloo inside which all could live well above the frozen ground. There remained the important post of interpreter to be filled. Armenians proliferated and, as their bush-telegraph informed them of what was afoot, they queued up for service. Of one thing, however, Toby was certain: no Armenian, be he ever so polyglot, would have any place in his entourage. Personal prejudices apart, if Toby were to penetrate to Kemal's lair, the chance of his interpreter's head parting company with his shoulders was not to be ignored. The problem was solved by the appearance in a street of "a miserable looking specimen of humanity in civilian clothes who addressed me by name and whom I at once recognised as a Russian who had been with me as interpreter on my last trip from Tiflis to Kars and Erzerum, whom I was very pleased to take on again in the same capacity".

Having gathered his force together, Toby prudently put it through a course of intensive training, in the forest of Belgrade, before setting out in search of adventure, a dozen miles north-west of Pera. That done, and with the assurance from Admiral de Robeck, the British High Commissioner, that if they got into trouble the Royal Navy would get them off from any Black Sea port at any time, Toby's party sailed for Trebizond, which they reached three days later. This time the port could boast all the modern conveniences of wooden wharf and steam derrick. The mission was expected to take about three months.

To begin with, it was necessary to obtain formal permission for the party to travel to Erzerum, and a telegram was despatched to Kiazim Pasha, still the military commander of the district. While the answer was awaited, Toby kept up his training marches and tried to find out what he could about the road. The passes would pretty certainly be under snow, possibly to an extent that would make them quite unusable or, at best, negotiable only with the greatest difficulty. To improve their chances, Toby obtained the use of a house at Gumush Khaneh, beyond the Zigana Pass but short of the worst part of the journey further inland. The authority arrived a few days later, with the additional and welcome information that another staging-post, a house at the foot of the formidable Khop Pass, was also at their disposal. This went beyond the demands of mere politeness and gave cause to hope that this further visit would not be unwelcome, in spite of the terms upon which Toby and Kiazim had last parted. His spirits rose, though he, alone of the party, was aware what the mountain journey ahead was likely to be. The message had added that the Khop was blocked but that men were being put to work to clear it. Toby knew what that meant.

The journey proved to be worse than even he had expected, largely because three of his four drivers were inexperienced and completely out of their depth in such gruelling conditions. Happily, the fourth man, the only one Toby had viewed with anything remotely approaching enthusiasm, turned out to be "a perfect hero". Corporal Ankers, whom he had made up to that rank on his own authority, was no tenderfoot. He had experienced the retreat through Serbia early on, before he had joined the Salonika Force, and any man who had shared the hardships of Voivode Putnik and his hardy men could have little to learn about mountain tracks, snow and freezing cold that deprives a man of his wits. His skills as a butcher, to which trade he had been brought up by his father, also proved invaluable to the little party. Between them, Ankers and Toby nursed the cars over the mountains, jollying the young men along and teaching them their business as they went. The tarpaulins were their salvation; with these draped over pairs of cars, firmly lashed down and weighted at strategic points and with the Primus stoves roaring out their promise of boiling cocoa, while the veterans regaled the youngsters with tales of adventures from a past that was already receding fast into history, the great winds outside seemed somehow remote. Two of the younger drivers were fired with the enthusiasm of their leaders, but the choice of one, an Irishman, had been plainly a mistake. Surly, frightened and querulous, he needed continual spoon-feeding and his demeanour promised no good for the future. Once more the cars had to be pushed up the Khop one at a time, and in this the party were assisted by twenty friendly Persians who happened to be travelling in the opposite direction; their noses blue with cold and Toby's long-suffering moustache once more transformed into a solid block, they pushed and shoved their heart-bursting way upwards through the snow to the elusive summit. Eventually the convoy reached Baiburt, where a telegram from the Commander-in-Chief was waiting; on no account was Toby to go beyond Erzerum. No reason was given but Toby's experienced nose had thawed out enough to smell trouble ahead. The rest of the journey was bad, but not as bad as it might have been, because the Turks provided working parties of snow-diggers and great numbers of oxen, enabling a dozen to be inspanned for each car. Thus preceded, the party and the cars eventually reached Erzerum.

Kiazim Kara Bekir Pasha was an honest man and seems to have liked rather than disliked Toby, however unwelcome his presence. Much had happened since their last meeting, and Kiazim was now a man with a secret. There had been a further conference, convened by Mustafa Kemal and held secretly at Sivas in September in defiance of Sultan Vaheddin, whose agents had done all in their power to arrest the moving spirits. In the middle of it news had arrived that the Sultan had ordered Ali Ghalib, governor of the province to the south, Malatia, to raise a levy of Kurdish tribesmen and with them to raid Sivas, capture the delegates and send them back to Constantinople in chains. This intercept rallied all the faint-hearts and the conference responded to the insult. Kemal, with all the speed and decision of his Gallipoli days, mounted a regiment of regular Turkish infantry on mules and rushed them, so far as mules can rush, into Malatia, where the assembling Kurds were rapidly dispersed and Ali Ghalib sent packing. The conference, backs to the wall, came out solidly with a programme of resistance to all foreigners and elected a provisional government with Kemal as its chairman. He had virtually taken over the state except for the environs of the capital, and the Sultan had yielded to his demand for an election. This had given the Nationalist Party a landslide of a majority (the deputy for Erzerum being Kemal himself) and the Congress, as it was now called, had moved to a more central position, at Angora (Ankara). With a proper respect for propriety, and regarding themselves, not without justice, as the elected government of a sovereign state, the deputies decided that they must assume their proper functions in the proper place, Constantinople. Kemal had told them that they were mad, for in Constantinople they would be in the power of the foreigner and would all be arrested at any moment they were found by the Allies to have misbehaved themselves. For once he was overruled, and the deputies set off for Constantinople at about the same time as Toby arrived there from England. The French government, with its customary talent for doing the spectacular thing when the price is not prohibitive, moved its troops into the Imperial Province of Syria. Every decent, patriotic, wavering Turk instantly fell in behind the Congress and the National Pact. It could hardly have been otherwise. Kemal, sensibly keeping out of the clutches of both Allies and Sultan, bent his ferocious energies to the preparation of armies against the crisis that was sure to come. Greeks in Anatolia with aspirations for a new Hellenic empire there, French in Damascus with more modest but still unacceptable plans for further dismemberment of the old Ottoman Empire, Armenians, Kurds and Bolshevik Russians provided enemies enough. Not a gun, not a rifle, not a donkey was to be handed over, nor was any unit to demobilize. Kiazim, as commander of a complete and undefeated army corps, was a most important cog in the machinery and was fully persuaded of it. A mission from the British army charged with ensuring that the terms of an armistice now almost forgotten should be scrupulously adhered to could hardly expect wholehearted help. The situation differed from that propounded to Lord Curzon.

After Toby had thawed himself out, he went to see Kiazim, who received him politely. They spoke long of the future of Turkey, and Toby, with complete sincerity, expressed himself as being personally sympathetic with the political aims of the Nationalists. Kiazim, having made the point that if they failed to come to some sort of sensible arrangement with the Allies, his people might find themselves unenthusiastically in the arms of Bolshevik Russia, undertook to try to arrange for a meeting with Kemal Pasha. The practical difficulties were obvious and he could promise nothing. In the meantime, would Toby care to come and inspect the orphanage that Kiazim had started up in Erzerum? At about the same moment, Turkish forces were enjoying minor successes against the French, besieging their garrisons at Aintab and Urfa, and had just carried out a successful raid on a French arms dump at Gallipoli itself. The British army, with the passing of every day, grew smaller and smaller.

Toby was kept fairly well informed of affairs by the cipher-wire to Constantinople; it was made plain to him that the Nationalists were *persona non grata* with the Allies, that the Angora Congress was not recognized and that only a parliament sitting in its usual place and in its usual manner could expect to receive diplomatic recognition. Nobody, it seemed, knew where Kemal had got to. It was clear to Toby that he was wasting his time in trying to carry out his official function as disarmament-supervisor, and the Admiral's promise to get him out from any Black Sea port sounded a little hollow in the stupefying cold of an Erzerum winter. As soon as there was a flare-up in Constantinople, Toby and his party would be held hostage and it was idle not to look this certainty in the face. Accordingly, at the first opportunity, he thinned out his party to an absolute minimum of four drivers, the interpreter and himself; the remainder were sent back to Trebizond by sleigh.

On 26 January 1920, the first Nationalist parliament opened in Constantinople, minus Kemal, and the Pact was formally published with a clear demand for a formal peace treaty in accordance with it. While the victorious Allies and their Associated Power led by its president talked at Versailles of the terms to be meted out to the defeated enemies, the delegates defied the occupying powers knowing perfectly well that, occupiers though they were, power was the one thing they lacked. Denikin had been routed in the Crimea and the rabble remnants of his army hung around the streets of the Turkish capital without hope of anything; the French had their hands full in Syria, and the British had theirs full in Ireland and India. Nobody bothered much about the Italians and the United States played the part of an inexhaustible soup-kitchen. Only the Greeks appeared to have the military power to influence events. The pomp of yesterday was, indeed, one with nearby Nineveh and Tyre as officers supervising the armistice conditions were insulted and disobeyed, obviously on orders from the new government. There was only one place where strength remained, and, on 16 March (two days before the anniversary of the most famous date in Turkish history: that, in 1915, when the Allied Navies had turned back from the Narrows), the Allies hit out as Kemal had prophesied. Their armies formally occupied Constantinople, every Nationalist deputy who could not get away was arrested, and they were shipped off smartly to an internment camp in Malta.

Before the sun set, the first ripple from these events reached Toby, just as he was writing a letter to his wife. A heavy tramp of boots, the rattle of arms and the flinging open of his door heralded the arrival of the governor of the fortress of Erzerum, followed by a full platoon of troops with fixed bayonets. Toby, not altogether surprised but determined not to seem out of countenance, rose politely and offered coffee. It was all very well-mannered and civilized: the Governor accepted the coffee and seated himself. He told Toby of the events in the capital, expressed Kiazim's regret that his many duties did not permit him the pleasure of visiting Toby personally, and went on to say that Kiazim considered that the surge of anger throughout Turkey would render unsafe so small a party. The troops which Toby had doubtless observed had, therefore, been assigned for his protection. He, the Governor, had to request that all the arms of Toby's men be handed over and the British flag which fluttered over the house be hauled down. The proposed indignity, though extremely disagreeable, mattered far less than gaining time in which to destroy cipher-keys and other extremely confidential documents which were in the room. Toby, therefore, after expressing an unfeigned regret for what had happened at Constantinople, took exception to the last part of the order while expressing gratitude for Kiazim's care for their safety. Would it not achieve the same end, he suggested, and at the same time salve his feelings if his command were to move under cover of the dark into the Citadel, where they would be quite safe? The Governor was regretful but firm: as a soldier, he quite understood how Toby felt, but his orders left him no discretion in the matter; it must, please, be done exactly as Kiazim Pasha had stipulated. At least, inquired Toby, the Governor would be willing to carry a written representation to his general to the same effect? The amiable Governor readily agreed that, as his general lived nearby, he would take with his own hand any letter Toby might care to write. "To this end I immediately began to put my suggestion in writing before any more could be said, using for the purpose, in my haste, the very paper I had before me, which bore as a heading the endearing terms in which it was my custom to address my wife, but in which it was by no means my intention to address the Pasha." As soon as the Governor had left, orders, cipher-keys, despatches and all the papers of Colonel Rawlinson's Establishment were crammed into the red-hot stove. On his return a few minutes later the Governor observed, unsurprisingly, that Kiazim could not consent to any change in his arrangements and advised Toby to accept the fortunes of war. He added a suggestion that Toby might look out of the window: around the four sides of the square were drawn up two complete Turkish battalions. Observing to the Governor that he held it a compliment that so great a force was needed to take five British soldiers, "with quite indescribably bitter feelings, such as I trust never again to experience, I proceeded myself to haul down the British flag, which I reverently folded and placed in the breast of my coat where it remained, in the only safe place I could command for it, until at long last I was eventually hoisted over the side of one of His Majesty's ships of war". All their arms, including Toby's two precious Colt machine-guns, were formally handed over and a receipt punctiliously given. He never saw the guns again. The officer left by the Governor pointed out that a strong guard had been placed round the house and that the ground-floor windows were being wired up to ensure their safety. Toby and his men must please consider themselves as confined to the house, but he, the officer, was authorized to purchase anything they might require with their money. It could not have been done with greater politeness, but the fact remained that Toby and his men were in prison for an indefinite term, with no certainty that they would even be fed once their small store of money had run out. The humiliation of it was the worst part, then the loss of his beloved guns. As to the party's incarceration, it was beyond doubt that the might of Britain and France, all others apart, would see to it that it did not long endure.

Within the first few days of their captivity it became plain that the reasons advanced for it by Kiazim were more than polite humbug. A roar of rage had gone up throughout Turkey, with the assistance of Kemal, as soon as the news of the action at Constantinople had got abroad. In Erzerum it manifested itself in the shape of a great demonstration outside the house in which Toby and his men were confined; as Toby, without moving from his chair, looked out of the window he was treated to the sight of "all the flat-covered roofs of the houses round about black with a collection of the most villainous looking ruffians that I had ever seen, who appeared capable of and anxious to commit at once unspeakable atrocities of every description and also that a crowd of several thousand other gentlemen of even more forbidding aspect were spread over all the open spaces amongst the ruins immediately surrounding our house". George demonstrated loudly what he would like to do to the hooting, cursing mob as they yelled for blood, but his master, as the only means of showing his contempt for the crowd, continued his writing in full view of them. As matters became worse, the Turkish officer of the guard burst into the room in a state of considerable excitement, imploring Toby to come down to the guard-room, as he felt no confidence in the reliability of his men and was personally responsible for the safety of the British party. Toby did as he wished and found that his men were already there, their composure being in strong contrast to the demeanour of their protectors. It was not until a strong force of armed Turkish police arrived on the scene and dispersed the mob that they were allowed to return to their quarters.

Next, Toby set himself to organizing activities to divert them and help keep them sane. His companions, with one exception, were men of the highest quality, as subsequent events were to show. Ankers was suffering from a wound to one of his hands that would later necessitate the amputation of the thumb; Carter and Leadbeater, both of the Machine-Gun Corps, were sound country-bred lads, a farmer's son from Norfolk and a watchmaker respectively. The weak link was the Irishman, Mahoney, for whose company the others had little taste. Nevertheless, he was there and had to be included. For a start, Toby decided to teach them to play chess. It was not difficult to make a board but the pieces presented a problem. He got over it with his usual ingenuity: Oxo cubes served as castles, corks as knights, ·45-inch pistol cartridges as bishops, machine-gun cartridges as queens, big Russian cartridges as kings and .38-inch pistol cartridges for pawns. The interpreter, Polakoff, possessed the usual Russian passion for the game and was appointed official instructor. By way of a change, and for entirely practical reasons, Toby taught them all Morse, both with makeshift flags and by tapping on the table, in place of a buzzer. Carter, the farmer's son, set himself the task of clearing the back garden and planting it with vegetable seeds, with an eye to the future. They were to be very grateful for his efforts. All the time they could not help being conscious of the arrival and departure of drafts of recruits, and the noise of machine-guns and rifle practice formed a permanent background music to their lives.

For the first few months they did not fare too badly, for Toby had quite substantial cash reserves hidden away and the guards translated these into food with moderate honesty. All the same, they were undernourished and growing daily weaker; at the end of May they saw under the windows the first Bolshevik Mission being received with great enthusiasm as it passed through on the way to Angora, on the same day as news arrived of the decision taken at Versailles to transfer large tracts of Turkey to the Armenians. It did little to add to their gaiety, even though the Turkish guards found it excruciatingly funny. At about the same time, Kiazim Kara Bekir Pasha was posted away to attend to this and the fortunes of the captives languished. His successor, also Kiazim but a mere bey, was an unattractive character, more German than Turk. With his arrival discipline deteriorated and the correct demeanour of the guards with it. It was this Kiazim who demanded that the Ford vans, still in the compound of the house, be handed over to the Turkish army. Toby replied with dignity that he must yield to overwhelming force and promptly, before the vehicles were removed, paid them a visit for the purpose of extracting and burying certain small but vital components. He made the mistake of having Mahoney help him; to his utter disgust, soon after the cars had been drawn uselessly away by the ubiquitous oxen,

> I became aware of the horrifying possibility that there might be found amongst our party any man who could prove capable of disgracing the uniform which we were all so proud to wear by giving assistance to the enemy; for although I pointed out to the Turkish expert the cause of the trouble in starting the cars was due to the worn-out condition of the electrical ignition devices of the motors,

replacements for which, I assured him, I had ordered from Constantinople, our one Irish driver, Mahoney, did his best in every way to assist the Turks in their endeavours to repair, though the other men quite properly refused to afford them any assistance whatever.

Fortunately Mahoney was not privy to the hiding places of all the missing bits and the cars remained *hors de combat*. Soon after this event, he wisely announced that he was feeling very ill and was admitted to the Turkish hospital of Erzerum. Toby was not absolutely certain of his guilt, though all appearances were heavily against him. Had he had no doubts about it, summary justice might well have been visited upon the scoundrel. As it was, he disappeared.

From this time on matters became much worse. The guards were no more than illiterate, ignorant recruits and the officers ceased to pay their visits. Nobody above the rank of corporal could be seen on any pretext, the prisoners were treated with a sullen rudeness, and money suddenly seemed to buy far less than in the time of Kiazim Pasha. In a while the health of them all, George included, began to deteriorate fast, and, in their now emaciated condition, dysentery afflicted them and they lacked the strength to perform even the smallest routine task. Their captivity had so far lasted five months and the future was a blank. Toby, now fifty-three and with all his old wounds and sicknesses come back to plague him, began in all seriousness to wonder whether they would ever see the outside world again. He wrote in his diary in the first days of September that he did not expect to last the winter out, but that the younger men might have some small chance of survival. As the avaricious guards, waxing fat on the prisoners' money, could no longer be trusted, Toby decided that he must hide the last small cash reserves he possessed and demanded that he and his men be issued with rations. The grinning corporal provided them: almost inedible black bread and the disgusting remains of the commissariat meat after the Turkish soldiers had had their issue from it. On this they were just able to remain alive; paraffin for the stoves and fuel for the fire ceased, though in plentiful supply for the guard-room. As the first of the winter snows came down, Toby was near death, his clothes hanging loosely over his shrunken frame, though his grizzled Captain Kettle beard proclaimed his defiance. Offers to the men of food and other luxuries if they would help to repair the cars were all treated with a splendid contempt that warmed Toby's heart as nothing else could have done. Judging from a photograph taken with one of his few remaining films, his six feet of skin and bone would have turned the scale at something like eight stone. For a time he did his best to keep up the games of chess and the little courses of instruction in Morse, the elements of French and any other subjects within his experience that seemed to him to be either useful or time-consuming; the men, none of whom counted much more than half his years, played up splendidly and it was as much a point of honour for them to keep their officer's mind occupied as it was for him to keep them from despair. As the dreadful winter drew on and the cold beyond description intruded into the marrow of their bones, even this became too much for him and Toby was compelled to concentrate all his powers of mind on one thing only. He knew himself to be dying, but he must not die. All personal feelings apart, he must contrive to stay alive somehow, for to yield to death, easy and even tempting though it must have seemed, would be a breach of duty. Life, always cheap in Moslem countries, was a very debased currency in Anatolia in 1920 and it was a certainty that, with the only British officer removed from the scene, the men would soon follow him. Only a little studied neglect would be needed to rid the guards of a nuisance and they could be trusted to supply it as soon as they realized that there was no more money to be had. Ankers, Leadbeater, Carter and Polakoff would soon be forgotten in a shallow grave under the snow and nobody would be troubled to ask any questions. Toby was known to have connections in high places, and, so long as some life remained in his wasted body, hope of eventual exchange would exist. On no account must he suffer death, for it would be an act of desertion. He had looked it straight in the face before without turning away and he would continue to do so for so long as the last atom of strength remained.

In this fashion the weary weeks of winter dragged on and men could have been forgiven for holding themselves forgotten and giving way to rage or despair. On Christmas morning 1920, after sixteen days without the smallest particle of meat and after six days with no food of any sort, Toby forced himself once more from the coma that passed for sleep.

> To my infinite surprise I heard a very weak and trembling voice addressing me, saying "A Merry Christmas, sir." My first thought, of course, was that this was as good a dream as I could expect but, on the words being repeated, I crawled from my little camp-bed and found my batman, Leadbeater, standing in the doorway supporting himself in his weakness by holding on to the post. I thanked him, of course, most heartily for his Christmas wishes and wished him the same in return, but all the while I was gradually taking in his appearance with the utmost astonishment. He

was dressed in full uniform (it is true that it was in some places in sad need of repair), but everything was scrupulously clean, to the last strap and fold of his puttees, whilst his boots and his brass buttons and badges shone like stars in the dim light of the winter's morning. As soon as I got over my astonishment I congratulated him upon the appearance of my "Army" (the men always spoke of themselves as such)· on Christmas morning. He then said, in rather quavering tones, that the "Army" wished to know at what time I would prefer to take my Christmas dinner, and again I gasped with astonishment and then begged him, for the Lord's sake, to tell me what it was all about for, as far as I knew, we had nothing to eat but a piece or two of black bread. He then told me that the "Army" had been preparing a surprise for me, and that each of tthe three of them had prepared a dish for my Christmas dinner and, please, what time would I take it?.

It was agreed that dinner should be at noon, Toby resolving to himself that he would eat as little of it as the chefs would permit so that something at least should be left for them.

As soon as Leadbeater was out of the room, Toby made his way painfully to the trunk which contained his one decent tunic, carefully preserved against the day of their eventual release. He found a brand-new set of medal ribbons to provide a touch of colour and got down to work on belt and boots, "determined to be in no way behind my comrades in showing our guards how the British Army turned out for their great national 'Bahram', as the Turks call their feasts". Punctually on the hour, arrayed in his very best, Colonel Rawlinson sat down to dine. As the midday gun went off, the door opened and there stood Corporal Ankers, resplendent to the last buckle and button, proudly bearing a dish "about which there was a certain suggestion of eggs". After the exchange of greetings, and a few words from Toby about the pride he felt in his men's pluck, he asked that he be allowed to come to see their dinner in accordance with the immemorial custom of the Army. Ankers, who had expected this, said that they would be delighted and they both moved to the men's quarters below, the dish still untouched. Carter, whose case was the worst of all, as untreated dysentery had made a skeleton of him, contributed a "plum pudding", "made, as I learned afterwards, from crumbs which they had swept up from the now very weevilly dust remaining from our tins of army biscuit, long since considered as finished, but at which he had been working for weeks to produce from them some semblance of a pudding. . . . Last of all came Leadbeater with a tart made I know not how but which he was graciously pleased to allow me to admire without detracting from its magnificent appearance or interfering with the elaborate motto of 'A Merry Christmas' which distinguished its truly wonderful crust." All the dishes were then borne off below and, as soon as the others were out of sight, Toby followed. As he had feared, the stairs were too much for him and he slowly made his way down backwards on hands and knees. The mess-rooms had been scrubbed scrupulously clean and they all sat down to the table before weakness should make them fall down. Toby catechized them keenly about the meal, for there were traces of such things as eggs and raisins to which they had long been strangers. It took a lot of coaxing to get it out of them; but eventually one of them admitted, in a whisper, that "they had sold their socks, sooner than be unable to keep up the traditions of the British Army, by some attempt, however poor, to celebrate their Christmas Day in their quarters. I then told them what I wanted to say to them, and did say, which cannot have differed much, I expect, from what those who read this story would have wished to say to such glorious men as tthese." The curious guards crowded round them, incredulous, uncomprehending, and "furious all of them at our undefeated aspect". For their benefit, one thing remained to be done, and "I asked the men if they would back me up if I tried to sing 'God Save The King'. Some very weak voices answered me that they were willing enough to try, if I so wished, but that they feared that it was beyond their powers to do themselves justice." Few people would call the melody an inspired one, and the words, banal enough when first written as an anthem for the first German Georges, have long lost what aptitude they once possessed. There are, however, occasions when together they make better battle-songs sound trivial; when quavered out by four feeble voices in a frozen prison in a far-off country they evoke memories of Blenheim and Minden, of Salamanca, the Somme and Ypres, and for a moment the strong wills of indomitable soldiers make a mockery of worn-out bodies. Even the Turkish guards stood silent. As for Toby, "I made my way back again to my room, thoroughly exhausted, but in a mood to defy and fight any Turk or any other man or beast, and so must have been feeling much the better for our glorious Christmas effort". The sentiments may not be exactly those appropriate to the occasion being celebrated, but the British Army has its own ideas on the subject.

Chapter Seventeen

The year 1920 had not been a conspicuously happy one for mankind in general, but for Kemal's henchmen, by that time the majority of his countrymen, it ended in a blaze of glory. The fortress of Kars had changed hands yet again and the crescent flag flew over its walls for the first time since 1878, when it had fallen to the Russians. Elsewhere, too, the Turks' fortunes were rising. However, for the forgotten prisoners in Erzerum this served only to render their lot even harder. On the pretext that he was a deserter from the Red Army, Polakoff, following the arrival of the Bolshevik Mission, had been taken away to an unknown fate, and for those left the future looked bleak indeed. Soon after, the Greek government of Venizelos fell and the last voice counselling moderation was silenced. Sir George Milne went home and was succeeded by Sir Charles Harington, once Plumer's brilliant Chief of Staff at Second Army Headquarters. The Twenty-Eighth Division, practically the entire Allied army left to enforce the terms of the absurd Treaty of Sèvres, had dwindled to six weak battalions, a cavalry regiment and a few guns. Many of the troops were pressed into service to feed Wrangel's refugees, with all the unfortunate women and children who accompanied them in headlong flight from the Red terror. In this work the Greeks, though nominally under Harington's orders, took no part. They had other plans.

There was only one event that lifted the unrelieved gloom about Toby. Three kind Americans, the representatives of that great organization that saved so many lives, managed to get to him a box containing a piece of bacon, "a delicacy carefully chosen as it was anathema to the Mussulman Turks who guarded him", and some equally abhorrent cigars. Heartened by the knowledge that they were not utterly forgotten, Toby and his men became even more determined not to die. Leadbeater, the watchmaker, busied himself with fabricating a tiny brass coal-scuttle out of old cartridge cases, while Toby decided to try his hand at wood-carving. He first prepared exact scale-drawings and then, with a broken pen-knife for his only tool, began work on a model of a motor-yacht of his own design. He had hardly begun it when, on 1 February 1921, the whole party were unceremoniously bundled out of the house and incarcerated in the common gaol of Erzerum. They had by then been prisoners for ten months and fifteen days, he noted with his usual precision. "All other sentiments were swallowed up in an overwhelming emotion of degradation and disgust that we, British soldiers who had done nothing but our duty, should be herded with the lowest prisoners in the common gaol." He had certain views on the political leaders of his own country and expressed them with a bitterness entirely understandable. "The bare fact itself brought home to me the immensity of the fall which the prestige of my country had suffered through the vacillating weakness of those into whose hands the custody of that priceless national heritage had fallen since the proud days, a short 28 months before, when our armies were everywhere victorious and the British uniform commanded respect throughout every country in the world." Even from the depths of humiliation, he demonstrated a selflessness of unusual quality. After remarking that the news would have been spread through every bazaar in the East to demonstrate how low the power of the British Empire had fallen, and after pondering upon what the consequences would have been in Lord Palmerston's day, he added, "In the feelings of sadness that then were mine there was never any thought as to what our own fate might be but only an abiding sorrow that our great country should be made to appear so cheap and powerless in the eyes of ignorant Oriental populations." It was, indeed, the worst loss of face endured by the Army since the First Afghan War eighty years earlier, but with the difference that this time there was unlikely to be an Army of Retribution. Though nobody condescended to furnish a reason for what had been done, it seems probable that the Turkish authorities had got wind of the Greek plans, for it was in the following month that the invasion of Anatolia by the troops at Izmid began.

As things turned out, the move to gaol was in some ways a change for the better, for although it was crammed with Armenian prisoners of war in the last extremities of filth and starvation, the arrival of the British compelled the appointment of an officer as commandant. Toby and Lieutenant-Colonel Emin Bey, the man appointed, had met before, when Emin had been commanding a brigade on the frontier. He was civil to Toby, though hardly cordial. He explained that all the hardships of the last months had been attributable to the slackness of Kiazim Bey, who had now been summarily dismissed. An officer named Salah-a-Din was detailed to be responsible for the British prisoners and proved himself to be a very decent man. When the money finally ran out, he obliged by selling Toby's fur coat in the bazaar and accounted honestly for the proceeds; he it was who also arranged for the prisoners to be able to buy the small quantities of fuel that kept them alive. His greatest service, however, was to permit one man at a time to go, under guard, to the market, so that they could lay out the remains of their money to best advantage and buy the cheapest food, instead of being dependent on the financial transactions of the guards.

From Salah-a-Din Toby learnt something of what was going on in the world and picked up hints of a possible exchange of prisoners, by which some of the Nationalist deputies held in Malta would return to Turkey. This was hope indeed, so much so that Toby abandoned himself to reading the plays of Racine and Fénelon's *Odyssey*. They were not the reading matter he would have chosen, but Salah had produced them and Toby did not want to offend him. From then on visitors began to arrive, apparently with the object of sounding him out to see what he would have to say about his treatment if such an exchange were to take place. As may be imagined, the callers got little change from him. Instead, Toby learned that they were particularly anxious to obtain the release of Raouf Bey, one of Kemal's closest associates, who had made the mistake of disregarding his leader's advice against going to Constantinople. Raouf was an important man and Toby spared no opportunity to make it clear that he himself was not exactly negligible. On 24 March, Emin called in person to break the news. The party was to be taken at once to Trebizond to await exchange. As the snow was still deep in the passes they would proceed by march route with an escort of six soldiers and two arabas (Turkish carts). Emin reckoned that the journey would take about ten days. As soon as Emin had gone, Toby tottered off to repeat the news to the others.

Naturally they were all elated, but they were under no illusions about the feat of endurance required of them. Crossing the Khop and the Zigana passes in March, on foot and with transport sufficient only to carry their kits and the mules' own forage, would tax strong men in good health. The men had had a little exercise in their excursions to the bazaar, but in the past two months Toby had not been out of the gaol at all and for the ten months preceding that he had been under house arrest. If it were truly necessary to make the 200-mile journey to Trebizond on foot in March, for him at least the result must almost certainly be death in the snow. However, in Toby's philosophy, that meant no more than that they must make their preparations as carefully as they could. With freedom round the corner, transport could certainly be found if only they tried hard enough. Salah-a-Din was invited to confer with them. He was tolerably sure that he could hire some sort of conveyance provided that the money for it could be found, and, being the good fellow he was, he set off to try and strike a bargain with the leading jobmaster of Erzerum. He brought "this interesting individual" back with him and they talked at length; the outcome of it was that the party could have what the jobmaster called a "victoria" and a large four-horse araba for the equivalent of £17, payable on arrival at Trebizond. Toby promptly agreed and wrote out the necessary undertaking. To meet the cost of food and lodgings *en route*, Toby's last and most treasured possession (apart from George) had to go, "a small carpet I had hung on to and slept on all the time, as a last resource in the case of urgent necessity". It realized less than a quarter of its value, but the amount raised was enough for the purpose. Salah's last act of kindness was to provide a transport officer, improbably named Hairie, to go with them; Toby found him "one of the nicest Turks it has been my lot to meet and a man I should be glad to see again at any time".

Early in the afternoon of 28 March the carriages arrived. The araba was more or less what they had expected, but the victoria was something out of the ordinary. Once upon a time, long ago, it had been just the kind of open carriage that bears the same name in England; but for entirely practical reasons, some previous owner had roofed it in after the fashion of a hen-house. Nobody complained of its lack of elegance, but practical difficulties arose when the passengers sought to enter it. Years of banging about, heavily overloaded, across indescribable surfaces had bent the side members of the chassis to an obtuse angle, with the result that the passengers in the back could stay in their seats only by perpetually leaning forward, hideously uncomfortably. Added to this, the capacity of the interior was so small that, by the time Toby, Hairie and Salah were aboard, there was no possibility of accommodating George as well. Salah-a-Din, indeed, who was travelling only as far as the gates of the fortress, wisely decided to remain standing on the step, though it threatened to part company with the rest of the carriage at any moment. As the plan was for them to cover only about eight miles to the first halt, Toby let George run beside them for that distance, reasoning that he should have no great difficulty in keeping up over the snow-covered plain.

Thus it was that the ancient, rickety conveyance set out from Erzerum, moving slowly through the deep snow, its creakings and groanings promising total disintegration at any moment. It took two and a half hours to cover the first stage, and the accommodation that awaited the travellers was better than they had expected. George, however, was not in good shape, for long months on short commons and with little exercise had had their effect on him. "Our poor old faithful George, who had never left me in the prison and whose loving sympathy had served on countless occasions to cheer and encourage me during the long and bitter nights, was obliged to follow afoot through the frozen snow, with the result that his poor feet were cut to pieces though he came on steadily without a falter even when lame in every leg and bleeding from all his feet." Toby's first task on arrival at their lodgings was to demand and obtain hot water with which to give George such first aid as he could; only then would he look at the tea and rolls provided, which made up their entire refection. In the morning, George was crammed into the victoria somehow; as Toby observed, "it must have been very uncomfortable for him but infinitely better than struggling through the frozen snow on his poor wounded feet", besides which "he kept me warmer than I should otherwise have been in the terrible wind which blows across that dreary, snow-covered plain". That day they advanced sixteen miles further towards freedom.

For the next stage George travelled in the araba. The party crossed the Euphrates and reached the entrance to the Khop Pass by nightfall. There the only shelter to be had was in an underground serai patronized almost exclusively by Persian camel-drivers, who filled every square inch of it. The *esprit de corps* would have made a goat feel unwell and it was convenient to have a Turkish officer with the party. Hairie, with the aid of his soldiers, cleared out a score or so of the Persians, leaving just enough space for the travellers inside the forbidding recess. Toby, whose tastes ran to fresh air whenever possible, waxed eloquent about the conditions there, such as the "natural effluvia which rose from the recumbent Persians, who alone remained motionless in that horrible place, where all else was literally moving with every species of verminous life."

The remaining stages of the journey were much as Toby had expected, but the travellers' lodgings never again approached the basic qualities of the serai below the Khop Pass. A sample of Toby's diary entries can speak for them all: "Left 5.30 a.m. Hell of a day. Over our waists in snow. Horses down. Cart overturned. Icy wind. Temperature below zero. Arrived Hamiskeui (18 miles) 7.30 p.m. All dead beat." The style may be that of Mr Jingle but it points the message that Erzerum was being left well behind and nothing much mattered apart from that. On the ninth day Toby and his men found, to their inexpressible joy, that a motor lorry had been sent from Trebizond to carry them over the last leg of the journey. The warmth of spring came with it and, as they drove past trees in full leaf, their winter clothing came off and they began again to feel like human beings. Home was now just around the corner. The first feeling of being back in civilization came with a visit to the Ottoman Bank's Trebizond branch, where an obliging manager cashed Toby's draft on the Command Paymaster at Constantinople, so providing the means of settling up with the jobmaster, buying clean clothes for all and laying in a small stock of edible food, razor blades and other half-forgotten luxuries. A beaming Turkish commandant found a doctor to attend to Toby, who was in low health and had kept going only by sheer will-power, and they were made comfortable whilst they waited the few days before the formalities of the exchange could be completed. A British ship, they were told, would be putting in any day now to convey them to Constantinople.

Their morning greetings to each other were exuberant. The Turkish authorities were unusually amiable and accommodating, even allowing them all to go into the town for baths and meals at restaurants. Toby at once sought out a barber and bade farewell to his year-old beard. After the fourth or fifth day without any news of ships the exuberance began to show signs of wearing thinner; every morning their first waking thoughts were of the "perhaps it will be today" order, but still neither ship nor news of ships arrived. After a fortnight of hope deferred, hearts were indeed becoming sick, and on 16 April the news arrived. It was not what they had been led to expect; the young Turkish officer charged with the duty of making it known to Toby clearly hated what he had to do; "however, I told him I was neither a child nor a man unable to face whatever adversity fate might yet have in store for me and begged him to tell me his news at once, as shortly and as plainly as possible". Though it was delivered with hesitation it was like a blow in the face. Orders had just been received by telegram from Angora that the prisoners were to be taken at once to some place in the interior; neither reason nor destination was given. All the young man knew was that the same old carts and guards were being got ready and that they were to start in the morning for Baiburt.

The shock of such a development when they felt themselves to be almost in sight of home was, of course, stunning, but "I trust that I received this sentence with proper courage and self-control, saying that it would be necessary to return at once to the fort to communicate this sad news to my men and to commence our preparations for the journey". The subaltern was genuinely distressed and he proved himself to be a better fellow than Toby would have believed possible by his next offer. There was an Italian ship in the roadstead due to sail for Constantinople in the morning and his duty required him to visit her that night; if there were any letter that Toby would like sent to his friends in the capital, he would at least engage to hand it personally to the Italian captain with a request that he deliver it, but that was as far as he could go. Toby thanked him with as much warmth as his frozen spirits permitted. His brain was working fast, for there was much to be done. The absolute priority was, plainly, to get all the money on which he could lay hands, and he went at once to the Ottoman Bank. Heroism is a quality not commonly associated with bank managers and it seemed as likely that one would risk his neck as that St Francis of Assisi would prove to be a judge of claret. It was common knowledge that, in accordance with the best revolutionary practice, the Nationalists at Samsun had recently shot the manager there for what they deemed improper banking transactions, very similar to the ones Toby was about to propose. All rules, however, have their exceptions and it turned out that the manager at the Trebizond branch and his assistant were not easily scared. They cashed him a draft for 1,000 Turkish pounds—about £120 sterling—and undertook to honour any more requests that Toby might manage to smuggle through from whatever place in the hinterland might be his destination.

With his pockets bulging with currency and his heart in his boots, Toby went to break the news to Ankers, Leadbeater and Carter. "I have had in all my life no harder task than that. Feelings were then stirred which were at the time and are even now far too deep for words, my one object being to do my utmost to assist and help them to meet the blow in a proper and soldier-like spirit and, as far as in me lay, to set them the example which it was my duty and privilege to do. But it was hard and if, as I fear was the case, my voice trembled, it was small wonder, as my physical strength was at a sadly low level and my own burden was a heavy one to bear." For a full minute one could have heard the traditional pin drop. Then, "I did my best to help them to face the music and to get busy with our preparations. Before concluding this account of that most painful scene, I wish to take this opportunity of thanking my comrades once again for their help and of saying, with deep respect and true appreciation of their courage, that these were fine men, tried and proved, and that I was proud indeed to be their commander."

For the next few hours Toby scribbled rapidly, eventually making up a parcel which contained a long letter to the Commander-in-Chief, a summary of the diary which had been taken from him at Erzerum, his diary of the last journey and, finally, with his usual punctiliousness, the accounts of Colonel Rawlinson's Establishment completed up to date. In a postscript to the letter he apologizes for, of all things, the informality of its language, "as I am still very weak, and today's news makes me so that I hardly know what I am doing and the officer waits while I write—so very disconcerting". Let one paragraph speak for itself:

> I wish to say in conclusion, Sir, that I can understand that it is more than possible and, in fact, only too probable, that the Turks may have put such a price on our exchange that it may not be the country's interest to pay it, and that, under those circumstances, we return to our prison readily and only trust that we may have the strength to carry out anything that our duty may demand of us, and we shall take pride in so doing, whatever it may be.

He had not, he added, the heart to write to his wife or brother.

The journey back was much the same as the journey out, save that the glare of the sun was substituted for the glare of the snow. An American of the Relief Mission who tried to speak to them at one of the halting places was hustled away by the guards; the party were not allowed to leave next day until the Mission had gone, but one of them had recognized Toby and managed to get a message through to Constantinople that they were still alive and, apparently, heading back for Erzerum. The guards, having no longer any incentive to behave in a way foreign to them, were rough and brutal, but, in the depth of misery, nobody cared very much. At the end of a week of travelling, they were back in the same old prison, feeling utterly forsaken.

Fortune gave them one small benison, for the officer placed in charge of them was an old acquaintance and friendly. It was he who warned Toby that they were to be subjected to a thorough search and gave them just time enough to conceal their stock of banknotes; the soles of slippers made out of old motor-tyres took some, the space between the felt and the metal of water-bottles absorbed more and the balance was concealed in the skin of Toby's dilapidated portmanteau of "good English leather about a quarter of an inch thick". As the authorities were sure to know exactly how much money he had drawn from the bank, Toby, for the first time in his life, "cooked" the accounts—which, as everybody knew, he kept meticulously—by entering a bogus purchase of furs for shipment to England which exactly covered the balance, except for some small change. The inquisitor, one Avni Bey, a major of artillery who had risen from the ranks and was known to be no fool, duly arrived. Toby, a stripling of fifty-five, kindly refers to him as "the old gentleman" but felt that "I had an opponent whom it would be a proud achievement to get the better of". He began by taking the bull by the horns and replied to

Avai's polite inquiries about their well-being by assuring him that the journey had been no hardship thanks to the money they had obtained from the bank. When asked whether he still had it, Toby replied that of course he had and produced his accounts together with the small cash balance, thanking his stars that he really had bought a few furs from a Greek to send home and for which he had been unable to pay because of the sudden move. Avni, unable to fault the accounts but quite certain that Toby would not have run himself so low on cash, demanded to search everything. Toby expressed himself to be injured by such behaviour but could not resist; nothing was found. His morale lifted a little by this, Toby wrote a well-phrased letter to the Commandant asserting that he and his men were almost penniless and asking whether Emin would cash him a cheque; he was not surprised to receive no answer.

For a time he had company beyond that afforded by George, for amongst the inmates of the gaol—still mostly the wretched Armenians—were the Prince and Princess Toumanoff and their small daughter; their escape from the frying-pan of Bolshevism had met the traditional fate and they were now penniless and nearly starving, their only money coming from such pitiful sums as the Princess could earn with her needle. With nothing to do, Toby went back to his wood-carving. The yacht was finished and he had started on a model house. Both of them were really professional pieces of work of which no Black Forest carver would have disdained authorship. He managed to buy a "very third-rate" Turkish–French dictionary with which to give work to his mind and "practically learnt it by heart".

Helped by this new accomplishment, Toby was able to carry on a conversation of sorts, in the way that prisoners acquire, with a Bulgarian officer who, unaccountably, was confined amongst the Armenians. The day came when his release was announced and Toby contrived to get to him a letter rolled up in a cigarette. It was addressed to the General Staff, Intelligence, at Constantinople and bore the date 1 August 1921. In it Toby gave an account of all that had happened since his previous letter (which, incidentally, had not arrived) and he permitted himself one line of rancour.

> One of my men, Mahoney of the ASC, joined the Turks and betrayed the fact of our having put our cars out of action and disclosed the hiding-place of the parts. *Look after him if you get him* as he has been the cause of our disgraceful treatment, solitary confinement, starvation and misery. Our health is wonderful, considering great privations and disgusting conditions, but we have kept our flag flying and

neither whined nor begged for anything. GOD SAVE THE
KING.

The Bulgarian picked it up and nodded, while Toby returned to his
cell to listen once more to Prince Toumanoff playing soulful Russian
music on his violin.

Suddenly he began again to have visitors, Turkish Intelligence
officers, who seemed surprisingly communicative. They openly
boasted of how their missions were stirring up trouble for the British
from Kabul and Delhi to Cairo and Baghdad—presumably in com-
petition with the Bolsheviks, although their aims were the same.
Toby felt inclined to believe them, for the questions he put to them
seemed to prove that the men had at some time been in the cities they
described. The object of their visit to him was far from clear. Even
more interesting was a call from Nuri Pasha, once one of Enver
Pasha's right-hand men and now in some sort of privileged captivity
himself. Nuri, who appeared to be well informed, was quite clear
about the reasons for Toby's incarceration. Kemal wanted him, first,
as a channel of communication with the Allies, and, second, as a
counterweight for the still-interned Raouf. He had come to the conclusion that the first purpose had been stultified but the second
remained; all the same, asserted Nuri, he was tolerably sure that
Raouf would be let out before long and Toby would doubtless then
be freed also. As for himself, he was hoping to go to Angora, as he
had some very interesting information which he was willing to make
available to Kemal, at a price. Then, one day, he disappeared.

At the beginning of September the same straws began to drift in
the wind as on the previous occasion. Rushdi Pasha, Kiazim Pasha's
second in command, paid a social call for no obvious reason; he left
assuring Toby that the exchange could not be far off and asked
hopefully what would be his attitude about his captors when he
returned home. Toby, not for the first time, turned the question, but
he could not help a feeling of hopefulness. Once more small privileges
were afforded them, including a dispensation to buy meat if they had
the money. The younger men were glad of it, but, for Toby, "my
digestion was too much destroyed to permit of my eating it". He did,
however, force himself to get a quantity of soup down every day, for
autumn was near and, although he did not rate very high his chances
of surviving yet another winter, he still had the duty of staying alive
as long as possible.

On 2 October Emin himself was announced. He brought with
him the order for their transfer to the coast, and announced that this
time vehicles would be provided for them. Three days later they
began again the familiar journey, furnished for the occasion with four

arabas and "a conveyance of a model unknown in Europe but in which one can lie down and which has a roof". In this primitive caravan Toby travelled over the passes for the last time, not troubling to make any record of anything beyond the facts that the snow was down and their escort had a skirmish with wandering banditti. At Trebizond all was unaccustomed sweetness and light and he was found a billet in the house of a kindly old Greek widow, who had also to endure the presence of a permanent guard over her emaciated guest. A Turkish naval officer presented himself with a letter from General Harington; the Bulgarian had been true to his promise and Harington had goaded the Foreign Office into giving him permission to organize the exchange. He entreated Toby, superfluously, to make no attempt to escape and added the news that his brother had achieved his heart's desire and was now Commander-in-Chief in India. He also added that Mahoney had shown up in Constantinople and was firmly under lock and key, a piece of news that cheered Toby almost as much as the rest of it. The greatest comfort of all was to learn that his future was now in the hands of soldiers instead of the despised politicians. He does not mention Lord Curzon by name but it would have been a work of supererogation. On the last day of the month, in his carefully-preserved decent tunic, with George at the head and the men marching as soldiers should, Toby embarked his Establishment for Constantinople.

Even there, it seemed, their troubles were not over. Colonel Baird of the Intelligence Staff came to meet them and explained the situation. He had just come in a destroyer from Ineboli, 500 miles to the west, where the Turkish internees who were being traded for Toby's party were now waiting on board ship. The bargain was that Toby and his men should not be released until the exchange was completed and that, if any hitch occurred, they would have to go back to Trebizond. After a moment of cold grue, Toby said that he accepted the situation and they made their way to the pier, where "the most glorious sight of all awaited us—namely a steam-launch manned by real British blue-jackets, with smiles all over their faces, and the White Ensign, that glorious emblem of the British Navy, floating proudly over the stern". Soon they were being piped on board HMS *Somme*, after which they went instantly to bed safely amongst their own people at last. Toby had not troubled to open the box that had been handed to him at the pier after having been forwarded by the Commandant at Trebizond. In it, instead of his pistols and all his valuables, were a few things of no account and the letter which had been handed to the Italian captain, with its seal still unbroken.

It was flattering to learn, in the morning, that over eighty Turks had been traded for Toby's party of four, but it was disturbing to be told that in Turkey there were still 140 British and Indian prisoners, of whom no news had been heard for a long time. Sir Horace Rumbold, the High Commissioner, authorized the transfer; Toby's feelings about it were mixed. "To our disgust we saw all the Turkish prisoners go over the side into their native boats, knowing that there were amongst them scoundrels of the deepest dye, whose crimes, committed against British prisoners in their hands, had been of indescribable barbarity." When HMS *Somme* weighed anchor, it was without Toby: he, knowing that Harington was authorized to make the exchange only for the full 140 named men, went aboard HMS *Centaur*, where General Franks, in charge of the exchange, had his headquarters. Toby had his reasons and had given them a lot of thought. The sea was getting much rougher, the roadstead was an exposed one and a ship of the *Somme*'s class could not safely remain. Toby was prepared, if he must, to go back to prison, but he was going to do his best to make sure that, if he had to, this time he would go alone. With the *Somme* out of the way and with his men aboard her, it did not seem likely that too much fuss would be made about a corporal and two private soldiers. In his weakened state he made a hash of jumping from the launch to the rope-ladder down the *Centaur*'s side and his leg was crushed between boat and ship. He was hauled aboard incapable of standing, but, as the surgeon was able to say that he had broken no bones, he refused all help and went straight to the General. Franks told him that the bargain was that Colonel Baird would surrender himself if the exchange did not eventuate and that there was no question of Toby's release being in jeopardy; he added that he was seriously thinking of taking Baird's place himself, as the duty of the senior officer present seemed to require it. Toby expostulated that he, if anybody, should be the sacrifice, as a lieutenant-colonel of artillery was a much poorer catch than a lieutenant-general. The main thing, he pointed out, was to hang on to Raouf at all costs: he was the man who mattered and Kemal would care nothing about the others. In the end Rumbold signalled, "Let all the Turks go", and the exchange was completed; a couple of gentlemen of indeterminate ancestry who claimed to be British subjects were thrown in for good measure. Toby landed at Constantinople on 5 November 1921, free from all conditions. The hospitable Navy readily offered him and his men, including George, a home on board their fine ship while Toby completed his reports and wound up the affairs of the Establishment. There was also the matter of Mahoney's court martial to be attended to.

The Commander-in-Chief, High Commissioner, Ambassador and other high dignitaries demanded to see them all, and Toby, Ankers, Leadbeater and Carter, plus George, were constrained to eat as much in a day as they had been used to eating in a month. On Toby's strong recommendation, all three of his men were immediately granted the Military Medal. The journey home was a triumphal progress. HMS *Centaur* carried them to Malta, where they were the guests of that great soldier Lord Plumer. Admiral de Robeck conjured up a destroyer to take them on to Naples (kindly producing their old friend the *Somme*, though it was not her turn for despatch work) and they cruised past Capri into the Bay. As there were some hours to kill before their train was due to leave, Toby dined all the ship's officers at the Hotel Excelsior, "as fine a hotel as can be found in Europe", and they saw the party off in great style aboard the Paris train.

It was near the entrance to the Mont Cenis tunnel that the horror occurred. The train stopped and George, who had been asleep at Toby's side, indicated a wish to go out. His master, in pyjamas and with feet bare, obliged. At the same moment as George's body touched ground, the train, without warning, moved off. Toby, fighting down the instinct to leap out and join him, managed only to yell "Otur"—the Turkish for "Lie down"— before they were away and into the tunnel. His frantic efforts to stop the train succeeded, but by then they had travelled for some miles and had reached the next station, where the only thing that could usefully be done was to enlist the help of the local *carabinieri*; their officer was most helpful and promised to find the missing member and send him under escort to Modane by the next train. At Modane Toby sought out Thomas Cook's representative, who engaged personally to bring George to the Rothschilds' house in Paris, to which the party was bound. Toby was more anxious and unhappy than he could ever remember, but all came well on the following day. All concerned had done their duty, and an impenitent hound was duly delivered just in time to be photographed with his friends, the Baron Robert de Rothschild's great house serving as a back-drop. Reunited and in the Calais train next morning, they set out on the last leg of the journey home. As soon as they had boarded the Channel packet, Toby went to look for his cabin; after a minute or two in possession a steward knocked on the door and told him with many apologies that he was in the wrong one, as this was reserved for another gentleman. As Toby turned round, the other gentleman came in. It was Bendor.

On 28 November 1921, at 7.30 p.m., an obsolete-looking officer stepped out of a train at Victoria station into a London that had almost managed to forget that there had been a war. His service dress was of a pattern disused for some years, with his rank indicated by braid on the sleeves, as it had been in 1914; khaki was, in any event, no longer a familiar colour at Victoria. The newspaper Toby bought there soon brought home to him the fact that England had returned to her genial peace-time habits, for the paper contained little beyond tales of strikes, shortages, economic crises and labour unrest, football results and accounts of Irishmen busily murdering each other and any British troops who might have the misfortune to provide them with targets. Lloyd George was still, for the moment, Prime Minister; and Sir Henry Wilson, not yet laid low by Irish assassins' bullets, was still CIGS. On the morrow after his arrival back in London, Toby reported himself to Sir Henry and for nearly two hours unburdened himself to him of all that he had seen and learned, taking great pains not to create a wrong impression or to give the smallest grounds for accusing himself of self-praise. This last ordeal completed his task, and, as he sat with his family at dinner that night, he collapsed. For a long time he lay in his bed unconscious, his nervous system completely exhausted now that that inflexible will allowed it to have its way. Though he was commanded to the Palace by the King himself, and though even the great Lord Curzon desired his attendance, his doctors would have none of it. Bendor probably saved his life by demanding that as soon as he was fit to travel Toby should go for a long rest to Mimizan, his estate in the Landes. It was not until the end of December that he was pronounced able to make the journey.

In the meantime Toby was to discover the gratitude of the nation to those who had defended it. He was commanded to a medical board, which granted him three months' sick leave, at the end of which he was to be examined again. As he intended to go abroad, he informed the War Office of the fact; the reply was "that no more sick leave was authorized under any circumstances unless an officer was actually detained in a military hospital" and that, unless he were re-employed, he would be granted only two months' leave and would then be demobilized. The War Office, when he questioned the accuracy of this pronouncement, granted him a further month, advancing the date of his release from both the Army and the Navy to 23 March 1922. Little comforted by this, he left for Mimizan, where he remained until the beginning of February 1922, for most of the time being confined to bed.

On his return, he kept the appointment at the Palace, where the King presented him with the insignia of a Commander of the British Empire, nearly three years after he had been selected for the honour. Lord Curzon also saw him and assured Toby that he had tried very hard to secure his release or exchange. Toby held his peace.

Towards the end of March it was all over. It was useless to point out that he had been on active service continuously since August 1914 without any leave whatever, and it was equally useless to ask for further employment in the Middle East, where his experience could be of great value; it was made clear to him that he was no more than a temporary officer and that this was the fashion in which temporary officers were treated. He would be demobilized on 23 March, and was advised that, if he had neither private fortune nor occupation, he should seek out the nearest Labour Exchange. On the matter of pay, he must understand that the special allowance which had been promised as an inducement for him to go to Turkey in the first place had ceased on the day he became a prisoner, because thereafter he had not been performing the duties contemplated when it was granted. This decision, at least, he forced the Paymaster to reverse, after much correspondence. Next there came a letter from the Ministry of Pensions; it arrived on 10 July and spoke of his "application". Toby, being unconscious of any application or, indeed, of the existence of such a Ministry, inquired what was meant. "In consideration of your disability [Toby supposed it to mean his ruined health], you have been granted a temporary pension from 23 March 1922 till 15 December 1923 at a rate of 34/7½ a week." Subsequently, after a battle royal, it was increased to £2 17s. 8½d. Toby thought of the able-bodied unemployed, many of them conscription-dodgers and irredeemably work-shy, who were receiving hand-outs far greater than this. He thought of the Hudson of First Ypres, of the "Toby" mortars and Aubers Ridge, of the Naval Mobile Anti-Aircraft Brigade, of London under bombing, of Baghdad and Baku, Kars, Trebizond and Erzerum. He was alive, and that was more than could be said of many of his generation. It was, perhaps, enough to be thankful for.

Envoi

In 1925 Sir Henry Rawlinson died suddenly in India after a game of polo, leaving no heir. His peerage died with him, but the baronetcy passed on and Toby became Sir Alfred. The title was of little practical use. On 1 June 1934, at 102, Elmhurst Mansions, Edgely Road, Clapham, died Lieutenant-Colonel Sir Alfred Rawlinson, Bart, CMG, CBE, DSO. His son, the new Sir Alfred, proved his Will at the Principal Probate Registry. Its total value was sworn at £115 7s. 0d.